Landscapes of Clearance
Archaeological and Anthropological Perspectives

Edited by
Angèle Smith and Amy Gazin-Schwartz

**Left Coast
Press** Inc.

Walnut Creek, California

Left Coast Press Inc.

LEFT COAST PRESS, INC.
1630 North Main Street, #400
Walnut Creek, CA 94596
http://www.LCoastPress.com

ISBN 978-1-59874-266-4 hardcover
ISBN 978-1-59874-267-1 paperback

Library of Congress-Cataloging-in-Publication Data

Landscapes of clearance : archaeological and anthropological perspectives /
Angèle Smith, Amy Gazin-Schwartz, editors.
p. cm. – (One world archaeology series ; 57)
Includes index.

ISBN 978-1-59874-266-4 (hardback: alk.paper)
ISBN 978-1-59874-267-1 (pbk. : alk. paper)

1. Landscape archaeology. 2. Ethnoarchaeology. 3. Landscape changes. 4.
Landscape assessment. 5. Cultural landscapes. 6. Geographical perception.
I. Smith, Angèle II. Gazin-Schwartz, Amy, 1952—
CC75.L333 2008
930.1—dc22
2008019850
5

Printed in the United States of America

∞™ The paper used in this publication meets the minimum requirements of
American National Standard for Information Sciences—Permanence of Paper for
Printed Library Materials, ANSI/NISO Z39.48—1992.

Contents

List of Illustrations 7

Preface 9

Part 1: Introduction 11

1. Landscapes of Clearance: Archaeological 13
and Anthropological Perspectives
Angèle Smith

2. Abandoned, Avoided, Expelled: 25
The Creation of "Empty" Landscapes
Amy Gazin-Schwartz

Part 2: Colonial Tools of Clearance 47

3. Written Off the Map: Cleared Landscapes 49
of Medieval Ireland
Angèle Smith

4. The Past Is Another Country: Archaeology 71
in the Limpopo Province, South Africa
Kathryn Mathers and Neels Kruger

5. Driekopseiland Rock Engraving Site, 87
South Africa: A Precolonial Landscape Lost
and Re-membered
David Morris

6. Constructing the Wilderness and Clearing 112
the Landscape: A Legacy of Colonialism in
Northern British Columbia
Brenda Guernsey

Part 3: Resistance and Revitalization 125

7. Ethnoarchaeological Study of Clearance in Palestine 127
Juliana Nairouz

8. The Domestication of Landscape through   139
    Naming and Symbolic Protection among
    the Batswapong Peoples of Eastern Botswana:
    Fullness and Emptiness of Landscapes in the
    Eyes of the Beholder
    Phillip Segadika

9. Enclosing the Spirit   154
    Peter Read

10. New Places for Old: The Reinhabitation   164
    of Cleared Landscapes in Northern Scotland
    Olivia Lelong

11. The Devonshires Held This Trench, They Hold   180
    It Still: Cultural Landscapes of Sacrifice and
    the Problem of the Sacred Ground of the
    Great War 1914–1918
    Jon Price

12. Archaeological Taxonomy, Native Americans,   190
    and Scientific Landscapes of Clearance:
    A Case Study from Northeastern Iowa
    Larry J. Zimmerman and Dawn Makes Strong Move

Index   213
About the Authors   219

List of Illustrations

Figures

Figure 3.1	*Mappa mundi* of Giraldus Cambrensis, from his *Topographia Hibernica* (1188)	59
Figure 3.2	Detail of Giraldus Cambrensis's *Mappa mundi* showing Ireland and England, from his *Topographia Hibernica* (1188)	63
Figure 4.1	Site of a twentieth-century farmhouse	78
Figure 4.2	Distribution of the archaeological sites identified by the survey	80
Figure 4.3	Characteristic palisade walls at Tshirundu's Kraal	80
Figure 5.1	Situation of Driekopseiland on the Riet River relative to other places and regions mentioned in the text	88
Figure 5.2	One of George Stow's Driekopseiland copies. The text reads, "From striated rocks at Blaauwbank on the banks of the Gumaap or Great Riet River, Griqualand West. GWS"	89
Figure 5.3	The site of Driekopseiland, early twenty-first century	95
Figure 5.4	A profusion of engravings spread across the glaciated surface at Driekopseiland	96
Figure 7.1	Qasr	133
Figure 8.1	Map of study area in east-central Botswana	140
Figure 8.2	Female Hill and Male Hill, with the Tswapong Hills in the background to the right	143
Figure 8.3	Ruins of the Bangwato church built in the 1890s at the foot of the Tswapong Hills, near Malaka village, east-central Botswana	146
Figure 8.4	Malaka village with the Tswapong Hills, location of Dimomo Cave and Tshekedi's Road, in the background	150
Figure 10.1	Location of project area, northern Sutherland, Scotland	165
Figure 11.1	Unofficial shrine at Sunken Lane, Beaumont Hamel, Departement du Somme	185

Figure 12.1   Effigy Mounds National Monument and Iowa's   191
              Neutral Ground

Figure 12.2   Aerial photograph of the Marching Bear group   195
              at Effigy Mounds National Monument, with
              bird and bear effigies and two linear mounds
              outlined in lime

Preface

This volume has its origins in a session on Landscapes of Clearance we organized for the Landscapes, Gardens, and Dreamscapes theme at the World Archaeology Congress meeting in Washington, DC, in June 2003. Most of the papers at that session are included in the book. Sven Ouzman, Matthew Kelly and Tracy Ireland, and Elizabeth Davis contributed interesting papers on South Africa, Australia, and Ireland to the session, but other commitments made it impossible for them to contribute to this volume. Following the conference, we sent out a call for further contributions to the volume and were very fortunate to receive papers from Jon Price, Phillip Segadika, Kathryn Mathers and Neels Kruger, David Morris, and Larry Zimmerman and Dawn Makes Strong Move. Their contributions extend the geographic and topical range of the book in valuable directions.

We would like to thank all the participants for sticking with the long process of getting the volume to publication. Mark Leone and an anonymous reviewer provided insightful comments on earlier versions of the chapters that helped the authors improve them. Elizabeth Schwartz helped to prepare the index. Lee Steadman's sensitive and careful editing, and patience coping with multiple time zones, helped to see this volume through to completion. Mitch Allen and Left Coast Press were helpful all through the process. We particularly extend thanks to Mark Leone for proposing the original theme at WAC, and especially for his extraordinary patience and encouragement throughout the process of getting the volume to press.

PART 1

INTRODUCTION

CHAPTER 1

Landscapes of Clearance: Archaeological and Anthropological Perspectives

Angèle Smith

Charles Orser writes that "to archaeologists, the way in which people abandoned their homes is as important as the activities they conducted within them" (2005:47). However, he continues that

> archaeologists have not yet studied eviction to any significant degree and that a full understanding of ... history will require archaeologists to consider the significance of eviction for numerous reasons, not the least of which relates to its effect on transcontinental migration and the modification of huge tracts of land. (ibid.:57)

He is referring specifically to the famine-era evictions in nineteenth-century Ireland, but his argument can most certainly be made for many places and social landscapes across the globe. Migration and movement through the landscape have always been part of human behavior and hence have shaped past landscapes and the way we view them. Indeed, as archaeologists, our specialty is generally the "abandoned place." Michael Schiffer's work (1972, 1987) on the process of site abandonment, defining the systemic and archaeological contexts, the latter the result of various processes/transformations of the "lived experiences" of the people, the landscape, and their material culture, is solidly part of the archaeological canon. And though empirically tested in terms of the reasons for abandonment and the likelihood of the inhabitants return to the site, what is less well explored is the impact and significance abandonment and clearance have on those who have been forced to move from their lands.

This book was the result of many discussions between the editors and with other archaeologists and anthropologists concerning the importance and meaning of place and landscape in people's lives. The topic of landscape has become a theme central to many archaeological and anthropological studies in the last decade and a half. Thus it was that at the World Archaeological Congress in 2003 (Washington, DC) the theme of a session organized by Mark Leone entitled "Landscapes, Gardens, and Dreamscapes" focused on "the lands around, between, and beyond human settlement" and explained landscapes broadly to include a growing range of definitions for the concept. While the focus on landscape has held much attention (Bender 1993, 1998; Hirsch and O'Hanlon 1995; Tilley 1994; Ucko and Layton 1999), less well explored are the social processes involved in clearing the landscapes of the past and the present and the significant and meaningful impact of these actions (although see Bender 2001; Bender and Winer 2001). Landscapes are made by the people that engage with them, and in making landscapes, the people themselves are made: their sense of place, belonging, and their social identity is constructed alongside the construction of the landscape. But the corollary to this is that landscapes are often highly political and contested, as different communities of people try to negotiate different interpretations of the same landscape. Thus landscapes can be dynamic and even volatile places that witness removals and clearances in the attempt to exclude and erase some inhabitants from the land.

Intrigued by the complexity of these issues, we organized a WAC session entitled "Landscapes of Clearance" to examine how landscapes, which by their very nature are meaningful, become artifacts of contestation when peoples are removed from or have abandoned their homes and homelands. We wanted to speak to issues of the colonial and post-colonial experience of eviction and forced removal from the landscape. Many of the papers, both those presented at the conference and those here in this volume, through richly detailed case studies, discuss various methods, means, and tools of removing people from the lands they occupy. In doing so, they reinforce the argument that landscapes are imbued with meaning and significance for those who live, work, and die in these places. The discussions in these chapters bring to light a poignant understanding of how rupture from one's sense of home, place, and belonging is a meaningful and often stark reality. This is also witnessed by acts of resistance against the forces that are clearing the lands and by attempts to revitalize the "emptied" landscapes. Such ruptures, resistances, and revitalizations have implications for understanding ideologies of landscape in the recent historical past (a colonial past), as well as the more distant (prehistoric) past, and should influence how we think about and interpret sites that have been "abandoned," "avoided," or from which people have been "expelled."

The discourse concerning "clearance" allows us to focus on the concepts of occupation and situatedness as well as abandonment. While we tend to concentrate more on sites and places, the discussion of clearance can also include the routes along which people left or are leaving. Further, beyond the simple physicality of the leaving, the concept of clearance allows us to look at the social and ideological processes it engages.

The papers in this book address the archaeology of apparently empty landscapes, demonstrating the complex and rich ways that cleared landscapes have been created, inhabited, and endowed with significance. Within the shared context of understanding the significance of landscapes, chapters in the book address such themes as the politics of memory and forgetting, individual and community experiences of clearance, and the ways ideology, identity, and diasporic experiences are linked.

LANDSCAPES AND CLEARANCE

"Landscape" has become a fashionable concept. While once perceived as the mere backdrop to human action and life, it is now recognized as having a more critical role in how people live and make sense of who they are and what is their identity. More than simply a physical place, landscape is now understood as also having social and ideological or cognitive elements. It has taken on a metaphorical quality in which people talk about the landscape as the general shape and lay of the land, as a body of knowledge, and most significantly as a body of lived experiences of the world. To know the landscape is to know and control the access to that knowledge or to those experiences.

Soja (1989) argued that "space" was simultaneously physical, social, and ideological. This, in part, accounted for his definition of spatiality: spatial relations are both produced by and are the product of social relations. Therefore, spatial/social relations are fraught with tension and conflict. For Soja, social space, along with material and cognitive space, is contingent on the cultural and historical context. The definition of material space is dependent on its topological configuration within a physical setting, i.e., its association to other physical spaces. Material space is also defined within and by a cultural context as being "physical" and "natural," measurable and tangible. Cognitive space has to do with ideas, ideologies, and interpretations of space, which in turn define the space. It involves human perception and cognition and is thus a product of its cultural, political, and historical context (see Downs and Stea 1977; Gould and White 1974; Ryden 1993 for discussions of cognitive space and mapping). Archaeologists have traditionally tended to focus on physical and material space (Clarke 1977a, 1977b; Hodder and Orton 1976). More recently, we have come to appreciate that no less important are the social and ideological dimensions of space (Bender 1993, 1998; Delle 1998; Hood 1996; Thomas 1993; Tilley 1994). We recognize in this multi-layered definition that space is at once material, social, cognitive, and ideological. In keeping with these explanations, the current understanding of landscapes similarly recognizes that the landscape is inherently connected to social relations, power, meaning, and social identity, and because of those connections it is often a site of contestation.

Yi-Fu Tuan wrote in the 1970s about the concepts of place and space—two terms often associated, even interchanged, with the concept of landscape. In *Space and Place* (1977), Tuan defines *place* as the fixed and static location of past actions, experiences, and memories or, as de Certeau (who later takes up the same oppositional positioning of these two concepts) writes, "place is time made visible" (1984:117). There is a physical tangibility to place because it marks past (and potentially continuing) actions and experiences with and in the landscape. Places in the landscape give meaning and identity to people, who have real emotional attachments rooted to the landscape through their memories and heritage (e.g., of their home or homelands). In contrast, *space* is dialectical and is about process, motion, and action; it is not tangible in the same sense as it is always in the process of becoming. Again to quote de Certeau, space "defines itself by action ... [and] is a practiced place" (1984:117); it is the journey between places. Without the actions and experiences of the process of space, places do not come into being; no spatial journeys can happen (take place) without places in which to take root. Perhaps more useful is to combine or bridge these two concepts in a dialectical relationship. Thus, in order to make sense of the lived experience of people we must link these two concepts of space and place within the landscape. That is, landscape bridges and encapsulates both the action and fluidity of space and the rootedness and memory/history of place.

Landscapes are imbued with meaning and significance for those who live, work, and die in them. Individual, as well as collective, senses of identity are inherently tied to a sense of belonging to a place or land-scape. Our sense of who we are and where we come from is linked to our experiences and memories of living in a place and acting in a landscape. In the phenomenology of landscape (Bender 1993; Thomas 1996; Tilley 1994), this is what is called "dwelling"; it assumes a long and lasting rootedness in the landscape, one that has a history and heritage that goes back through generations. But as Ingold (1993) would rightly argue, dwelling in the landscape is a product (and process) of living in, working in, and acting in the landscape; it is these dynamic processes and actions that make the memories and histories that continually shape and reshape our landscapes. Landscapes are thus meaningful not only to individuals but also to collective groups that share a commonness of experiences and memories.

Lovell talks about this meaningful experience as belonging and locality (the term she uses in lieu of place), and argues that a sense of identity can never be divorced from a sense of place/locality:

> Locality often appears subsumed within the notion of belonging itself, which serves to provide collective identity and a sense of cohesion and cultural commonality (although conflict and differentiation can also emerge out of these processes) ... Yet belonging itself also appears at least partly predicated upon locality or a memory of locality ... [that is] belonging to a place is viewed as instrumental in creating collective identities. (1998:4)

She continues by arguing that a "placedness" is also represented and reified in the discipline of anthropology. As anthropologists go to "places" to study communities, the people themselves become synonymous with their geographical locality, ultimately constructing a heightened sense of the meaning of place while also creating a boundedness (and hence boundaries) to the social unit on the landscape.

I would add that archaeology too focuses on "placedness." In archaeology, material culture and actions are always contextualized in locale. Indeed it is the provenience, whether at a general site level or at a more specific within-site positioning, that makes material culture meaningful. Archaeology is often the documentation of people's lived experience in place; it marks both the temporality and the spatiality of living. Maps, profiles, and other spatial tools abound in archaeological texts as "proof" or "evidence" of the archaeological past (or present, if we expand our understanding of archaeology to also encompass the analysis of spatiality and process in the contemporary context). In this way, the process of archaeology further reifies the "placedness" of human life, though it is often uncritical and sometimes unaware that it does so.

It is ironic, then, that archaeology "clears" the landscape of the very cultural information it is simultaneously trying to retrieve and interpret. However, archaeology is also a valuable tool for understanding the social processes by which a landscape is cleared of people, their past, and their meaning or understanding of that place. Clearance can have many forms, including removal by a peaceful evolution as people's use of the land changes, the eviction or the forceful removal of people by some external force, or the abandonment of sites as a process of changing perceptions of place. This latter is witnessed in Barbara Bender's work *Stonehenge: Making Space* (1998), in which she richly details the historical evolution of the Stonehenge landscape, including the periods of time when people abandoned or stayed away from the site due to its supernatural power. The Christian Church promoted the idea that the stones were the work of the devil and that the place was evil. This, however, does not mean that during these periods of nonoccupation Stonehenge lost its power of place or its meaningful impact on the local population. In fact, the power of Stonehenge was so strong that it influenced people's actions to stay away.

THE MEANING OF CLEARANCE

What is the impact of clearance and removal of people from their homes and lands? If the meaning of landscapes in terms of a sense of place and identity is so great, then what must be the terrible impact on people who have had to leave, for whatever reason? Archaeologists can turn to the research conducted on placelessness, homelessness, and diaspora to better understand the personal and collective sense of grief, defeat, outrage, and resistance that often follows on clearing people from their landscape.

Featherstone describes the place of *home* as that sustained by the collective memory, dependent on ritual performances, bodily practices, and commemorative ceremonies, or as the "batteries which charge up the emotional bonds between people and renew the sense of the sacred" (1993:177). Hence, homelessness is the loss of wholeness, moral certainty, and genuine social relationships.

Neil Smith (1993) writes about the scales of spatiality, beginning at the smallest scale of the body. The next scale is concerned with home and is associated with family, identity, and safety. The next scale again is community, which defines the collective sense of a people's daily lived experiences. The scales continue to include urban, regional, national, and global.

Clearance as an act of colonialism is an act of ethnocide, perhaps even genocide—rupturing people's sense of place and thereby destroying some part of the people themselves. Short of killing and doing bodily harm, this is one of the worst and most effective acts of cruelty and violence against a people. We tend to imagine that acts of clearance (especially when linked to colonialism) might be situated in the scale of the global, that it is the outsider that seeks to lay claim to new lands and thus is the cause of the dispossession. But can there be other circumstances where clearances might occur? The case of the Palestinians and Israelis provides an intriguing example of a contested landscape in which all parties stake their identity, heritage, and right to stay and live, in their connection to those lands (see Abu El Haj 2001). In this way, the landscape and the people who have been cleared from it are linked too to the national scale and to ideologies of nationalism and belonging at a larger scale of the politics of space.

Removing people and communities from the landscape, and thus their sense of belonging and identity, has drastic impact. In British Columbia,

Canada, for instance, the early colonial government sought to remove the First Nations communities from the supposed "wilderness" lands through the creation of reserves, which corralled diverse communities into land-zones set aside for them. The creation of reserves was an act of dispossessing the First Nations of their claim to land, family, and their identity. It was simultaneously an act of creating the Canadian nation and claiming the land and its rights for the newcomers. Today, these acts of clearance still haunt the British Columbian landscape as treaty negotiations center around territorial rights. To lay claim to the land, local First Nations must "prove" that they had occupied the lands. In his book *Making Native Space—Colonialism, Resistance, and Reserves in British Columbia*, Cole Harris (2002) describes the process of dispossessing Native peoples from their land and relocating them on reserves in an attempt to fracture their connections with the land (and subsequently fracture their community and culture). The very simple and yet powerful act of mapping the Native and non-Native space separately finalized and formalized the removal of the peoples from their lands. Thus the book deals with the local tactics and strategies of land clearance as well as the consequence of this clearance: resistance and the struggle for repossession through extensive and enduring treaty negotiations.

The essays in this volume explore the meaning of landscapes and their clearances. This book allows us to examine the material expression of clearance—to grasp whether local variation can be seen in different kinds of clearance—so as to appreciate better the social and ideological implications of clearing the landscape. To begin, part 1 examines the basic processes of clearance. In part 2, the chapters are concerned with the tools of clearance, especially the tools of colonial clearances, including mapping, archaeology, and tourism. The inhabitants, however, do not succumb easily to being removed from their landscapes, and the chapters in part 3 deal specifically with resistance and the revitalization of cleared landscapes.

In the chapter 2, Gazin-Schwartz examines the underevaluated complexities of the processes of clearance. Arguing that the reasons for land clearance may be economic, environmental, sociopolitical, or combinations of these, she explores three categories of emptying the landscape: abandonment, avoidance, and expulsion. Within each of these categories, clearance may vary according to the cultural or environmental changes that caused the landscape to be cleared, the ways people responded to those changes and the reasons they chose particular responses, and the locus of decision making around leaving a landscape. These variations then influence the ideology and later conceptions of the landscape, and the archaeological consequences or correlates of these processes. Using case studies of abandoned, avoided, and expelled landscapes in Raasay,

Scotland, Gazin-Schwartz illustrates that these processes have been shaping landscapes (and the archaeologies of these landscapes) from prehistoric into historic and contemporary times.

Part 2 explores the various tools used in the practice of clearing the landscape. Although the previous chapter suggests that emptying of lands surely occurred all through prehistory, the chapters in this section deal primarily with colonial tools of invaders and settlers (including mapping and rezoning of lands into marginal reserve lands). Historically, clearance is often associated with a colonial force removing the people from the landscape both physically and ideologically. The tools that are used include military force, but also include the reshaping of the ideology of the place by "reconfiguring" and re-presenting the place through maps, literature, and official documentation. Smith (chapter 3) outlines such a case as the Anglo-Normans colonize Ireland in the late twelfth century. Based on the colonial writings of the priest Giraldus Cambrensis and the map that accompanies his *Topographia Hibernica*, Ireland was represented as a newly colonial place, a wild, empty land that was both terrifying and bountiful. The colonial map topographically removed the people from the landscape, focusing on (and legitimizing) the areas of the Anglo-Norman intervention in order to distance the colonizer from the colonized. As well as colonial tools, there is evidence in the following chapters of tools of clearance that continue into the present, including tourism, policies of land conservation, and even archaeology itself.

Like Smith, Mathers and Kruger (chapter 4) also explore the power of mapping in the northern Limpopo Province of South Africa to support a modern identity of a presettler empty landscape. While this form of clearance has its roots in the colonial period, the current State's goal of giving land back to the people who were forcibly removed from their lands conflicts with the economic goal of attracting tourists to a pristine African past and landscape. This chapter considers the ways the region has been mapped, first by missionaries but more recently by conservationists and archaeologists, who are also implicated in the myth of an empty landscape.

In chapter 5, Morris considers the Driekopseiland rock engraving site in the Northern Cape of South Africa in recounting the colonial evictions and forced removals of the Khoe-San people from this area. Early colonial settlers played a role in this disenfranchisement, and a century's worth of agricultural practices further added to the Khoe-San people's sense of alienation. That the archaeological interpretations of the enigmatic engravings have failed to draw on the insights of the indigenous people and to communicate findings outside of the discipline suggests that archaeology too plays a role in absenting the Khoe-San people from their links to this site.

Guernsey's chapter (chapter 6) on the colonial process of land appropriation in British Columbia, Canada, outlines how the ideology of wilderness was at the heart of the land clearances, and how the First Nations peoples were removed from their lands and forced on to marginal reserve lands that were mapped as separate from the lands of the colonial settlers. Guernsey argues that these evictions still have contemporary implications as land treaties between the First Nations peoples and the government continue to negotiate the rights to the land and its resources.

It cannot be assumed that these attempts to colonize peoples and places went unresisted. To do so would be to assume that the local populations were agentless in their sense of place, belonging, and identity. Thus in part 3 of this volume the chapters represent the ways in which the aims to clear landscapes were contested and resisted.

In chapter 7, Nairouz provides, through an ethnoarchaeological study, a powerful account of how the writing of the archaeological record itself can be an act of resistance to the clearing of people from their homes. Nairouz argues that Palestinians have been ignored in the writing of their own history and that Palestinian archaeologists never seriously had the chance to participate in excavating their past, or interpreting it from their own perspective. This study of stone structures in the central West Bank of Palestine highlights the necessity of including indigenous people in archaeological research in order to rethink the past based on the living archaeology of the people who are still adding to the material archaeological record.

Segadika (chapter 8) attempts to include the indigenous Batswapong people back into supposedly empty landscapes through his rich exploration of folklore and place-names. Using two examples, the Tswapong Hills and the Dimomo Cave in East Central Botswana, Segadika illustrates that though archaeologists would presume this land to have been empty of past human occupation, it is nevertheless rich in cultural meaning often linked to ancestral spirits. Far from being empty, creation stories, folklores, and myths are land markers in defining and contesting territoriality and gender relations. Segadika argues that emptiness and fullness is, therefore, in the mind of the beholder.

In chapter 9, Read paints the complex story of evictions and clearances in Australia as indigenous urban camps are bulldozed overnight, streets are destroyed by freeways, suburbs by "slum clearance," and towns by inundation for irrigation dams. Read, a historian, reviews the shattering psychological impact of Australian human clearances where often there is nothing left to remind survivors or later generations of what once had been. However, there is a sense of resisting this loss as Read looks at the revitalization of cleared landscapes and the reoccupation (and simultaneous remaking or restructuring) of these lands. This is done through a variety of means, including heritage management and tourism as well as through doing archaeology and making public the findings.

The focus in the final chapters is also on the revitalization of cleared lands, either by the original indigenous people or by newcomers. In chapter 10, Lelong illustrates, through the ethnography of an archaeological survey, the links between the past and the present. The nineteenth-century Highland Clearances of northern Scotland emptied the land now perceived as romantic wilderness. However, Lelong argues that these lands are far from blank: they carry multiple layers of meaning. Peppered with archaeological remains, they continue to attract the attention of archaeologists. Moreover, people living on and around the cleared lands endow them with significance and, in some cases, the depopulated landscape becomes a monument to the past. People are also reinhabiting these lands by engaging with them as crofters, fishermen, or artists, or as those involved in tourism or interested in natural science. They respond to the land's aesthetic qualities, topography, natural resources, and habitats as well as to its history to create new and different senses of place, and therefore living landscapes in the present.

Price (chapter 11) also engages in a discussion of the complexity of revitalization. At the end of the Great War (1914–1918), the land along the western front in France and Belgium, devastated by bombardment and containing the unlocated bodies of millions of soldiers from around the world, was meant to be preserved as an uninhabited memorial "Red Zone." However, new resettlement has seen the eradication of the war landscape in favor of economic stability. While British descendant groups make accusations of sacrilege, the problem arises from the treatment of human remains as state property by both the French and British governments that excludes descendants from any decisions concerning the recovery and reburial of their ancestors. Archaeological recovery of the bodies of individual soldiers is an act of reclaiming the individuality of the nameless dead.

In chapter 12, Zimmerman and Makes Strong Move explore first the removal and then the restoration of the Siouan-speaking people, the Ioway, from the Effigy Mounds area of northeastern Iowa (USA). Once a ritual center of 195 mounds, this area sits on lands near what in the 1830s became Iowa's "Neutral Ground," where the government forced three groups, the Ho-Chunk (Winnebago), the eastern Dakota, and the Meskwakis to reside, thus pushing out the Ioway from the area. Ultimately all these groups were removed to open the land to white settlement. In 1999, there was an official reestablishment of an indigenous presence at the Effigy Mounds National Monument (EMNM) in the form of an Indian Heritage Festival, and in 2004 by a Sacred Sites Symposium.

Using historical memory, archaeology, and commemoration, the authors examine the symbolic nature of the restoration.

The clearance of landscapes, then, is about the material and social expression of ideologies and of community and/or individual experiences. Clearance of landscapes is about rupturing the sense of belonging, home, identity, and meaning; it is about the politics of remembering and the politics of forgetting; it is about violence, colonialism, forced movement, and removals; and it is about postcolonialism, diaspora, migration, asylum seekers, and refugees. The clearance of landscapes is a constant in both the past and the present. All landscapes are constantly "occupied" and simultaneously "cleared" from the past and into the present. In this book we are able to think about the impact of studying clearance in a postcolonial world, and in doing so, work towards understanding contemporary diasporic people and their experiences.

While anthropologists, among others, today focus on the effects of losing that sense of rootedness in the attachment to one's home landscape, archaeologists might do better at thinking critically about the impact and significance of cleared landscapes; they might think about how and why the archaeological landscapes they study were cleared of habitation and how the act of archaeology might help to further remove or help to revitalize the lived experiences of the landscapes as they were.

REFERENCES

Abu El Haj, Nadia. 2001. *Facts on the Ground: Archaeological Practice and Territorial Self-Fashioning in Israeli Society.* Chicago University Press, Chicago.

Bender, Barbara. 1993. *Landscape: Politics and Perspectives.* Berg, Providence.

———. 1998. *Stonehenge: Making Space.* Berg, Oxford.

———. 2001. Landscapes On-the-Move. *Journal of Social Archaeology* 1(1):75–99.

Bender, Barbara, and Margot Winer (editors). 2001. *Contested Landscapes: Movement, Exile and Place.* Berg, Oxford.

Certeau, Michel de. 1984. *The Practice of Everyday Life.* University of California Press, Berkeley.

Clarke, David. 1977a. Spatial Information in Archaeology. In *Spatial Archaeology*, ed. by D.L. Clarke, pp. 1–32. Academic Press, New York.

Clarke, David (editor). 1977b. *Spatial Archaeology.* Academic Press, New York.

Delle, James. 1998. *An Archaeology of Social Space.* Plenum Press, New York.

Downs, Roger, and David Stea. 1977. *Maps in the Minds: Reflections on Cognitive Mapping.* Harper and Row, New York.

Featherstone, Mike. 1993. Global and Local Cultures. In *Mapping the Futures: Local Cultures, Global Change*, ed. by Jon Bird, Barry Curtis, Tim Putnam, George Robertson, and Lisa Tickner, pp. 169–187. Routledge, London.

Gould, Peter, and Rodney White. 1974. *Mental Maps.* Penguin Books, New York.

Harris, Cole. 2002. *Making Native Space—Colonialism, Resistance, and Reserves in British Columbia.* University of British Columbia Press, Vancouver.

Hirsch, Eric, and Michael O'Hanlon (editors). 1995. *The Anthropology of Landscape: Perspectives on Place and Space.* Clarendon Press, Oxford.

Hodder, Ian, and Clive Orton. 1976. *Spatial Analysis in Archaeology*. Cambridge University Press, Cambridge.

Hood, Edward. 1996. Social Relations and the Cultural Landscape. In *Landscape Archaeology: Reading and Interpreting the American Historical Landscape,* ed. by R. Yamin and K. Berscherer Metheny, pp. 121–146. University of Tennessee Press, Knoxville.

Ingold, Tim. 1993. The Temporality of the Landscape. *World Archaeology* 25(2):152–174.

Lovell, Nadia. 1998. Introduction. In *Locality and Belonging,* ed. by N. Lovell, pp. 1–24. Routledge, London.

Orser, Charles E. 2005. An Archaeology of a Famine-Era Eviction. *New Hibernia Review* 9(1):45–58.

Ryden, Kent. 1993. *Mapping the Invisible Landscape*. University of Iowa Press, Iowa City.

Schiffer, Michael B. 1972. Archaeological Context and Systemic Context. *American Antiquity* 37:156–165.

———. 1987. *Formation Processes of the Archaeological Record*. University of New Mexico Press, Albuquerque.

Soja, Edward. 1989. *Postmodern Geographies*. Verso, London.

Smith, Neil. 1993. Homeless/Global: Scaling Places. In *Mapping the Futures: Local Cultures, Global Change*, ed. by Jon Bird, Barry Curtis, Tim Putnam, George Robertson, and Lisa Tickner, pp. 87–119. Routledge, London.

Thomas, Julian. 1993. The Politics of Vision and the Archaeologies of Landscape. In *Landscape: Politics and Perspectives*, ed. by Barbara Bender, pp. 19–48. Berg, Providence.

———. 1996. *Time, Culture and Identity: An Interpretive Archaeology*. Routledge, London.

Tilley, Christopher. 1994. *Phenomenology of Landscape: Places, Paths and Monuments*. Berg Publishers, Oxford.

Tuan, Yi-Fu. 1977. *Space and Place: The Perspective of Experience*. University of Minnesota Press, Minneapolis.

Ucko, Peter, and Robert Layton (editors). 1999. *The Archaeology and Anthropology of Landscape: Shaping Your Landscape*. Routledge, London.

CHAPTER 2

Abandoned, Avoided, Expelled: The Creation of "Empty" Landscapes

Amy Gazin-Schwartz

People today so intensively occupy the land, filling inhabited places and investing every inch of those places with cultural meanings, that we have come to associate empty landscapes with nature. We contrast occupied land with wilderness, and productivity with barrenness. Yet archaeology and anthropology demonstrate that few empty landscapes were historically empty or devoid of cultural meaning. Where today we may see only low rock foundations, postholes, cold hearths, and quiet, forgotten tombs people once prepared meals, built shelters, raised children, negotiated kinship and other social relationships, buried their dead, and dealt with the supernatural.

Most archaeological thinking about empty landscapes emphasizes the environmental, economic, and sometimes political causes of what is usually referred to as abandonment or regional depopulation (for examples, see Burgess 1980; Cameron and Tomka 1993; Cordell 1984; Cunliff 2000; Nelson and Hegmon 2001). Yet archaeologists can not only address the reasons why landscapes become empty, but also develop formulations to understand the lived experiences of people in those landscapes. Economic, environmental, and political analyses may help to explain why landscapes become empty, but they are not adequate to describe the variations in the lived, social experiences of the people who once lived in those landscapes. In this chapter, I aim to further develop and make more textured the processes of emptying that are currently condensed into a single category of abandonment (Cameron and Tomka 1993; Cobb and Butler 2002; Nelson and Hegmon 2001; Orser 2005). I will distinguish three processes through which people might create empty landscapes: abandonment, avoidance, and expulsion. These processes are thought of as differentiated responses by people living in a particular context in a particular landscape. I will develop an understanding of these processes in terms of several variables that serve to develop a more textured understanding of how a particular landscape was emptied: the cultural or environmental changes that underlie clearance; how people responded to those changes and why people responded in the ways they did; and the locus of decision making around leaving a landscape. I will then consider archaeological signatures of the three categories and use examples from the landscapes of the Isle of Raasay in Scotland to illustrate these processes and their ideological consequences.

EMPTY LANDSCAPES

The complex and contested term *landscape* has been defined elsewhere in this volume (Smith, chapter 1). Empty landscapes seem to be landscapes from which human activity has disappeared. They may be considered natural, as in wilderness regions uninhabited by people, dominated by wild animals and seemingly natural flora. Often these "wilderness" regions are actually modern social or political creations. National parks in the US or areas of Natural Heritage in Scotland are such landscapes. We tend to think they are remnants of original nature, often not recognizing the profound changes that past human activity left on the land (Ralston 1998).

The assumption is often that empty landscapes are depopulated and no longer part of the cultural world. They appear either to be remnants of nature or to be in the process of returning to nature. That this interpretation is often invalid has been documented in many places, including the other papers in this volume (for other examples, see Basso 1996; Carmichael, Hubert, Reeves, and Schanche 1994; Smout 2000). As these studies demonstrate, many apparently empty landscapes are the foci of mythological, religious, or historical meanings. What appears empty to a visitor or to someone unfamiliar with the landscape may be full of meaning to local people, or to descendants of people who once lived there.

ARCHAEOLOGICAL PARADIGMS OF ABANDONMENT AND THE PROBLEM OF NEW CATEGORIES

Much archaeological analysis seeks to explain why landscapes are empty (Cameron and Tomka 1993; Cobb and Butler 2002; Nelson and Hegmon 2001). It is not my intention to explicate these models in depth here, but rather to offer a brief summary of their characteristics as a background to my discussion of a different question, what are the different social experiences of different routes to emptying a landscape?

Current models link demographic change, environmental degradation, and social instability to explain why landscapes are depopulated. Archaeological evidence for subsistence systems and practices, settlement patterns, regional continuities and discontinuities in artifact styles or production, and environmental changes support these models in a number of places. In North America, for example, these changes have been studied particularly with regard to the later prehistoric Southwest, where movements of Ancestral Pueblo peoples have been linked to periods of drought and conflict (Cameron and Tomka 1993; Cordell 1984; Cunliff 2000; Nelson and Hegmon 2001). In Britain, depopulation of upland regions in the later Bronze Age of southern England has been linked to increasingly wet climatic conditions and human-induced environmental degradation (for examples, see Barrett 1994; Burgess 1980). Climate and environmental degradation are also suggested as the cause for the seventeenth- and eighteenth-century abandonment of upland farms in southern Scotland (Parry and Carter 1985).

In archaeology, the study of formation processes details the material expression of site depopulation (Schiffer 1987). By interpreting the processes through which material culture is deposited at a site, we can better understand how a site was created and, by extension, how the site came to be empty. Case studies in Cameron and Tomka (1993), for example, use Schiffer's analysis of refuse to distinguish between sites abandoned intentionally over a short period of time, sites abandoned only seasonally, and sites abandoned slowly over a long period of time.

These studies provide valuable insight into some of the reasons why people leave a region, and point to the complexities of understanding population movements. Environmental changes, economic changes, and sociopolitical changes interact in complex ways and may provide the impetus for the emptying of landscapes. However, a focus on the economic, environmental, and sociopolitical causes of depopulation tends to reduce the differentiated historical processes into one seemingly rational, but also inevitable, course of action. It does not adequately describe the variations in the social experience of depopulation. If we accept that people in the past, as well as in the present, were active participants in constructing their cultures, then we want to understand how they negotiated the complex problems of environment, economy, social relationships, and landscape use. By further analyzing the category of abandonment, and considering that landscapes may be emptied through a number of more narrowly defined processes, we may develop a more nuanced approach to the cultural meanings of empty landscapes.

DISTINGUISHING ABANDONMENT, AVOIDANCE, AND EXPULSION

Abandonment, avoidance, and expulsion are three different processes by which people might leave a landscape. These processes can be differentiated by a matrix of variables that serves to describe the experiences of the people leaving a particular landscape. This matrix is comprised of three variables: the precipitating cause, the particular response people make to the cause, and the locus of decision making about the response. I will first characterize these variables before discussing how the three processes differ.

Cause of Emptying

Inhabited landscapes become empty due to environmental or cultural changes. The models for depopulation described above mostly deal with the causes for emptying. They provide formulations about what happened that made people leave or avoid the landscape. They serve to account for the objective conditions, the events, changes, or continuities that led to the landscape becoming (or remaining) empty. The cause is what happened to make people change how they engaged with the landscape.

Response

How people choose to respond to these changes is a second variable to consider. As the studies cited above discuss, depopulation may be a rapid process or may be the result of a slow decline in population. It is necessary also to consider why people decide to respond to environmental or cultural change in one way rather than another—why empty the landscape rather than develop another way of coping with the changes? In considering how and why people respond to changes by emptying a landscape, we might consider what they were seeking, what they were escaping, what they wanted to accomplish through emptying the landscape, and how they experienced the process of emptying.

Locus of Decision Making

A third variable is who decides how to respond to environmental or cultural changes. Investigating the locus of decision making recognizes that people's decisions about how to respond to changes may be autonomous, may be entirely imposed by outsiders, or may be constrained by forces both internal and external to individuals and the community. While environmental, economic, and political models postulate the seemingly rational or empirically objective nature of landscape depopulation, we know historically that the locus of decision making varies. Decisions may be made on the individual, household, or community level, or they may be imposed from outside the community. Decisions are rarely uncontested. Further, rational decisions are subject to cultural rules. People may take action based on emotional responses, or their actions may be governed by beliefs about supernatural powers or about social and cultural rules.

These variables interact differently in the context of the three processes through which landscapes may be emptied. In the following sections,

I will consider how these three variables differ in the cases of landscapes that people abandoned, those that people avoided, and those from which people have been expelled.

ABANDONED

Abandonment involves leaving home, a known landscape invested with meaning, for somewhere else. It can be distinguished from avoidance and expulsion most clearly in terms of the locus of decision making and people's responses to change.

The cause of abandonment is generally formulated in terms of economic, social, biological, and environmental change. Economic change can include changes in the use or production of particular resources. For example, shifting from foraging to agriculture will make some landscapes more useful and lead to the apparent abandonment of others where the resources are no longer as valuable; a shift from agriculture to pastoralism or to foraging will again change the economic value of particular kinds of landscapes.

Social changes may also lead to abandonment of landscapes. Population increase or decrease, internal social conflict, and changes in the intensity of social networks may lead to abandonment of parts of settlements, whole settlements, or entire landscapes. These social changes may be tied also to economic and environmental changes. Population increase beyond the economic capacity of the environment would require either intensification of production or the abandonment of that environment for somewhere more productive. Population decrease may lead to abandonment because there is no longer a need to occupy an expansive region, or because there are not enough people to perform the work required to live on that landscape. Changes in the intensity of social networks might lead to settlement aggregation, with people abandoning a landscape of dispersed settlements in favor of more aggregated settlements (Evans 2003:111). Conflict within communities, on the other hand, may lead to the dispersal of a population and the abandonment of one landscape for another.

Sometimes settlements can be abandoned for biological reasons. Disease may depopulate a settlement, and people may abandon landscapes because they associate them with the presence or virulence of disease.

People choose to respond to environmental, social, or cultural changes by abandoning landscapes because they believe that the situation will be better somewhere else. Different landscapes are understood and explained as better or worse for particular economic activities in part based on the ecological qualities of those landscapes, and in part based on cultural values associated with the landscapes and the activities that take place in them. For example, movement and use of pastures may be contrasted with permanent settlement and differently valued depending on how intensely people want to maintain social integration (Evans 2003:111). Abandoning a landscape may then be chosen because of cultural values surrounding population density or social changes.

The variable that most distinguishes abandonment as a process of emptying landscapes from other processes is the locus of decision making. Abandonment should be understood as an act undertaken by people themselves, rather than something imposed on them by others. The locus of decision making may be individuals, families, households, or communities, and there could well be conflict among individuals and within the community about what decision to make. The cause of abandonment may indeed be external environmental and cultural change, but how to respond to change is experienced as an autonomous decision. Think of dairy farmers in New England, for example. External realities of the market for milk, the cost of feeding animals, transportation costs, property values, the pressure of development, and the structure of bank loans all may be external factors in the economic pressures farmers face in trying to continue farming. The decision to sell the farm and take up other employment, however, is an individual and family decision. It is certainly overdetermined, and the farmer may experience the decision as the only one that makes sense, but it is still an autonomous and considered decision. Similarly, eighteenth-century farmers in the Lammermuir Hills of Scotland faced a number of external pressures, including in this case the fact that they probably did not own the land they farmed but owed rents to absentee and increasingly demanding landlords. Yet they do not seem to have been evicted from their farms, as was to happen later in many parts of Scotland. Rather, they seem to have evaluated their varied opportunities, varied pressures, and social contexts and to have decided to abandon the uplands for other occupations elsewhere (Evans 2003:111–112).

AVOIDED

Avoidance is differentiated from the other forms of emptying by some continuity in cultural beliefs about features or elements of the landscape that prohibits its use. People avoid a landscape because they continue to hold to memories, beliefs, or experiences that are associated with the causes and motivations for avoiding it.

Avoiding landscapes is often a response to beliefs about their inherent natural or supernatural danger. With cultural factors like taboos and biological factors like death and illness as causes for avoiding landscapes, people respond for self-protection from the natural and supernatural forces that are believed to inhere to those landscapes. Such areas have ritual significance, and access may be strictly limited or prohibited altogether.

Rules about access may be reinforced with ideology about danger from supernatural forces or from natural elements, or both. Places associated with death may be avoided because they are thought to be haunted by the spirits of the dead, and therefore dangerous. These places may also be avoided because only certain individuals have the ritual authority to engage with the dead ancestors. Other places, like cliffs, swamps, or caverns, may be avoided because the places pose physical dangers to people.

While the explanation for deciding to avoid such landscapes is found in ideology, the locus for decision making may be restricted to individuals with particular authority or may be available to any member of the community. Decisions made by individuals endowed with ritual authority may be enforced by that authority. On the other hand, rules about access and avoidance may be part of everyday knowledge, subject to the same variation in individual adherence as other cultural norms. Avoidance is thus not always absolute. Different individuals may have the authority to use avoided landscapes, or different individuals may decide they don't have to follow cultural rules about avoiding those landscapes.

EXPELLED

Expulsion is another process caused by cultural and economic change. In all cases, expulsion is the product of conflict through which people lose their rights to land. People may be expelled through two main processes: the first is warfare or colonization, actions in which people lose their right or ability to occupy the landscape through being conquered by another group that claims the land. Conquest brings with it the subjugation of indigenous peoples (Guernsey, this volume; Read, this volume; Zimmerman and Makes Strong Move, this volume). It is often accompanied by the replacement of an indigenous population by a new population. Colonial enterprises across the globe demonstrate this process.

The second process through which people may be expelled involves economic and social changes that produce shifts in land ownership or in how the landscape is perceived by landowners. This process can lead to changes in how the landscape is used and to depopulation through eviction. Eviction legally eliminates people's rights to land.

In response to these changes, people often have quite limited choices. Emptying the landscape (or leaving it for others to inhabit) may often be the only response possible. In the case of conquest, people may choose to flee or to stay and fight, but their range of choice is strongly restricted. They experience the choice as a choice of life or death, not as a choice between different ways to live. Eviction implies legal and coercive authority behind emptying, which again limits the ways people might respond. People often attempted to resist eviction in nineteenth-century

Ireland (Orser 2005) and Scotland (Richards 2000), but they almost never managed to stay on the land.

In these cases of conquest, warfare, and political-economic change, the locus of decision making about whether to leave a settlement and landscape or to stay is external to the community of people who live there. Once land is claimed, either through warfare, colonization, or legally, residents are subject to the will of others primarily because they do not own the land they inhabit. Expulsion implies the presence of a coercive agent that decides to remove people from the landscape.

CASE STUDY: ABANDONED, AVOIDED, AND EXPELLED LANDSCAPES IN RAASAY, SCOTLAND

The three variables (cause, response, and locus of decision making) function as a matrix of factors that can be used to think about the particular nature of a given landscape and the experiences of the people who left the landscape.

Economic, environmental, and political analysis may provide a causal impetus for these emptying processes, but they are not adequate to describe the variation in social experiences these processes represent. By developing a matrix of data organized by the three variations of experience and drawn from archaeological, historical, and oral traditional sources, we can generate questions and formulations about the lived experiences of the processes of emptying landscapes. Using examples from the Isle of Raasay, Scotland, I will demonstrate how this matrix approach can be used to develop a more textured understanding of emptying processes.

The Isle of Raasay, off the northwest coast of Scotland, provides examples of all three of the processes through which landscapes may be emptied. Raasay is a small island, approximately 4 miles east-west by 12 miles north-south, located between the Scottish mainland and the Isle of Skye. Raasay has been occupied since the Mesolithic period about 10,000 BP. Today, however, most of Raasay is empty of occupation. The current population of about 200 people lives mostly along the southern and western shores of the island. A few individual holiday houses are scattered throughout the rest of the island, often at the location of earlier settlements, but these are occupied only seasonally or occasionally. To the casual visitor or tourist, and to archaeologists, Raasay is largely an empty landscape.

Since 1994 the island has been the subject of annual archaeological surveys by the Association of Certificated Field Archaeologists under the direction of John Macdonald and Scott Wood (Macdonald and

Wood 1995–2000, 2002–2006). As of 2006, these surveys have identified over 900 features and sites from all periods of prehistory and history. These features include rockshelters inhabited by Mesolithic foragers, Neolithic chambered tombs, prehistoric hut circles and field systems, medieval chapels and carved stones, and medieval and postmedieval farmsteads, settlements, shielings, and field systems. Nearly all of these are in landscapes that are now empty of human habitation, though they may still be used for grazing some sheep and cattle. I will describe three particular areas of Raasay and how they may have become empty.

The Abandoned North End

The northern part of Raasay is geologically distinct from the southern part, being formed of Torridonian sandstone and Lewisian gneiss, some of the oldest rock in Scotland. The thin soils that form on these rocks have little potential for agriculture, and it would never have been easy for farmers to make a living there (Golightly 2002). Nevertheless, the remains of six townships (Torran, Arnish, Umachan, Doire Dubh, Kyle Rona, and Tigh an Achaidh) are visible on the ground. Arnish, the most southerly of these townships, is the only one named in a 1596 charter of James VI (Sharpe 1977). Most of them seem to have been founded in the eighteenth and nineteenth centuries by people who had previously lived in the southern part of the island; Arnish, Torran, Umachan, and Kyle Rona are all marked on an 1846 estate map of Raasay, Fladda, and Tighe (National Archives of Scotland: Register House Plan 1308). It is worth noting that, in contrast to the southern portion of the island, none of the hills or lochs in the northern part are named on this map.

Testimony by residents to the Royal Commission of Inquiry into the Condition of Crofters and Cottars in the Highlands and Islands (commonly referred to as the Napier Commission) speaks to the bleak and difficult living here.

> .We would take the example from those who were in bondage, and who were sighing in their bondage, and wishing for liberty. The Israelites before were in bondage, but there was One above who heard the sighing of those in bondage, and fixed the time for coming for their deliverance. We are oppressed with cultivating bad land, which yields no crop, which does not return to us the value of our work. There are many reasons for that, the way the island is circumstanced. (Charles McLeod, crofter and fisherman, Arnish, testimony to the Napier Commission, 1883)
> I have only to say what the rest have said, that it is poverty sent me here—that I am situated on bad ground, and little of it, and too dear, and that for a long time. In my own memory, it was five families who were in the township numbering twenty-nine individuals, and to-day there are ten families and eighty individuals. (Donald M'Leod, crofter, Kyle Rona, testimony to the Napier Commission, 1883)

These townships were abandoned beginning in the early twentieth century, and finally in the 1960s. The cause for the abandonment was cultural change. Some of the crofters from the northern part of the island, returning from the First World War, claimed the better lands their ancestors had been evicted from around Eyre on the southern tip of the island. Subsequently known as the Raiders, these men were at first arrested and charged with trespassing; later they were awarded the tenancy of the land, on which they built houses and established crofts. The land reforms that came about as a result of the Napier Commission's recommendations gave crofters heritable rights to their holdings. Changing economic conditions, along with changes in the ownership of the island, made it possible for crofters to move onto the better agricultural lands of the southern half of the island. Perhaps the most important change, however, was the increase in the availability of jobs elsewhere, including off the island, during and after the Second World War. Many young people who grew up in Kyle Rona, Tigh an Achaidh, Torran, and Arnish left the island to join the military during the war and to work in the cities of mainland Scotland afterwards. While people had periodically left Raasay for work elsewhere, it seems that after the Second World War more of these young people spent much of their adult life abroad. This emigration of young people meant that the population in the northern townships was aging. It was always difficult to make a living there. In addition, it was hard for residents to travel to other parts of the island to work or to attend school or church. There were no roads to this part of the island until one man, Calum MacLeod, built a road to Arnish himself in the 1960s. As the population dwindled and aged, they also lost facilities like churches and schools, making it more unlikely that young people would return to their childhood homes. Thus, cultural changes off the island, as well as on the island, created different conditions under which people made decisions about where to live.

People responded to these cultural changes by abandoning the northern part of the island because they desired an easier or better life elsewhere. Despite attachment to the landscape they grew up in, documented not only in the building of Calum's Road but in recent memoirs (Mackenzie 2000; Nicolson 1989; Raasay Heritage Trust 2001), it was certain that the poor lands of the northern part of the island would not support the number of people who would have had to make a living there. As they had done throughout history, people chose to stay or to emigrate depending on what they thought would be best for their families.

> The family left Achadh in 1942, as father could not manage on his own; we had all volunteered for the forces: John, Chrissie, Sheila and myself. He sold his motor launch. It was easier to get home when we lived at Rudha na Cloicheadh, which was right beside the pier. (Mackay 2001:36)

The locus of decision making in this case was with local individuals and their families, who decided to abandon these settlements and landscapes at the north end of Raasay. Later they are remembered with nostalgia, but also with recognition of how hard life was.

> On reflection it seemed like quite idyllic times, yet life was hard, but having no comparison then, we were very content with our lot. Now we have hot and cold water, flushing toilets, electricity and all the appliances that go with it, yet we seem to have less time to enjoy the short life that we have. (Mackay 2001:39)

Avoided: The Prehistoric Plateau at Doire Domhain

Doire Domhain refers to a farmstead on the western slope of Raasay. More generally, I am using the place-name to refer to an area extending from this farmstead north towards the deserted townships of Manish More and Manish Beg. This area is characterized by a series of plateaus running roughly north-south, stepping down from the central ridge of hills to the west coast of the island. ACFA surveyed this section of the island in 1997 (Macdonald and Wood 1997). The survey identified both historic and prehistoric sites, including dispersed houses, enclosures, a small historic period settlement, and prehistoric (Bronze Age or Iron Age) hut circles, field systems, and possible cairns. Prehistoric and historic period sites may be distinguished by the structural forms (prehistoric houses being circular and historic ones rectangular in plan) and perhaps by the preservation of the structures and field walls, assuming that the older prehistoric walls are more denuded than the more recent ones. In addition, it is generally assumed that the prehistoric fields are characterized by narrower rig (ridge and furrow) than historic fields.

Taking these dimensions to distinguish prehistoric and historic sites, the survey suggests a discontinuous pattern of settlement in one area of Doire Domhain. Bronze and Iron Age sites are distributed along the highest, most easterly plateau, while medieval and postmedieval historic sites are scattered along the two plateaus to the west (and downslope) from this plateau.

Although two to three thousand years ago, the easterly, more elevated plateau was clearly occupied, three factors may have caused this plateau to be avoided in historic times. One is environmental: microclimatic conditions at the higher and more exposed elevation may have made settlement and agriculture there more difficult in historic times than in the generally warmer prehistoric periods. A second impetus might have been economic. If later people were more involved in fishing than earlier settlers had been, we would expect their settlements to be located closer to the sea. A third impetus can be found in Scottish folklore referring to prehistoric sites. Often people believed that fairies or other supernatural folk inhabited these sites. Folklore specifically warns against disturbing prehistoric cairns (Gazin-Schwartz 1999).

People might have avoided this higher plateau in historic times for both practical and supernatural reasons. They may have sought sites that offered more protection from the elements, as is suggested by the fact that later houses seemed to be tucked behind knolls rather than in the open areas where prehistoric houses are located. Secondly, if people were fishing for part of their living, then the focus of their attention would be the sea rather than inland. Not only would they choose to settle closer to the sea, but they may have avoided more exposed areas that would also be more visible from the sea. In this case they may have desired not only protection from the elements, but also perhaps from the attention of unfriendly people on the sea. Finally, if the higher, easterly plateau was avoided in historic times because it was associated with supernatural beings or powers, then the motivation for this avoidance (and the historic emptiness of the landscape) could be fear of the unknown. The prevalence of prehistoric sites on this plateau may have made it a dangerous place for settlement. Though the area would then be devoid of historic settlement, it would not have been empty of cultural meaning. Folklore speaks of people pouring milk or other offerings onto chambered tombs, or engaging the power of prehistoric sites to seal agreements or provide cures (Gazin-Schwartz 1999). The lack of archaeologically visible settlement remains may disguise ongoing cultural engagement with the landscape.

The locus of decision making about whether to avoid the landscape, then, would be individuals, but strongly influenced by cultural values and family rules. Especially in contexts where an area is viewed as dangerous, decisions about using that landscape would be strongly conditioned by ideology.

In contrast to the north end, or to the interior and eastern half of the island, the area around Doire Domhain remains largely unmarked by historically known names. This suggests that the area was more lightly used in historic times. However, the people who last lived there left the island in the nineteenth century, and they may have taken the place-names and stories with them. It would be unwise to assume that the lack of names reflects a lack of historic significance.

Expelled: Hallaig and the Raasay Clearances

The township of Hallaig was located on the east coast of Raasay, on quite steeply sloping ground below cliffs. To the east, the ground drops abruptly to the sea. Along with twenty other named places on the southern half of the island, Hallaig first appears as a named settlement in a 1596 charter (Sharpe 1977), and it is recorded as a settlement in all later enumerations until 1891. In the 1830s, the township built a school and petitioned the Gaelic School Society for a teacher, saying they would have 60 scholars in the schoolhouse (Macdonald and Wood 2004:8). An 1846 estate map of Raasay (National Archives of Scotland: Register House Plan 1308) shows upper and lower Hallaig and indicates 26 inhabited houses in lower Hallaig, and two in upper Hallaig. In the 1871 and 1881 census returns, only one shepherd and his family are recorded living at Hallaig; by 1891, the township and the lands surrounding it are empty (Macdonald and Wood 2004:8).

Hallaig became empty because landowners expelled people from the settlement. According to the 1841 Census Enumeration, upper Hallaig had been "cleared" by the last MacLeod chief of Raasay in 1841, and most of the people emigrated. Following poor harvests in the 1840s (perhaps due to the same potato blight that also caused the famine in Ireland), more people emigrated from Hallaig. Five families sailed on the ship Edward Johnstone from Liverpool to Australia in 1854. By 1861, the township was entirely cleared, the lands used for a sheep farm, and the people removed to Skye and to the northern part of Raasay (Macdonald and Wood 2004:8).

Throughout the Highlands of Scotland, landowners in the first half of the nineteenth century were evicting people from townships, forcing them to emigrate or to move to other regions. The impetus for these evictions can be found in the political and economic changes among the elite lairds and landowners in the eighteenth and nineteenth centuries and changes in concepts of land ownership which disrupted the social understanding between chiefs and tenants. In the Middle Ages, the chiefs were believed to hold the clan or community land in trust for all clan members. As the chiefs began to participate in urban, lowland elite society, they began to consider themselves landlords and to gain documented legal rights to the land. They then thought of the people who occupied their land as rent-paying tenants rather than tribute-paying clan members and turned to them for the money necessary for urban life (Dodgshon 1998). These legal changes happened relatively rapidly, and may be juxtaposed to the tenants' longstanding traditional model of rights based on mutual interdependence. Tenants like the residents of Hallaig thus had to change some of their own practices in order to raise funds for rent. By the nineteenth century, most landowners believed they could gain more profit from their lands by running them as sheep farms, and they used their newly documented legal rights to land to evict their tenants in favor of thousands of sheep managed by one or two shepherds, who often were lowlanders.

In addition, however, it seems clear that by the 1830s Hallaig, like many other Highland townships, was quite severely overpopulated. Combined with poor harvests in the 1830s and 1840s and increasing demands for cash rent, this overpopulation meant that people found it increasingly difficult to support themselves. Economic changes, social changes, and demographic changes combined to legally expel people from the lands their families had inhabited for hundreds of years.

The response to these cultural changes depends on whether we are considering the landlords or the people of the townships. Landowners desired to become "modern" and to participate more fully in urban, elite society and politics. The landowners increasingly were absent from island life. Their connections to the traditional paradigms of interdependent natural rights to the land weakened, and they took up the model of landlord/tenant, the rights of each defined by law. On the part of the people removed, responses and the reasons they made those responses were more complex. At least in the early part of the clearance of Hallaig, it seems that removal was at least partially voluntary, a response to the pressure and hardships of life in the township. In that case, the removal was more like abandonment, with the exception that people did not initially choose to leave their homes, but were either ordered to leave or strongly encouraged to leave. Later evictions, however, were less voluntary, and in those cases people did not want to leave; they were removed to other, less hospitable parts of the island where it was much more difficult to make a living. After people had left upper Hallaig, it must have decreased the overcrowding. People in lower Hallaig would then have had more land to farm and on which to graze their animals, and they would have had little motivation to move to the northern part of the island where land was so much poorer. One method to force these removals, imposed by the later nineteenth-century landlord Mr. Rainey (also spelled Rainy), was to prohibit people from marrying.

> Mr. Rainy enacted a rule that no one should marry in the island. There was one man there who married in spite of him, and because he did so, he put him out of his father's house, and that man went to a bothy—to a sheep cot. Mr. Rainy then came and demolished the sheep cot upon him, and extinguished his fire, and neither friend nor any one else dared give him a night's shelter. He was not allowed entrance into any house. (Donald MacLeod, crofter, testimony to the Napier Commission, 1883)

Particularly when conducted by the clan chiefs, eviction must have been experienced as betrayal. The cultural changes that produced the urbanized elites destroyed the traditional ties between chiefs and people, creating instead ties between landlords and tenants (Dodgshon 1998). The chiefs were no longer thinking of themselves as protectors of their people, and the people experienced the evictions as the chief's forsaking traditional social ties.

While the landowners continued to be motivated to get a better cash return on their land, the residents of Hallaig had little motivation to move away. These decisions were largely imposed from outside. Testimony from the Napier Commission report is consistent about this:

> Did the people out of these fourteen townships that Rainy cleared go of their own accord?
> No, not at all. The people were very sorry to leave at that time. They were weeping and wailing and lamenting. They were taking haudfuls of grass that was growing over the graves of their families in the churchyard, as remembrances of their kindred. (Donald MacLeod, crofter, Kyle Rona, testimony to the Napier Commission, 1883)

John Munro, the minister in Raasay in 1883, also stated to the Commission that people were not willing to leave their homes, even though life was difficult for them. Even when the lands were over-crowded, many people did not choose to leave their homes, but had those choices made for them.

Today the Highland Clearances are a powerful symbol of oppression of the Scottish people, of loss, and of memory. The hardships imposed by landowners and the betrayal of traditional social relations is empha-sized; overpopulation and voluntary emigration are not. On the track to Hallaig, descendants of the residents have erected a monument with a plaque engraved with Sorley MacLean's poem "Hallaig." Today, Hallaig is a symbol of loss. (see http://www.sorleymaclean.org/english/poetry. htm for the text of the poem.)

As the case study of Raasay illustrates, the emptying of landscapes, which has generally been termed abandonment by archaeologists, may take place through a number of different processes. In Raasay, abandon-ment can be distinguished from avoidance or expulsion primarily through attention to the reasons people chose to leave a landscape, and through the locus of decision making about leaving. These two factors require archae-ologists to consider the personal and social experiences of depopulation and the social meanings attached to empty landscapes. Ideas about ances-tors, homelands, social orders, politics, and religion may all be attached to empty landscapes. The distinction between abandonment, avoidance, and expulsion contributes to a more textured understanding of how landscapes became empty in Raasay, and in other areas of Highland Scotland.

DISCUSSION: IDEOLOGY AND ARCHAEOLOGY

The condensed single category of abandonment can be further de-veloped and analyzed to understand the more textured processes that produce empty landscapes through consideration of a matrix of factors, including the changes that cause emptying, how people respond to those changes and why they respond in the ways they do, and the locus of decision making about those responses. This analysis suggests that abandonment is only one way landscapes are depopulated and that it can be distinguished from avoidance and expulsion, two other processes leading to empty landscapes. Such a distinction brings to the fore the experiences of people who create the empty landscapes.

People's experiences also have implications for how the landscapes are viewed after they become empty. The meanings people impose on or experience through the landscape are dynamic (Ingold 2000). Emptying the landscape may change those meanings, intensify them, or lead people to create entirely new meanings. The processes through which landscapes become empty will have different effects on how those landscapes are later conceived.

Ideologically, abandoned landscapes may become both places of memorialization and places that are rejected. Evans (2003:112) suggests that they can be remembered as ancestral landscapes and become sites of veneration. They may also become sites to be avoided as places now occupied by the ghosts or spirits.

An abandoned landscape may continue to serve as a resource base, so that we may find some evidence of continued use even when settlements are no longer inhabited (Cameron 1993). This use may be "practical," as in landscapes used for the procurement of resources, for farming, or for pasture. They may, alternatively, become ritual landscapes, as in sites for burials, seasonal ceremonies, or gatherings (Burgess 1980; Cordell 1984). Different segments of the previous populations may think of them in different ways, depending perhaps on what their experiences are after abandonment. People who chose to leave the Scottish island of St. Kilda seemed to think of it in both these ways—as their homeland and as a place that was harsh beyond bearing (Steel 1988). In this context, reuse of the empty landscape may be appropriate, or may be considered sacrilege.

We would expect that avoided landscapes would not show evidence of reuse as a resource base. Rather, continued use might be more ritual in nature and possibly restricted by belief, practice, or other social taboo.

When they have been expelled, people may regard the empty landscape as their lost homeland, and ideology surrounding it will include memorialization and political reinterpretation of the meanings of the landscape. Folklore and oral traditions may cast the conflict in heroic terms, excoriating the victors and valorizing the ancestral heroes who resisted the expulsion. The landscape may become the site for political action and the symbol of resistance.

Archaeologically, these processes produce overlapping and ambiguous material correlates. Because most archaeology to date has condensed these categories into one, the archaeological signatures of abandonment, avoidance, and expulsion require further research. The lack of excavation in Raasay means that understanding these processes from archaeological evidence is limited to interpreting the presence and condition of surface remains.

Abandonment, avoidance, and expulsion can theoretically be expected to produce differing archaeological evidence in the landscape and in any archaeological sites contained in that landscape. The materials left behind when settlements and landscapes are emptied, what Schiffer (1987) calls de facto refuse, should vary depending on the processes that led to the depopulation of a site or landscape.

The complexities of the process of abandonment, diverse motivations, and varied postabandonment ideals mean that archaeological signatures of abandonment are also likely to be varied and complex. When people decide to leave their homes and to move elsewhere, they are likely to take their most useful materials with them, leaving behind only those items they consider refuse and those items that are too heavy or difficult to carry, along with the permanent features of the settlements. Thus, we would expect to find midden materials, building foundations, field walls, pits, and items of little value or use. When the landscape was viewed as a source of curated resources, as described by Cameron (1993), fewer and fewer useful materials will remain over time. Archaeological remains of abandoned landscapes should be expected to favor features over artifacts, except for those artifacts that may have already been deposited as secondary refuse.

Avoided landscapes may be actually empty of archaeological features and materials (Bradley 2000; Segadika, this volume). Alternatively, there may be evidence for ritual attention to natural and cultural features of the landscape. When associated with ancestral homes, buildings and other structures that were once features of the landscape may continue to exist and be protected from damage by taboos on visiting, use, or modification. Evidence of the range of materials found in abandoned settlements may point to their being avoided. A full range of domestic and special artifacts may be found at such sites. In addition, such sites may have "odd" deposits (Bruck 1999) such as structured midden deposits or artifacts placed in unusual positions at the bottom of pits or in the entrances to enclosures. Such closing deposits are the products of ritual acts that seal the settlement and make it out of bounds for other people. Their continued presence in the archaeological record, particularly in the case of usable or valuable items, speaks to the avoidance of the site.

Archaeologically, landscapes from which people were expelled should contain evidence of conflict. While people who flee may leave behind most of their possessions, invaders may well loot sites, removing valuable goods for their own use. The conquerors may also reoccupy sites, showing up archaeologically as cultural change.

We would expect that people who were evicted would take most of their possessions with them. They were not going to return, and probably would not be allowed to return, so it would be unlikely that they would leave materials as caches for later use, as has been documented for other depopulated areas (Cameron 1993). Instead, as we know from the Napier Commission report, people even took clods of earth with them to remember their homes and their ancestors. All that should be expected to remain in landscapes from which people have been expelled would be those things they could not manage to take with them: their houses, the graves of their ancestors, and their fields. However, Orser's excavations of houses from which people were evicted in Ireland revealed that many possessions were left behind. Small-scale excavations in Ceinnabeinne in Sutherland, Scotland, also produced thimbles, buttons, and pottery (Lelong, personal communication 2007). In both of these places the houses seem to have been intentionally destroyed after people were evicted, and the processes of expulsion may have involved significant conflict, limiting people's abilities to take all their belongings with them.

Both conflict and eviction will often be accompanied by destruction of sites and materials, including burning or deliberate demolition of buildings and intentional destruction of fields, cemeteries, and other features.

Further research attempting to distinguish the signatures of abandonment, avoidance, and expulsion will provide better archaeological correlates of these processes. In addition, each of these processes can be further analyzed, and finer-textured distinctions made. Expulsion, for example, includes both eviction and conquest. Abandonment and avoidance also condense more nuanced dimensions of landscape emptying. Finally, research on the processes through which landscapes outside of Highland Scotland were emptied may suggest new categories altogether.

ACKNOWLEDGMENTS

I would like to thank John and Anne Macdonald, Scott and Ann Wood, and the members of the Raasay survey teams for welcoming me and sharing Raasay archaeology with me. Rebecca Mackay, Calum Don Mackay, and other residents of Raasay have generously offered hospitality and shared stories and local knowledge during my visits to the island, and I am grateful to them. Lastly, I am grateful to Ave Schwartz for his incalculable help.

REFERENCES

Barrett, John C. 1994. *Fragments from Antiquity: An Archaeology of Social Life in Britain 2900–1200 BC.* Blackwell, Oxford.

Basso, Keith H. 1996. *Wisdom Sits in Places: Landscape and Language Among the Western Apache.* University of New Mexico Press, Albuquerque.

Bradley, Richard. 2000. *The Archaeology of Natural Places.* Routledge, London.

Bruck, Joanna. 1999. Houses, Lifecycles, and Deposition on Middle Bronze Age Settlements in Southern England. *Proceedings of the Prehistoric Society* 65:145–166.

Burgess, Colin. 1980. *The Age of Stonehenge.* J. M. Dent, London.

Cameron, Catherine M. 1993. Abandonment and Archaeological Interpretation. In *Abandonment of Settlements and Regions: Ethnoarchaeological and Archaeological Approaches*, ed. by Catherine M. Cameron and Steve A. Tomka, pp. 3–7. Cambridge University Press, Cambridge.

Cameron, Catherine M., and Steve A. Tomka (editors). 1993. *Abandonment of Settlements and Regions: Ethnoarchaeological and Archaeological Approaches.* Cambridge University Press, Cambridge.

Carmichael, David L., Jane Hubert, Brian Reeves, and Audhild Schanche (editors). 1994. *Sacred Sites, Sacred Places.* Routledge, London.

Cobb, Charles R., and Brian M. Butler. 2002. The Vacant Quarter Revisited: Late Mississippian Abandonment of the Lower Ohio Valley. *American Antiquity* 67:625–641.

Cordell, Linda S. 1984. *Prehistory of the Southwest.* Academic Press, San Diego.

Cunliffe, Barry. 2000. *Danebury Environs Programme: The Prehistory of a Wessex Landscape.* Volume 1, Introduction. English Heritage and Oxford University Committee for Archaeology Monograph No. 48. Institute of Archaeology, Oxford.

Dodgshon, Robert A. 1998. *From Chiefs to Landlords: Social and Economic Change in the Western Highlands and Islands, c. 1493–1820.* Edinburgh University Press, Edinburgh.

Evans, John. 2003. *Environmental Archaeology and the Social Order.* Routledge, London.

Gazin-Schwartz, Amy. 1999. Constructing Ancestors: Archaeology and Folklore in Scotland. Ph.D. dissertation, Department of Anthropology, University of Massachusetts, Amherst.

Golightly, Roland. 2002. *An Archaeological Survey of the Geology & Soils of Raasay*, ed. by J. Scott Wood. Association of Certificated Field Archaeologists Occasional Paper No. 58. Glasgow University, Glasgow.

Ingold, Tim. 2000. *Perception of the Environment: Essays in Livelihood, Dwelling and Skill.* Routledge, London.

Macdonald, John, and J. Scott Wood. 1995. *An Archaeological Survey of the Townships of Oskaig and Holoman on Raasay, Portree Parish, Skye and Lochalsh District, Highland Region.* Association of Certificated Field Archaeologists Occasional Paper No. 13. Glasgow University, Glasgow.

———. 1996. *An Archaeological Survey of Four Townships at Balachuirn, Balmeanach, Inbhire and Brae on Raasay, Portree Parish, Skye and Lochalsh District, Highland Region.* Association of Certificated Field Archaeologists Occasional Paper No. 18. Glasgow University, Glasgow.

———. 1997. *An Archaeological Survey of the Township of Glame, Manish More, Brochel and Doire Domhain on Raasay, Portree Parish, Skye and Lochalsh District, Highland Region.* Association of Certificated Field Archaeologists Occasional Paper No. 26. Glasgow University, Glasgow.

———. 1998. *An Archaeological Survey of the Township of North and South Screapadal on Raasay, Portree Parish, Skye and Lochalsh District, Highland Region.* Association of Certificated Field Archaeologists Occasional Paper No. 32. Glasgow University, Glasgow.

Macdonald, John, and J. Scott Wood. 1999. *An Archaeological Survey of the Township of Manish Beg with a Survey of the Surrounding Area on Raasay, Portree Parish, Skye and Lochalsh District, Highland.* Association of Certificated Field Archaeologists Occasional Paper No. 43. Glasgow University, Glasgow.

———. 2000. *An Archaeological Survey of the Townships of Arnish and Torran on Raasay, Portree Parish, Skye and Lochalsh District, Highland Region.* Association of Certificated Field Archaeologists Occasional Paper No. 47. Glasgow University, Glasgow.

———. 2002. *An Archaeological Survey of the Township of North Fearns on Raasay, Portree Parish, Skye and Lochalsh District, Highland Region (Part 1).* Association of Certificated Field Archaeologists Occasional Paper No. 59. Glasgow University, Glasgow.

———. 2003. *An Archaeological Survey of the Township of North Fearns on Raasay, Portree Parish, Skye and Lochalsh District, Highland Region (Part 2).* Association of Certificated Field Archaeologists Occasional Paper No. 62. Glasgow University, Glasgow.

———. 2004. *An Archaeological Survey of the Townships of Hallaig and An Leac on Raasay, Portree Parish, Skye and Lochalsh District, Highland Region.* Association of Certificated Field Archaeologists Occasional Paper No. 71. Glasgow University, Glasgow.

———. 2005. *An Archaeological Survey of the Townships of Suisnish and South Fearns Plus the Surrounding Area on Raasay, Portree Parish, Skye and Lochalsh District, Highland Region.* Association of Certificated Field Archaeologists Occasional Paper No. 80. Glasgow University, Glasgow.

———. 2006. *An Archaeological Survey of the Township of An Lon Ban and the Coastal Area from An Lon Ban to Oskaig on Raasay, Portree Parish, Skye and Lochalsh District, Highland Region.* Association of Certificated Field Archaeologists Occasional Paper No. 84. Glasgow University, Glasgow.

Mackay, Margaret I. 2001. Suil air Ais. In *Duanagan, Dain is Dualchas a Eilean Ratharsair, Fladaidh is Eilean Tighe (Songs, Poems, Stories and Prose Emanating from the Rich Treasure of History and Traditions of Raasay, Fladda and Eilean Tighe)*, pp. 28–39. Raasay Heritage Trust, Raasay, Scotland.

Mackenzie, Julia. 2000. *Whirligig Beetles and Tackety Boots.* Blaisdon Publishing, Bedale, North Yorkshire.

Napier Commission (Royal Commission of Inquiry into the Condition of Crofters and Cottars in the Highlands and Islands). 1884. *Report of the Commission.* http://www.highland-elibrary.com/7.html, accessed July 15, 2007.

National Archives of Scotland. 1846. Map of Raasay. Register House Plan 1308. Edinburgh.

Nelson, Margaret C., and Michelle Hegmon. 2001. Abandonment is Not as it Seems: An Approach to the Relationship between Site and Regional Abandonment. *American Antiquity* 66:213–235.

Nicolson, John. 1989. *I Remember: Memories of Raasay.* Birlinn, Bedale, North Yorkshire.

Parry, M. L., and T. R. Carter. 1985. The Effect of Climatic Variations on Agricultural Risk. *Climatic Change* 7:95–100.

Orser, Charles. 2005. An Archaeology of a Famine-Era Eviction. *New Hibernia Review* 9(1):45–58.

Raasay Heritage Trust (Urras Dualchas Rathersaidh). 2001. *Duanagan, Dain is Dualchas a Eilean Ratharsair, Fladaidh is Eilean Tighe (Songs, Poems, Stories and Prose Emanating from the Rich Treasure of History and Traditions of Raasay, Fladda and Eilean Tighe).* Raasay Heritage Trust, Raasay, Scotland.

Ralston, Ian B. M. 1998. National Parks: The Cultural Dimension. In *Protecting Scotland's Finest Landscapes Session II: National Parks—The Opportunities*, ed. by Scottish Wildlife and Countryside Link, pp. 8–10. SWCL, Perth.

Richards, Eric. 2000. *The Highland Clearances: People, Landlords and Rural Turmoil.* Birlinn, Edinburgh.

Schiffer, Michael B. 1987. *Formation Processes of the Archaeological Record.* University of New Mexico Press, Albuquerque.

Sharpe, Richard. 1977. *Raasay: A Study in Island History.* Grant and Cutler, London.

Smout, T. C. 2000. *Nature Contested.* Edinburgh University Press, Edinburgh.

Steel, Tom. 1988. *The Life and Death of St. Kilda.* 2nd ed. Fontana Press, London.

PART 2

COLONIAL TOOLS OF CLEARANCE

CHAPTER 3

Written Off the Map: Cleared Landscapes of Medieval Ireland

Angèle Smith

INTRODUCTION

Archaeological landscapes are assumed to be those that, while once lively, have since been abandoned. How these lands have been abandoned or cleared of human society varies; abandonment can be the result of a slow and gradual decline of the population, or it can be the result of a forceful and even violent removal of peoples from their lands and homes as a result of pestilence and disease, economic expansion, warfare, or colonization. In this chapter, I will explore the colonial clearance of the Irish landscape in the late twelfth century, not so much by the physical removal of peoples from their land, but by removing them ideologically from the landscape. In doing so, the colonizer is able to justify and authorize their place by portraying Ireland as a barren, empty landscape. This strategy is not uncommon and certainly has been examined elsewhere, for example, in the case of colonizing North American lands and the removal of First Nations or indigenous peoples (Axtell 1981; French 2003; Harris 2002). In this study, however, I explore how the Anglo-Normans ideologically "cleared" or removed the early medieval Irish society from their lands by writing them off the map of Ireland.

It is important to note that this chapter is not so much about the archaeology of this early medieval landscape or about the archaeological evidence of the colonial act of clearance. Rather this chapter aims to explore the complex process of ideologically removing the Irish from their landscape and remaking that landscape—a process that has not been examined through archaeology, yet has great implication for understanding the gap in the archaeological record of this period (a gap which further serves to reinforce the notion of an empty Irish landscape). In examining the colonial process through the artifacts of Giraldus Cambrensis's early texts and his single map, which represent the newly colonized Ireland, I seek to illustrate and analyze how the landscape is refashioned cartographically and ideologically. It is clear that a robust archaeological plan to reinvestigate this period of early colonization is necessary. The analysis in this chapter sets the stage for and allows such archaeological inquiry to now be possible.

Ireland's colonial history comprises various periods in which the landscape was literally cleared of its local inhabitants to reshape it as British space (Andrews 1985; Brady and Gillespie 1986; Canny 2001). The late twelfth century "invasion" by the Anglo-Normans into Ireland is the earliest evidence of colonialism in the island. However, it was not the first time that peoples from Ireland and Britain had interacted: trade, culture, and religious ties forged close links between the two islands. The new political relationship created through the Anglo-Norman intervention required a process of justification. It was a paradoxical process through which the long-standing friendly connections were severed, the sense of "sameness" replaced by "otherness," and the landscape reimagined and re-presented as barren, yet bountiful and profitable for colonization; uninhabited, yet inhabited by wild beast-like people. The fact that clearance was necessary for colonization presupposes that the land had indeed been occupied and used. To legitimize intervention, more than just the people had to be evicted: the landscape itself had to be made barren. This was accomplished in several ways through physical, cartographic, and ideological removal and/or distancing.

In this chapter I will first outline how Ireland was part of the social, political, and religious landscape of Christian Europe; how early medieval Gaelic Ireland was a stage set for the late twelfth-century Anglo-Norman intervention or "invasion"; and how this invasion resulted in drastic changes in the sociopolitical relationship between Ireland and England. These changes included the physical clearance of the Irish as Anglo-Norman lords seized their lands and built motte fortifications, altering the very look of the landscape. The process of colonialism also resulted in ideological clearances of the Irish from their lands, especially through the writings of the colonial supporter, the priest-scholar Giraldus Cambrensis. Accompanying Giraldus's *Topographia Hibernica* (written in 1188) is an early medieval map of Ireland within Europe. Examining this map and Giraldus's writings, I explore the spatial and social colonial representations of Ireland and the Irish people that attempted to distance and "other," and thus legitimize, the colonial process.

Special attention is paid to the image of the map as a means to understand the process of removing the Irish from their lands. Monmonier (1991) writes that maps are distortions of the world. Maps, as two-dimensional representations, cannot be accurately representative of the three-dimensional world. Indeed, maps have more to do with selection, highlighting some features of the natural and cultural landscape while omitting others. Cartography reveals how the landscape is/was perceived, understood, and even manipulated and contested. Maps are cultural artifacts that reflect the choices about and the interpretations of the land, the people, and their culture. Maps are both produced by and help to produce the social and political relations and contexts of their day, reinforcing the perceptions held by the mapmakers.

Maps are often regarded as the product of politically unstable times. Brody (1989:135) comments that an interest in maps reflects a state of historical uncertainty, turmoil, and contestation. This explains the strong mapping tradition in Ireland, since Ireland has been a contested land for centuries. Mapping was a means for Britain to maintain colonial control over the island, making the landscape known and quantifiable. Mapping is a tool of the state for legal appropriation of land, for military security (both offensive and defensive), and for economic purposes such as taxation and resource exploitation (Anderson 1991; Black 1997; Harley 1989; Kain and Baigent 1992; Monmonier 1991; Scott 1998; Smith 2001). As will be seen, the map that accompanies Giraldus's propaganda writings is a good example of such a tool of the colonial state.

SOCIAL HISTORICAL LANDSCAPE: ELEVENTH- AND TWELFTH-CENTURY EUROPE

The eleventh and twelfth centuries were a time of population growth and increased economic activity leading to an increase in size and number of towns throughout all of western Europe. One result of this population pressure was a colonial movement in which both lords and peasants of central Europe began to resettle in, among other places, the Celtic lands of the British Isles. As part of these developments, the Normans had by AD 1100 gained control of southern Italy and England as well as lands in France. It was a period of heightened intellectual pursuits that saw the rise of the first universities in western Europe at Paris and Bologna. These centers drew people from all over Europe and thus had the affect of reaffirming a sense of a Christian European community.

Especially after the Church Schism in 1054, the papacy sought to strengthen its overall authority as a powerful leader within Europe. Religious reform was at the forefront of social and political life during this time. New religious orders, including the Augustinians and the Cistercians, were founded. Heightened Church authority was felt throughout Christian Europe and beyond. This was both cause and effect in the launching of the First Crusade (1095) by Pope Urban II to liberate Jerusalem. But even before that time, the Church reforms were reinforcing the connection between Rome and the local churches.

In Ireland these reforms (at the Synods of Cashel in 1101, Raith Bressail in 1111, and Mellifont in 1152) sought to forbid simony, lay abbots, and clerical marriages, and to introduce a diocesan system dividing the country into four ecclesiastical archbishoprics (Armagh, Cashel, Tuam, and Dublin). It is important to note that the Irish Church had begun to reform itself, but reform took on a different light when the English Pope Adrian IV (1154–1159) granted King Henry II (1154–1189) of England and part of France, permission to go to Ireland "to reform its Church." King Henry II had long considered conquests in Ireland. He went so far as to seek (and receive) papal sanction, as John of Salisbury, a member of the papal embassy, wrote in 1159:

> It was at my request that he [Pope Adrian IV] granted to the illustrious king of the English, Henry II, the hereditary possession of Ireland, as his still extant letters attest; for all islands are reputed to belong by a long-established right to the church of Rome, to which they were granted by Constantine, who established and endowed it. He sent moreover by me to that king a golden ring, adorned by a fine emerald, in token of his investiture with the government of Ireland; and this ring is still, by the king's command, preserved in the public treasury. (*Metalogicon*, Book IV, Chapter 42, edited by Webb 1929)

Henry did not go to Ireland until 1171, and by then it was for quite different reasons. But Adrian IV's earlier papal sanction and that of Pope Alexander III helped to justify the process of colonization that began with the Anglo-Norman "invasion" into Ireland. That England had papal permission to interfere in Ireland's affairs sets the relations between England and Ireland into the larger European context.

SOCIAL HISTORICAL LANDSCAPE: EARLY MEDIEVAL GAELIC IRELAND

Gaelic Ireland was not an isolated island, despite being on the western margin of continental Europe. It was well embedded in the European system in terms of trade and a shared Christian religion. Trade between Ireland and the British Isles was regular and frequent (there are only 21 kilometers separating Ireland and Scotland across the North Channel). Beyond connections with England, we must keep in mind that Ireland had long been involved in European trade relations. The Viking cities (Dublin, Waterford, and Wexford) had been considered international trading ports for some two hundred years. Christian Ireland in the seventh and eighth centuries was clearly a part of the European world and not an insignificant one:

> Ireland had contacts with the Mediterranean world, with Egypt, Italy and especially Spain although the links were even closer with her immediate neighbours across the sea, Gaul and Britain. Ireland exerted its strongest

influence on Britain; Northumbria and Ireland were part of one and the same cultural area. (Richter 1988:95)

At home, what was the Irish society like? How did the Gaelic society live on the landscape? According to O'Conor:

> The settlement pattern throughout Gaelic-dominated parts of medieval Ireland seems to have been predominately dispersed, with most of the population living in scattered farmsteads or small house clusters. The economy was largely pastoral, with transhumance or booleying being practised as part of the yearly agricultural strategy ... Although native Irish lords did possess fortifications, castles of the types seen elsewhere in western Europe were not common across the landscape of Gaelic Ireland during the twelfth, thirteenth, and fourteenth centuries. (1998:109)

O'Conor cautions that these are broad generalizations. For example, it is known that there was regional diversity amongst Gaelic settlement patterns across the landscape (before and after the Anglo-Normans arrived). Gaelic lords lived almost exclusively in crannogs, natural island fortresses (especially in Connacht and Ulster), cashels, and possibly ringforts (see O'Conor 1998). Large houses were not built, even for the lords. This can be explained with reference to their military tactics, which used the landscape as their best means of offense and defense. In other words, houses would not be defended in war; rather mobility across and through the landscape was their best strategy.

In addition to this Gaelic settlement pattern, the Irish landscape was dotted with monastic sites and their associated local communities. Some of these settlements, such as Armagh, Cashel, Clonmacnoise, and Glendalough, were large and well established. Numerous other settlements with smaller populations represented permanent and stable communities throughout the countryside. Some settlements established early in Ireland's history had by the late twelfth century a uniquely Irish-Norse flavor to them, having experienced Viking colonization in the ninth and tenth centuries. Dublin, Waterford, Wexford, Cork, and Limerick were important Viking towns, and each had a thriving economy based on international trade and a prosperous community.

It is clear that much needs to be learned, both about the Gaelic lords and, particularly, about the common population. Study in the last ten years has begun to address these questions. Archaeology will surely add to this discussion in a period when the Irish perspective is not well presented in the extant literature. Until now, archaeology has been distinctly quiet in the study of medieval settlement (Barry 1987), focusing its efforts instead on the prehistoric or Early Christian periods. Barry argues that archaeology has focused on a time that Irish nationalists would regard as before Norse interference or Anglo-Norman and English domination

(Barry 1987:1). The early medieval period was seen as an extension of English archaeology (but see Kenyon and O'Conor 2003; O'Keefe 2000, 2004; Sweetman 2000 for examples of works focusing on the Irish archaeology of this period).

At the end of the 1100s the ruling family dynasties of Uí Nèill, Uí Chonchobhair, and MacMurchada were competing for land and power. This internecine struggle was further fueled because there was no established system of succession to kingship. When the Anglo-Normans arrived in Ireland at the request of MacMurchada, they were able to play off faction against faction and thus secure their own independence from the native Irish kings.

THE INVASION

Dairmait MacMurchada (ca. 1134–1171), king of Leinster, was involved in a long and bitter dispute with Ruaidrì Uí Chonchobhair, king of Connacht, and his ally Uí Ruairc. When in 1166 Uí Chonchobhair became the high king of Tara, MacMurchada found himself surrounded by enemies and driven from his kingdom, and he sought help abroad from England. He traveled to France and pledged his loyalty to King Henry II as his lord. In early medieval Europe, national boundaries were much more fluid; it was far from unusual to call for foreign aid.

Henry was reluctant to expend any of his own energies on the infighting of Ireland, but he granted MacMurchada leave to recruit his knights in England to intervene and help recover his position in Ireland. It was among the marcher lords of south Wales that MacMurchada found his supporters, especially when they were promised rights to land in return for a successful campaign. These men (including the FitzHenries, FitzGeralds, and Barrys) were also keen for the intervention since, having supported Henry's opponent King Stephen in England's civil war in the 1130s and 1140s, they did not receive patronage from Henry. The knights were led by Richard FitzGilbert de Clare, earl of Pembrooke, better known as "Strongbow" (ca. 1130–1176). To him MacMurchada offered his daughter Aoife in marriage and succession in the kingdom of Leinster. On May 1, 1169, Strongbow landed in Wexford, and through a series of victories, the Anglo-Normans gained control in southeastern Ireland, taking Waterford, Wexford, and Dublin.

The situation escalated with the intervention of King Henry II himself in 1171. While Strongbow and the other knights, along with the Irish kings of the southeast and the Irish clergy, vowed allegiance to Henry, the king's authority was still not secure. The following years were marked by conflict among Irish chieftains and with the new Norman settlers. In 1177, Henry named his son John "Lord of Ireland" and in 1185 urged him to lead a second invasionary force into Ireland. This was in part motivated by the events of the Crusades. In 1185 Jerusalem fell, and Henry was petitioned for funding and requested to participate in person or send one of his sons. Henry gave generously but refused to go himself or send his sons. He declared that he meant to send his favorite son John to visit Ireland (much to his son's displeasure), perhaps to protect him from the Crusades. Prince John's visit to Ireland was intended to fully secure English rule in Ireland. The mission, however, was far from successful; John achieved only the alienation of the church and those Irish rulers who had originally supported Henry. Fortunately for the English crown, John's men ruled more temperately and diplomatically than did their prince.

While the events of the late twelfth century in Ireland have been likened to later colonial projects in Ireland, there is legitimate debate regarding whether the Anglo-Normans' arrival in Ireland was as an invasion or conquest. One tends to associate such terms with new contact with lands and people unfamiliar to the colonizer. Yet that was clearly not the case. This first colonial encounter between Ireland and England was unique and begs the question, what had really changed? First, there was the physical clearance of Irish lords and locals from territories, especially in the southeast, of Ireland. This had the effect of reshaping the appearance of the landscape. But in addition to this physical clearing, there was also an ideological reimaging of Ireland that removed existing understandings of what was Ireland-the-place and who were the Irish people. This ideological colonization was brought into effect by the revisionist writings of Giraldus Cambrensis, the priest-scholar who accompanied Prince John and wrote the *Topographia Hibernica* and the *Expugnatio Hibernica* (the Irish Topography and the Conquest of Ireland).

PHYSICAL CLEARANCE OF THE LANDSCAPE

The invasion originated in the southeast of the country. Yet within the short period between 1168 and 1171, Anglo-Norman lords had taken extensive tracts of land throughout all of eastern Ireland and had invaded the neighboring provinces into the north and west.

These lords took control of the lands, building motte- and bailey-style castles that were quick to erect (within a week) and easy to defend. This led to a drastic change in the Irish landscape: the local Irish lords and their followers were removed from the southeastern portion of the country and replaced by the Anglo-Norman lords. The newcomers overwhelmed former Viking-Irish towns and seized the fertile lowlands, leaving the rough mountainous areas in the west and northwest to the native Irish chiefs. The motte fortification—a uniquely Norman style—consisted of a stronghold erected on an artificial flat-topped circular mound with steep sides. The mound itself was constructed using the earth removed from a surrounding encircling ditch (for archaeological and historical discussions of these structures, see Barry 1987; McNeill 1997; O'Keefe 2001). Later, the original building was replaced with more permanent stone castles. These defensive sites liberally dotted the countryside throughout the east of the island and were an obvious symbol of Anglo-Norman control over the landscape, as well as a symbol of the new relationship between Ireland and England.

This military emphasis soon changed to one of colonization with an emphasis on economic exploitation. An imported English agricultural system based on a mixture of arable and pastoral farming techniques required more than the local Irish peasants as laborers, and so resulted in a marked increase in English migrant farmers and artisans settling into these lands. This colonial movement dramatically changed the look of the Irish landscape. In the countryside, the expansion of arable cultivation meant the clearance of woods and forests. In addition, many new market towns were built, with impressive city walls and stone castles as a reminder that these transformations were the product of the Anglo-Norman conquest.

IDEOLOGICAL CLEARANCES

Colonialism is in part the physical removal of a people from their place along with the infilling of outsiders into that same place. But colonialism is also an act of the ideological clearance of people from place in order to justify and authorize the physical acts of clearance on the landscape. In the late twelfth century this ideological colonialism was cunning and complex. There were extensive economic, political, and religious relationships already well forged between the two countries, as well as much shared cultural custom. In order to legitimize the invasion and colonization, the image and understanding of Ireland and the Irish people had to be drastically changed.

I examine Giraldus Cambrensis's *Topographia Hibernica* and the accompanying map as acts and artifacts of this process of colonizing the representation of the place and the people of Ireland. The new representation had to create and support a novel relationship between the two countries that justified colonialism; it needed to transform what was sameness between the two into an otherness. But first, it needed to make the landscape appear as an empty, barren wasteland. I particularly focus on the map as the key to painting Ireland in a new light, as "a country so remote from the rest of the world, and lying at its furthest extremity, forming as it were another world" (Giraldus Cambrensis 1982 [1188]).

GIRALDUS CAMBRENSIS: COLONIAL REVISIONIST AND PROPAGANDIST

Who was the author of this revisionism that reinvented Ireland and the Irish people? Accompanying Prince John on his visit to Ireland was the priest-scholar Giraldus Cambrensis, or Gerald of Wales (also known as Giraldus de Barri), who compiled information about Ireland and its people. As a result of his observations, Giraldus wrote *Topographia Hibernica* (1188), a description of the country and its people, and *Expugnatio Hibernica* (1189), an account of the Norman Conquest.

Giraldus, born in 1147, was kin to the FitzGeralds and Barrys who had fought during the original invasion of Ireland. Little is known of his education, save that he studied in Paris in the 1160s, where he devoted himself to the study of Latin, law, philosophy, and theology (O'Meara 1982:11–18). In 1185 he was employed as a member of Prince John's entourage in Ireland, partly as a diplomatic negotiator with the Welsh lords, and partly as a tutor to Prince John himself. After John's return to England, Giraldus was "left with Bertrand of Verdun, the Seneschal of Ireland, to be his comrade and the witness of his deeds, and remained in the island to the following Easter, that he might pursue his studies more fully, not merely gathering materials but setting them in order" (Giraldus Cambrensis 1937 [ca. 1196]:65).

His travels through Ireland at this time could not have been extensive, perhaps only traveling from Cork to Waterford and from Waterford to Dublin. It is clear that he did not travel far inland, since he erroneously wrote, "On the whole the land is low-lying on all sides and along the coast, but further inland it rises up very high to many hills and even high mountains" (O'Meara 1982:14). Norman-Welsh colonists likely described to him most of the island that he did not visit himself, although their knowledge too was limited to the southeastern portions of the island. This bias suggests the familiarity with the regions having the greatest Norman influence. Giraldus was a royal propagandist and his writing was extremely biased against the Irish. But A.B. Scott and F.X. Martin, the latest editors of the *Expugnatio*, maintain it must be remembered what limitations faced the twelfth-century chronicler:

> There was so much of Gaelic culture which Giraldus could not be aware of, simply because it was an orally transmitted rather than literate culture ... [Giraldus] had no Irish, and therefore, presumably little or no contact with the Irish other than the small group of ecclesiastics who knew Latin ... Very often it seems as if Giraldus had got to hear just enough about Irish customs to misunderstand them and give a travestied account of them. (1978: xvii-xviii)

Nevertheless, Giraldus was regarded as an expert and his manuscripts were widely circulated and well known, particularly since the *Topographia Hibernica* was dedicated to Henry II and read publicly at Oxford in 1188. In this way, Giraldus may have directly (or indirectly) affected popular opinion concerning the Irish. The views that were disseminated, then, were that the land itself was praiseworthy, but not so were its inhabitants. It is clear that he had a powerful influence on how Ireland and the Irish were represented in the writings of the thirteenth through the fifteenth centuries.

Giraldus's works were the most widely circulated pre-Renaissance accounts of Ireland and influenced how later chroniclers understood the Irish and their landscape. Giraldus's own words and opinions of those features and characteristics he deemed "Irish" were often repeated verbatim in later accounts. While other, often ancient classical, accounts might also be cited (including Solinus, Strabo, Tacitus, Julius Caesar, and Hector Boethius, among others), it is Giraldus who provides the principal source of information. The Renaissance period may be crucial for the founding of an English sense of national identity (Helgerson 1992) as well as an Irish identity springing from their united efforts during the Nine Years' War (1594–1603). Much recent interest in Renaissance colonial literature (Bradshaw, Hadfield, and Maley 1993; Morgan 1999; Murphy 1999; Rambo 1994) has focused on the writings of Spenser, Shakespeare, and Geoffrey Keating. However, I argue that emergent national identities had their foundation much earlier, in the twelfth century. Although some have dismissed Giraldus's work as simply royal propagandist literature, close examination illustrates the creation of the ideologies of colonialism in Ireland. Mapping Ireland as the "world beyond" and defining Irish identity as "the other" controlled the image of England's western neighbor and lay the foundation of the long process of colonization in Ireland.

In the essay "Anglo-Irish Attitudes" Declan Kiberd remarked that "the English did not invade Ireland—rather, they seized a neighbouring island and invented the idea of Ireland" (1986:83). Geographer Brian Graham argues that "because political activity often—if not necessarily—depends on concepts of territoriality, validated through legitimising images of place, landscape texts are frequently central to processes of empowerment" (1997:4). Thus the works of Giraldus Cambrensis in the *Topographia Hibernica* and in *Expugnatio Hibernica* help to reshape Ireland and remap its people. In the former treatise we also find one of the earliest medieval maps of Ireland. It is in these representations of Ireland and its people that Giraldus creates a framework for subsequent generations, writing about and mapping that other world which was/is Ireland. The map and the texts are artifacts of the social process which helped to create the image of Irish place and identity within the colonial relationship with England, and within a more global Christian Europe engaged in the Crusades (1095–1271).

I am particularly interested in the map of Europe that accompanies Giraldus's *Topographia* (Figure 3.1). Giraldus did not draw this map himself; however that does not take away from its significance nor does it diminish the importance of examining the map in detail. It is a

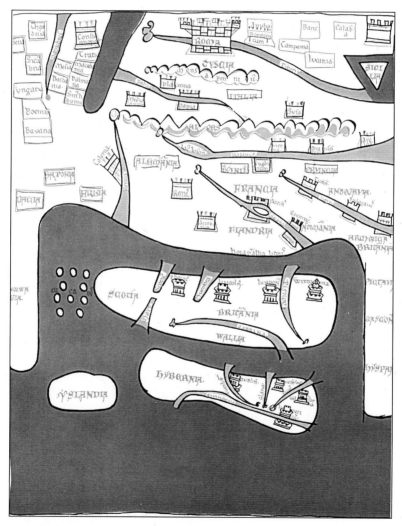

Figure 3.1 *Mappa mundi* of Giraldus Cambrensis, from his *Topographia Hibernica* (1188). The map is oriented with southeast at the top. (Courtesy of the National Library of Ireland, MS 700).

twelfth century map (MS 700 of the National Library of Ireland) and is likely to be the one that Giraldus himself comments on in his autobiography (O'Meara 1982:16–17). Further, it is the map that, because it accompanied the earliest copies of the text, has long been associated with Giraldus's *Topographia* and thus has made an impact on the British Renaissance colonial texts concerning Ireland. It is important to ask how this single map and the geographic literature as artifacts demonstrate the negotiation of constructing identities and social relations of power through the representation of the Irish landscape.

Maps work because they "give us reality, a reality that exceeds our vision, our reach, the span of our days, a reality we achieve no other way" (Wood 1993:4–5). It is interesting to note that, as in the colonial literature, scholars who study the history of mapping in Ireland tend to also begin with maps of the Renaissance period. Notable cartographic historian John H. Andrews's book *Shapes of Ireland: Maps and their Makers* (1997) begins its detailed examination of historical maps with Mercator's depiction of Ireland dated 1564, and Swift's *Historical Maps of Ireland* (1999) starts its discussion with the circa 1558 sketch map of the island. However, in this discussion of Giraldus Cambrensis's early medieval map we are provided with a unique opportunity to closely examine the contestation in the process of identity and place formation in the representation of a newly colonized land, and to illustrate the shaping of difference and other out of what was previously considered sameness.

This is accomplished through the manipulation of social and spatial ideologies. Spatial and social relations have long been recognized as important in understanding archaeological landscapes and thus the following analysis draws from that literature to examine the spatiality of Giraldus's map and historical texts.

THE SPATIALITY OF MAP AND TEXT

In looking at this medieval map of Ireland and its place within the wider context of Christian Europe, I have employed the spatial categories used by Andrew Murphy (1999) in his analysis of the two geographical writings of Giraldus Cambrensis. These spatial categories establish the link between place/space on the one hand, and identity and social relations of power on the other. This is not simply a spatial metaphor. Rather, as Soja (1989) and Foucault (1984) have argued, spatial relations and social relations are dynamically linked, such that social relations produce and are simultaneously produced by spatial relations. In this case, spatial proximity is likened to social/cultural sameness and hence familiarity and acceptance. In contrast, spatial distancing is associated with the process of othering, thereby legitimizing power inequalities in the form of colonization and colonial ideologies. Said (1978, 1993) suggests identity is about the discourses of inclusion and exclusion articulated against a hostile other. I argue here that spatiality is also understood in terms of inclusion and exclusion defined by boundaries, whether they be physical (e.g., a body of water), social (e.g., a national border), or cognitive (e.g., ideological differences), or all of these combined. Yet space is, by its very essence, fluid. The sense of boundedness is arbitrary and always in the process of being created, torn down, or recreated. Similarly, identity is fluid and always shifting in the process of being defined, and redefined. Thus in analyzing the spatial artifact of the Giraldus map, it is important to see that the spatial/identity categories that seem to be rigidly defined are actually determined by their borders and boundaries; yet these are permeable and (often) crossed. Boundaries are breached as Ireland-the-place is simultaneously depicted as proximate and distant, and the Irish identity as simultaneously the same and the other. This creates problems for installing the dominant colonial ideologies, for justifying political actions of inequality, and for legitimizing new power structures because such crossing of boundaries (spatial and identity) creates a liminal state which is, in actuality, much more representative of the complexity of the social and spatial relations.

In inventing a colonial Ireland and the colonial Irish, England has a difficult task: it must fashion out of a sense of spatial proximity and cultural sameness, a distant other. Set against this background of geographical proximity and cultural sameness, the writing of Giraldus and the *Topographia* map sought to justify the colonial endeavor of Britain in Ireland. Murphy (1999:36) argues that

> in writing about the Irish in this period, Giraldus had not only to strive to evoke a sense of Irish otherness, but also needed to engage with an account for the fact that, within that otherness, there resided a certain profound and enduring element of proximate alignment. We can trace in [Giraldus's] work the strategies he employs both for engaging with and disengaging an Irish sense of proximity, and also the residual inscription of the proximity within his narratives.

Proximity and Sameness

Giraldus did not create a new map for the *Topographia*. He merely copied an existing map, but he put his mark on his rendering in the changes and additions he made. It is a part of a *mappa mundi*, a map of the world, which was the tradition of that period. The *mappae mundi* differed from the earlier maps of Ptolemy in significant ways. For example, on Giraldus's *mappa mundi* there are no longitudes and latitudes, nor is there a north orientation (conventions which we use today). It was not meant to be an accurate geographic depiction of the world. The aim of the *mappae mundi* was to reflect a Christian worldview. It is not surprising that maps that supported the Christian worldview coincided with the Crusades in the Holy Land, and that at the center of these maps was Jerusalem. In this way they were also pilgrimage maps; east was situated at the top of the map.

Giraldus's map in *Topographia* is set within the context of the Crusades (1095–1271), a time in which the concept of pilgrimage held great significance. During this period hundreds of thousands of men, women, and children marched on pilgrimage paths, especially to the Holy Land or, for those who could not travel so far, to sacred religious sites within Europe itself. Chief among the European destinations was, of course, Rome, the seat of the Roman Catholic Church. It could be said that Giraldus's map is best regarded as a pilgrimage map from England to Rome, illustrating a route connecting churches, castles, and other stopping points along the way. The route on Giraldus's map (see Figure 3.1) can be traced via the Seine River (written as Secana on the map) and Paris, crossing the Rhone River at Lyon (Lugdunum), traversing the Alps to Pavia (Papia), from there to Piacenza (Placentia), and finally to Rome. That this is a pilgrimage map to Rome can account for some of the manipulations to the traditional *mappa mundi* style of representation that are apparent in Giraldus's map. The map definitively places Ireland within the Christian realm of the West.

While the map of *Topographia* is clearly based on European sources, the representation of Ireland specifically suggests the Norman influence. The relations of Ireland, England, Wales, and Scotland to one another are roughly accurate; however, there are some key features which distort the look and thus the message of Ireland's place on the map. The features provided in Ireland are scant, and yet when looked at carefully they provide information about an Ireland that was recognized as being in many respects similar to England. We see that the map was creating the image of Ireland within the context of sameness. While this may seem contrary to the colonial act of physically clearing the landscape of the Irish, this was a significant first step in ideologically removing the people and thereby justifying the invasion.

The beginning of Giraldus's *Topographia* provides an account of the geographical location and primary physical features of the island: "Ireland, the largest island beyond Britain, is situated in the western ocean about one short day's sailing from Wales ... This farthest island of the west has Spain parallel to it on the south ... Greater Britain on the east ... and only the ocean on the west" (1982 [1188]:33). In addition, he notes the "nine principal rivers," likening them to Britain. The various flora and fauna he compares to Britain and continental Europe,

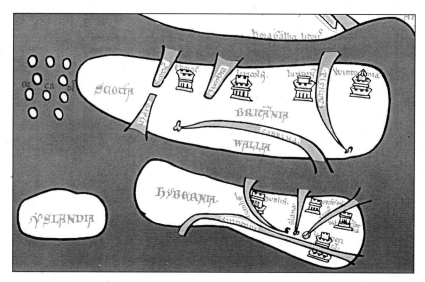

Figure 3.2 Detail of Giraldus Cambrensis's *Mappa mundi* showing Ireland and England, from his *Topographia Hibernica* (1188). (Courtesy of the National Library of Ireland, MS 700).

stating that "Ireland has almost all the kinds of wild animals that are found in the western regions" (1982 [1188]:47), but highlights those which are novelties or absences.

Giraldus's map (see Figure 3.2) depicts only some of the physical features of the island—four named rivers and the cities at the mouth of each. The four rivers are the Auenliffus (transcribed from Abhainn Liffus, indicating the River Liffey), Slana (the Slaney River), Suirus (the Suir River), and Sinnenus (the Shannon River, which is combined as one river with the Erne River). The four fortified cities are at the mouth of each of these rivers: Dublin on the Liffey, Waterfodia (Waterford) on the Slaney, Weiseford (Wexford) on the Suir, and Limericum (Limerick) on the Shannon.

These fortified cities are depicted similarly to those found on the *mappae mundi* as well as on the merchants' road maps, which are laid out in straight strips (Thrower 1996). They appear as turreted multi-storied buildings depicted at eye level. The lower levels of the buildings have three tall, thin windows. These strongholds are situated on banked-up mounds. Are these not representations of the Norman motte and baileys then, rather than some Irish-Norse settlement? The Wexford and Waterford castles are the simplest of the four; the Dublin castle appears to have an additional level (perhaps an encircling wall around its base) and Limerick, the most complex structure, has a double level of turrets. The base of the Limerick castle appears separated by the Shannon River.

All of these are Viking towns. All are situated on rivers and are coastal towns, emphasizing their role as trading ports. Interestingly, Cork, arguably an important Viking town, is not marked on the map. Many earlier pre-Viking settlements situated at inland monasteries (e.g., Kells, Roscrea, Armagh, Kildare, and Cashel) were still thriving at the time of conquest. They, however, are not represented on Giraldus's map. The difference is that all the towns on the map were taken during or soon after the initial Anglo-Norman invasion.

That only rivers are marked as a topographical feature suggests an emphasis on mapping movement through and access into the interior of the country. This, of course, reflects both the importance of trade and movement, and also charts the flow of the Anglo-Norman invasion; Henry II landed at Waterford and sailed up the Suir River in 1171 to claim the city—and Ireland—for the crown. The Slaney River runs through Wexford, where Henry II stayed at Selskar Abbey in 1172 doing penance for the murder of Thomas à Becket. Thus the map shows more about the connections between Ireland and England in reference to the events of the invasion, than it does about Ireland's geographical exactitude. This also may explain why cities, such as Cork, that were not central to the invasion were not represented.

While no longitudes and latitudes are depicted, it is still obvious that Ireland is placed too far south, such that both Ireland and England appear to be parallel at their southern base. The effect of this is that Ireland appears to look like a smaller version of England. That is, Giraldus's map successfully depicts Ireland as like England, as within that context of sameness with England. That sameness had to do with the interconnections of Ireland, England, and the European continent through trade and religion.

Beyond laying out the geographical information of Ireland, which by its very nature presents Ireland as close or proximate to Britain, Giraldus's text provides additional evidence for spatial proximity and cultural sameness between the two neighboring countries. The connection between Ireland and Britain focuses on the commonness of their Christianity. Through Saint Patrick, Ireland is bound in a relationship with Britain, for it is this missionary saint that brings Christianity to the island. Giraldus is careful to reinforce Patrick's origins: "Particus ... natione Britannus" (1982 [1188]:104, note 62). This is evidence that not only Patrick, but Christianity itself, came to Ireland *from* Britain. Thus Ireland, incorporated into the realm of the West, is distinguished from that of the iniquitous East in the usage of the terms *here* and *there*. In such manner, Giraldus opens the *Topographia* by acknowledging the proximal sameness of Ireland and Britain positioned against the different East.

Indeed, Ireland is (initially) represented as the direct opposite of the East, first because of its geographical positioning and second because of Ireland's ability to fend off such evils as reptiles and all poisons. Giraldus writes, "The well of poison brims over in the East. The farther therefore from the East it operates, the less does it exercise the force of its natural efficacy. And by the time it reaches these farthest parts, after having traversed such long distances, losing its force gradually, it is entirely exhausted" (1982 [1188]:56). Thus Ireland is set up as the absolute West. However, Murphy (1999) argues that in doing so, Ireland is made out as an anomalous, unique place where no poison prevails, and is thus disjoined from a "continuous East-West realm." He writes, "where at the close of part 1 [of the *Topographia*] he unites Ireland with the West against the East, Gerald now, continuing to invoke the East-West dichotomy, turns to aligning Ireland with the East by presenting both realms as anomalous territories lying outside the central Western domain" (1999:39). The bounded spatiality that is represented creates cultural distancing, thus signifying the final step in ideologically removing Ireland from England and thus justifying the colonial process.

Distance and Othering

Giraldus's map represents Ireland as a newly colonized land, a representation which helps to justify the invasion and conquest. Hitherto regarded as part of the same world, the map also serves to create images of difference, of a distanced, othered wasteland.

Giraldus's map shows only part of the known world of the *mappa mundi* tradition. Rome, as the place of European pilgrimage, is located at the top of the map. This skews the traditional *mappa mundi* orientation such that the southeast (Rome) and not true east is at the top (see Figure 3.1). (If true east were at the top, Rome would be at the upper right of the map and Ireland at the bottom left.) With the orientation given in Giraldus's map, Rome is at the top center, which thus shifts Ireland to the center of the bottom of the map. The map therefore sets up clear spatial oppositions between Rome at the top and Ireland at the bottom. Also, since this is only one part of the *mappa mundi* that refocuses the orientation to the pilgrimage site of Rome at the top of the map rather than Jerusalem in the middle, Giraldus's map has the added result of situating England in the center of the page. England, not Jerusalem, becomes the center of the Christian worldview.

The resulting message, then, is that Ireland and the Irish Catholic Church are far from Rome and the papal seat of the Church. This underscores the

Church reform movements that sought to make the Irish Church more compliant with the doctrines of Rome. It also underscores English involvement in this reform as a result of Pope Adrian IV's papal bull that charged England with the responsibility for these reforms in Ireland.

There is other evidence of distortion in the map that has the effect of distancing Ireland from England and the rest of continental Europe. This distortion is that Ireland and Iceland are placed parallel to each other at the bottom of the map. In actuality, the distance between Iceland and Ireland is almost as far as the distance between Ireland and Rome. Yet in Giraldus's map, Iceland is placed as a near neighbor to Ireland, as close to Ireland as it is to England. This could be interpreted simply as "squishing in" Iceland to fit the map. Or, it could be attempting to create the image that Ireland is as far-flung and distant from Rome as is Iceland. Whether intentional or not, the result of distancing Ireland is the same. It is at the outer limit of Christian Europe.

This geographical distancing represented in the map is also reinforced in Giraldus's *Topographia* as a social distancing or othering of Ireland. While clearly part of Christian Europe, Ireland is depicted as the "Far West," the farthest from the un-Christian dangers and evils of the East. Yet, this means that Ireland, like the East, is far removed from the center of Christian Europe (whether that be considered Jerusalem, Rome, or in this case, England). In this way, Giraldus is able to align Ireland with the East: "Just as the countries of the East are remarkable and distinguished for certain prodigies peculiar and native to themselves, so the boundaries of the West also are made remarkable by their own wonders of nature ... and in these remote parts [nature] indulges herself in these secret and distant freaks" (1982 [1188]:31). By emphasizing in Ireland "such things marvelous in themselves" and "those exceedingly wonderful and miraculous deeds done through the merits of the saints" (1982 [1188]:57), Giraldus invokes an image of Ireland and the Irish as "unnatural," effectively creating a sense of spatial distance and cultural otherness.

The marvels of Ireland are recorded in the many accounts of bestiality and the resulting offspring of such couplings—creatures that are half human and half animal. These progeny are neither one thing nor another: they, like Ireland, bridge two realms of nature, producing repellent monsters. Ireland is thus painted as a "marvelous" place filled with weird creatures (not the least of which are the barbarian, "wild" Irish themselves).

Giraldus's description of the saints also effectively creates a sense of the Irish other. While on one level the saints might be read as indicators of Christianity, the stories themselves are more marvelous and wild than are they miraculous. Often these are tales of wrongdoers banished by the saints. The saints, having created places of exclusion, mete out severe, even brutal, punishment for crossing the boundaries. In this way Christian Ireland is made to appear less than Christian in the perverse actions of the vindictive and cruel saints. The Irish and Ireland are represented as having a liminal status: good, pure, and "lacking all poisons and snakes" (1982 [1188]:50–51), while at the same time evil and ugly, filled with wild and monstrous beings. Like the East, Ireland has been reimagined as an "otherworld," a mystical, dangerous, and threatening place. This works in a number of ways: justifying a Christian colonization that would subdue the evils of the land; glorifying the leadership of any people able to conquer that hostile otherworld; bringing order out of chaos; and protecting the known world from threat of danger. What is created is an ideological image of Ireland and the Irish as the "distant other," thereby legitimizing the colonial process that began in the twelfth century and continued into the twentieth century.

But the key means of distancing and thereby othering Ireland is through its representation as an empty place, a wasteland. Ptolemy in the second century AD only mapped three continents—Europe, Asia, Africa—even though he thought it likely that there was more of the world than he portrayed (Wilford 2001). Yet he held fast to his belief that only those parts of the world that were known to be inhabited and had been visited and measured ought to be included in the map. Giraldus did not hold the same conviction to map only what was known. Indeed, the map of Ireland speaks largely of what is not known of Ireland. The limited number of features (only four rivers and four towns, mostly in the east and southeast part of the island) and the large open space in the north and west portion of the map suggest that Ireland was not known and yet was depicted as if it were known to be an empty uninhabited place.

Filling gaps in the maps with monsters and marvelous creatures was a common practice for early mapmakers, as centuries later, in 1733, Jonathan Swift proclaims:

> So Geographer, in Afric-maps,
> With savage-pictures fill their gaps;
> And o'er unhabitable down
> Place elephant for want of towns. (quoted in Just 2004)

Although Giraldus's map did not fill in the blank space of the north and west portion of Ireland, his writings of the land, the wildlife, and the people of Ireland in *Topographia Hibernica* amply provided filler for the gaps of what was known in Ireland. This had the effect of illustrating an inhumanness about Ireland, effectively clearing the landscape of the Irish.

WRITTEN OFF THE MAP: CLEARED LANDSCAPES OF MEDIEVAL IRELAND

This is a unique act of colonialism, and as a result allows for a critical analysis of the ideological process of clearance and othering that works to justify and authorize colonization. It is unique because it is the *first* colonial episode that initiates and influences the subsequent long history of colonial relations between Ireland and Britain. It is also unique in that unlike most colonial experiences, this invasion and conquest was not the meeting of unfamiliar peoples from different cultures in lands foreign to the colonizer. Rather, Ireland and the Irish were well known to the colonizing Anglo-Normans. Economic and political, as well as cultural and religious ties, had linked the two countries prior to the 1169 invasion. Thus the act of colonialism was much more than the physical act of removing people from their landscape, it was an ideological reimaging of Ireland and the Irish people.

While this colonial "invasion" has yet to be extensively examined using an archaeological approach, the implications of the analysis made here of Giraldus Cambrensis's contemporary map and texts are significant for archaeology and the historical reconstruction of the early medieval Irish landscape. As noted by Barry earlier in this chapter, the relative absence of archaeological inquiry into the Anglo-Norman period simply reaffirms the colonial control (still) by assuming this period to be more a part of English rather than Irish history. By examining the spatial and social relations mapped out by Giraldus in the twelfth century, it becomes clear that archaeological investigations of the colonial process and the colonial landscape are necessary to examine and critique the map and texts for their reimaging of Ireland and the Irish people.

The new image of Ireland was that of a barren wasteland, "unoccupied" especially in the sense that the Irish did not live in cities. The depiction of Ireland represented in the map is not of an Irish-inhabited landscape but of the colonial landscape of the Anglo-Norman lords. By mapping Ireland as a "world beyond," at the extreme West of Christian Europe, Ireland and Irish identity becomes the other. This is in contrast to (and ideologically transforms) the previous close relationship and social sameness and proximity between the two countries. Controlling the image of Ireland and its people helped to lay the foundation for an ideology of colonization that cleared the landscape of shared commonness and wrote the Irish off the map of medieval Christian Europe.

REFERENCES

Anderson, Benedict. 1991. *Imagined Communities: Reflections on the Origin and Spread of Nationalism*. Verso, London.

Andrews, John H. 1997. *Shapes of Ireland: Maps and their Makers 1564–1839*. Geography Publications, Dublin.

Andrews, 1985. *Plantation Acres: An Historical Study of the Irish Land Surveyors and His Maps*. Ulster Historical Foundation, Omagh, Co. Tyrone.

Axtell, James. 1981. *The European and the Indian: Essays in the Ethnohistory of Colonial North America*. Oxford University Press, Oxford.

Barry, Terry. 1987. *The Archaeology of Medieval Ireland*. Methuen, London.

Barry, Terry, Robin Frame, and Katharine Simms (editors). 1995. *Colony and Frontier in Medieval Ireland: Essays Presented to J.F. Lydon*. The Hambledon Press, London.

Black, Jeremy. 1997. *Maps and History: Constructing Images of the Past*. Yale University Press, New Haven.

Bradshaw, Brendan, Andrew Hadfield, and Willy Maley (editors). 1993. *Representing Ireland: Literature and the Origins of Conflict, 1534–1660*. Cambridge University Press, Cambridge.

Brady, Ciaran, and Raymond Gillespie. 1986. *Natives and Newcomers: Essays on the Making of the Irish Colonial Society, 1534–1641*. Irish Academic Press, Dublin.

Brody, Hugh. 1989. Maps and Journeys. In *Togail Tir, Marking Time: The Map of the Western Isles*, ed. by Finlay Macleod, p. 135. Acair Ltd. and An Lanntair Gallery, Stornoway, Scotland.

Canny, Nicholas. 2001. *Making Ireland British, 1580–1650*. Oxford University Press, Oxford.

Edel, Doris (editor). 1995. *Cultural Identity and Cultural Integration: Ireland and Europe in the Early Middle Ages*. Four Courts Press, Dublin.

French, Laurence. 2003. *Native American Justice*. Burnham, Chicago.

Foucault, Michel. 1984. Space, Knowledge, and Power. In *The Foucault Reader*, ed. by Paul Rabinow, pp. 239–256. Pantheon Books, New York.

Giraldus Cambrensis. 1937 [ca. 1196]. *The Autobiography of Giraldus Cambrensis [De Rebus a se Gestis]*. J. Cape, London.

———. 1978 [1189]. *The Conquest of Ireland [Expugnatio Hibernica]*. Royal Irish Academy, Dublin.

———. 1982 [1188]. *The History and Topography of Ireland [Topographia Hibernica]*. Penguin Books, London.

Graham, Brian. 1997. Ireland and Irishness: Place, Culture and Identity. In *In Search of Ireland: A Cultural Geography*, ed. by Brian Graham, pp. 1–15. Routledge, London.

Hadfield, Andrew, and John McVeagh (editors). 1994. *Strangers to that Land: British Perceptions of Ireland from the Reformation to the Famine*. Colin Smythe Press, Gerrards Cross, England.

Harley, John B. 1989. Deconstructing the Map. *Cartographica* 26(2):1–20.

Harris, Richard. 2002. *Making Native Space: Colonialism, Resistance, and Reserves in British Columbia*. University of British Columbia Press, Vancouver.

Helgerson, Richard. 1992. *Forms of Nationhood: The Elizabethan Writing of England*. University of Chicago Press, Chicago.

Just, Melanie. 2004. *Jonathan Swift's On Poetry: A Rhapsody*. Peter Lang, New York.

Kain, Roger, and Elizabeth Baigent. 1992. *The Cadastral Map in the Service of the State: A History of Property Mapping*. University of Chicago Press, Chicago.

Kenyon, John R., and Kieran O'Conor (editors). 2003. *The Medieval Castle in Ireland and Wales*. Four Courts Press, Dublin.

Kiberd, Declan. 1986. Anglo-Irish Attitudes. In *Ireland's Field Day*, by the Field Day Theatre Company, pp. 81–105. University of Notre Dame Press, Notre Dame.

Lydon, James (editor). 1984. *The English in Medieval Ireland. Proceedings of the First Joint Meeting of the Royal Irish Academy and the British Academy*. Royal Irish Academy, Dublin.

McNeill, Tom. 1997. *Castles in Ireland: Feudal Power in a Gaelic World*. Routledge, London.

Monmonier, Mark. 1991. *How to Lie with Maps*. University of Chicago Press, Chicago.

Morgan, Hiram (editor). 1999. *Political Ideology in Ireland, 1541–1641*. Four Courts Press, Dublin.

Murphy, Andrew. 1999. *But the Irish Sea Betwixt Us: Ireland, Colonialism, and Renaissance Literature*. University Press of Kentucky, Lexington, Kentucky.

O'Conor, Kieran. 1998. *The Archaeology of Medieval Rural Settlement in Ireland*. Discovery Programme Monograph No. 3. Discovery Programme, Dublin.

O'Keefe, Tadhg. 2000. *Medieval Ireland: An Archaeology*. Tempus Press, Dublin.

———. 2001. Concepts of "Castle" and the Construction of Identity in Medieval and Post-Medieval Ireland. *Irish Geography* 34(1):69–88.

———. 2004. *Ireland's Round Towers*. Tempus Press, Dublin.

O'Meara, John (translator). 1982 [1188]. *The History and Topography of Ireland [Topographia Hibernica] by Gerald of Wales [Giraldus Cambrensis]*. Penguin Books, London.

Rambo, Elizabeth. 1994. *Colonial Ireland in Medieval English Literature*. Susquehanna University Press, Selinsgrove, Pennsylvania.

Richter, Michael. 1988. *Medieval Ireland: The Enduring Tradition*. St. Martin's Press, New York.

Said, Edward. 1978. *Orientalism*. Pantheon Books, New York.

———. 1993. *Culture and Imperialism*. Knopf, New York.

Scott, A. Brian, and Francis X. Martin (translators). 1978 [1189]. *The Conquest of Ireland [Expugnatio Hibernica] by Gerald of Wales [Giraldus Cambrensis]*. Royal Irish Academy, Dublin.

Scott, James. 1998. *Seeing Like a State: How Certain Schemes to Improve the Human Condition Have Failed*. Yale University Press, New Haven.

Soja, Edward W. 1989. *Postmodern Geographies*. Verso, London.

Smith, Angèle. 2001. Mapping Cultural and Archaeological Meanings: Representing Landscapes and Pasts in 19th Century Ireland. Ph.D. dissertation, Department of Anthropology, University of Massachusetts, Amherst.

Sweetman, David. 2000. *Medieval Castles of Ireland*. Boydell and Brewer, Rochester, New York.

Swift, Michael. 1999. *Historical Maps of Ireland*. Parkgate Books, London.

Thrower, Norman. 1996. *Maps and Civilization: Cartography in Culture and Society*. University of Chicago Press, Chicago.

Webb, Clement C. (editor). 1929. *Metalogicon of John Salisbury: A Twelfth-Century Defense of the Verbal and Logical Arts*, Book IV. Clarendon Press, Oxford.

Wilford, John Noble. 2001. *The Mapmakers*. Vintage Books, New York.

Wood, Dennis. 1993. Maps and Mapmaking. In *Introducing Cultural and Social Cartography*, ed. by Robert A. Rundstrom, pp. 1–9. *Cartographia* 30:1, Monograph 44.

CHAPTER 4

The Past Is Another Country[1]: Archaeology in the Limpopo Province, South Africa

Kathryn Mathers and Neels Kruger

Archaeology in South Africa has changed less than was hoped for since the official demise of apartheid. African archaeology in general was closely linked with colonial projects, and South Africa, like other settler nations, built its "official" national identity on a myth of an empty landscape waiting to be filled with the civilizing structures, institutions, and people of the north (Andah 1995; Kinahan 1995; Shepherd 2002; Trigger 1989). Today South African archaeologists struggle to come to terms with their role in creating representations of a past that is invoked for political purposes, as well as with the legacy of studying past landscapes inhabited by "others." Archaeology in South Africa remains implicated in discourses of nation building and identity construction, but this is happening largely without much participation in these discussions from archaeologists themselves (Hall and Bombardella 2005). Shepherd has shown how much of South African archaeology has tended to conform to a practice of "looking through the present landscapes, with their clutter of political aspiration and cultural change, to find the traces of an imagined past lying below" (Shepherd 2003:839). This is particularly the case when archaeology is invoked to serve the needs of tourism or land claims. Archaeologists can easily get caught in the middle of a struggle caused by the tension between the State's goal of giving land back to the people who were forcibly removed by colonial and apartheid legislation and the often overlapping economic goal of attracting tourists to landscapes that represent a pristine African past. Where the same land is identified for these seemingly conflicting goals, it becomes even more imperative for archaeologists to pay attention to issues of reparations and restitution, projects of memory, education and development, and to experiment with new and accessible formats (Shepherd 2002). To achieve this, archaeologists have the challenging task of mediating between folk and academic archaeologies, engaging with issues of culture and identity, and, rather than looking through present landscapes, finding "the signs of a poetic sensibility by thinking deeply through the past" (Shepherd 2003:844). By drawing on a combination of oral histories and an archaeological survey in the northern Limpopo Province of South Africa, we critically examine a landscape in which archaeology sits in the middle of a conflict over whether land should be given over to tourism-motivated conservation or to people.

In South Africa a tension has developed within the discipline as to whether archaeology is a science or the voice of the people (Shepherd 2003). A claim to scientific authority is one reason that archaeology risks remaining at once disconnected from public discussions and the creation of representations of the past, while simultaneously being invoked in these discussions by others with little foundation. Among the practices that can stand in the way of a postcolonial archaeology is archaeology's increasing dependence on technologically sophisticated mapping tools such as GIS. Mapping effectively clears landscapes of the messiness of present conflicts and of the everyday lives of people who inhabited the landscape before or after those being mapped. Thus, the mechanisms and tools used by archaeologists can contribute to the production of images of the past that are conducive to the manipulation of the local landscape in the interests of the tourist industry or land claims. These technologies can allow tourists and conservationists to interact only with a particular past landscape, one without the tensions, traumas, and change of the present. Much as early cartographers produced images that allowed imperial powers to somehow own and possess lands that they had not yet settled, so archaeologists risk producing images of past landscapes that appear neutral but that allow them to be claimed by one or other group. We argue that the ways landscapes are used and represented by archaeology, especially in a discourse of heritage tourism and ethnic ownership, can generate representations that produce colonized landscapes (Asad 1973; Keesing 1994; Trouillot 1991).

Landscape studies in archaeology, as in anthropology, generally recognize that a landscape is the product of dynamic and complex interdependent relationships between physical, social, and cultural dimensions of social life across time and space. They have moved substantially away from simply providing the backdrop for the plotting of material traces and from the determinism that assumed past lifeways were the product of their environments (Anschuetz et al. 2001; Green 2004). Archaeological landscape studies now work hard to integrate nature and culture, dismissing neither the physical nor the symbolic meaning of landscapes. In this way studies of archaeological landscapes should be able to reveal the way in which people turn physical spaces into meaningful places through daily activities, beliefs, and values (Anschuetz et al. 2001;

Ashmore 2004). Such an approach requires recognizing the multiple layers of meaning created by different actors within a particular landscape. What is often missing, however, is the meaning created by archaeologists in a practice that is ultimately effective at producing an imagined geography of the past and that risks being just as damaging of contemporary people's lives as past colonial discourses (Lowe 1991; Mitchell 1988; Said 1979; Shepherd 2002).

When Lowenthal incorporated into landscape studies an understanding that the environment and nature are individually and culturally perceived phenomena that are historically constituted, he emphasized the importance of representations (Olwig 2003). Archaeologists, however, have increasingly expressed impatience with the stress on perception within landscape studies and emphasized the need to understand the way humans move through, exist, and are in the world (Ashmore 2004; Bender 2001; Ingold 1993; Olwig 2003; Spiegel 2004). Yet archaeology's dependence on features and things that can be seen lends itself to "rendering people in the past mainly as enactors of a script of cultural rules in material form" (Lazzari 2003:197). Although it is essential that archaeologists pay attention to the practices of everyday life as marked on landscapes, we argue for a renewed focus on representations in all their multiplicity. In fact, given the slippage in much anthropological discourse between landscape as representation and landscape as the reality that is represented, it is even more important to pay attention to the relationship between the representation and the land it is meant to represent (Spiegel 2004). Ironically, it is archaeology's emphasis on taking what can be seen—the material remains that can be plotted—and using them to imagine what cannot be seen that leads to the creation of representations that "tend to flatten out the diversity of human actions and practices" (Lazzari 2003:201). This flattening out of everyday practices continues, we suggest, to characterize South African archaeology. By downgrading the way landscape studies produce visual representations, no matter how useful or valid, archaeologists risk establishing a relationship of unequal power between themselves, as authors of the script, and the inhabitants of a landscape in the past and present.

TECHNOLOGIES OF MAPPING: POSSESSING A SOUTH AFRICAN LANDSCAPE

The past is always constructed by the present, and technologies (such as museums and maps) and social sciences (such as archaeology) were and continue to be instrumental in building, for example, an image of a nation as if firmly entrenched in the past (Anderson 1991). Maps have often been particularly effective at quite literally wiping people off the landscape in the interest of colonial expansion or even putting people on the map in order to legitimate ownership of new territories (Carruthers 2003; Duncan and Gregory 1999; Green 2004; Olwig 2003; Sluyter 2001; Wheeler 1999). Maps are slippery because they appear to be so scientific, especially as computers increasingly generate them. Maps are received with trust; they construct taken-for-granted worlds in which geographies and identities are naturalized. Mapping contributes to the ease with which archaeology can be used to create particular images of past landscapes that suit the agendas of heritage tourism practitioners and others interested in controlling the way we perceive the past. New mapping technologies are especially seductive as they appear to be able to reflect different perspectives and multiple landscapes both past and present. For example, in mapping the temple district of Vijayanagara from different points in order to show a range of possible perspectives on the temple in the past, Mack's use of a sophisticated and interesting technology hides the extent to which the mapping was framed by the questions of an archaeologist in the present and that what is produced is a representation (Mack 2004). Anschuetz, Wilshusen, and Scheik write unquestioningly of the power of such representations in their review of landscape archaeology.

> The analytical power, the widespread availability, and the comparative ease of computerized applications of geographical model-based paradigms within geographical information systems (GIS) packages is providing archaeologists now with a new set of quantitative tools for research of spatial patterns at macro- and microscales. (Anschuetz et al. 2001:170)

We do not suggest that there is no value in archaeologists tracking and mapping the actions of people across a particular space. But the paean above forgets that in doing this labor, archaeologists produce representations, and like all representations these risk becoming fixed, leaving out different interpretations of the past. There is a need to consider, beyond the technology, how archaeological practices give meaning to any particular landscape.

The primacy of the visual in encoding and legitimating economic expansion and empire was fundamental to the way travel writing emptied landscapes for imperial appropriation and is clear in the monarch-of-all-I-survey description of landscapes (Pratt 1992). The Victorians' verbal paintings used this trope to produce geographical discoveries for the audience at home (Pratt 1992). They depended on descriptions that were "extremely rich in material and semantic substance" and contained a "proliferation of concrete, material referents" to create a density of meaning that translated, through "estheticization," a scene into a painting (Pratt 1992:204). GIS and contemporary forms of mapping provide archaeologists with just such a monarch-of-all-I-survey perspective especially through the density of "concrete material referents" provided by the sophisticated computer technology described above that creates a pretty picture for the archaeologist's use. Visualization is also one of the defining qualities of tourism (Bruner 1995; Galani-Moutafi 2000; Ntarangwi 2000; Urry 1990). Archaeologists can, we suggest, be compared to tourists, much as anthropologists are because of ethnography's travelogue-as-technique for establishing the place of the other in another time as well as another space (Crick 1985; Fabian 1983; Kaspin 1997; Van den Abbeele 1980). Not only, therefore, are archaeology and tourism intrinsically linked through an industry of heritage tourism, but the archaeologist is to some extent a traveler in a foreign country, one that the archaeologist actually creates. The archaeological past becomes a space, a landscape that risks being colonized (recolonized) by the archaeologist. The past is no longer just another country but another colonized country.

Anschuetz, Wilshusen, and Scheik argue that a landscape approach in archaeology can "bridge the division between archaeological practice and the concerns of archaeology's many publics, including the people of indigenous communities who are increasingly vocal participants in discussions on the interpretation and management of their heritage" (Anschuetz, Wilshusen, and Scheik 2001:159). But the power of this approach cannot be seen as inherent; technologies, which are always products of specific sociotechnic worldviews and, therefore, never neutral, can be no more or less capable of cross-cultural dialogue than any other. What is necessary is finding ways to pay attention to and engage with multiple versions and multiple representations of any one area by, to some extent, re-asserting the importance of time within a study of space. By "thinking deeply through the past" as suggested by Shepherd, we want to show how a landscape mapped by archaeologists and others cannot stand in isolation from the centuries of activity and engagement that produced multiple landscapes over time, nor can it stand apart from the present landscapes (Shepherd 2003).

Archaeology cannot simply see through this to an untainted past, and we cannot indulge the whims of tourists or those in land disputes by producing images of the past that take no account of the passing of time. We will attempt to do this through an analysis of a landscape over the last 200 years in an area that lies north of the Soutpansberg in the Limpopo Province of South Africa, near Musina, where the tensions between science and myth, politics and community are being played out.

TSHIRUNDU: WRITING DIVERGENT LANDSCAPES

Shirbeek is 30 miles east of Messina, and on the kopjes[2] at the back of the kraal near the main road there are many ruined walls, generally following the Dzata tradition, though admittedly of more recent date. The headman of the kraal, Tshirundu, who hospitably received me and gave me all the help I needed, informed me that his family once occupied the ruin nearby, and that he himself was born in it. (Fouché 1937:22)

Here we focus on the Kwinda Tshirundu, Venda-speaking farmers who settled north of the Soutpansberg in the Limpopo Province of South Africa in the last 200 years. This area is near what is now the city of Musina and is dominated by the Nzhelele River, a tributary of the Limpopo, and the Ha-Tshirundu Mountains. Oral histories[3] and historical sources suggest that the Tshirundu's ancestors trekked into southern Africa with the Lembethu from the Great Lakes district during the seventeenth century (Stayt 1968). The first headman of the Tshirundu, Nyadembe, settled in the vicinity of Mt. Dowe, which was used as a ceremonial centre, a function that it continues to fulfill. He set up a kraal (cattle enclosure) at Ama Madala, in the vicinity of Mt. Dowe close to the Limpopo River, but later moved to the Ha-Tshirundu Mountains where he built elaborate stone structures, including a site commonly known as Tshirundu's Kraal (Site number TSH 40[4]), in approximately 1860. Nyadembe was a renowned miracle maker and was wealthy, owning large herds of cattle. He died in the second half of the nineteenth century, but tradition is unclear about whether he was buried in a stone-filled rock shelter near Tshirundu's Kraal or at Mphathele (the farm Framton). Although White South African cartographers mapped the Soutpansberg and the Sand River–"Sterkstroom" (Nzhelele River)–Nuanetsi River areas in the nineteenth century, these Tshirundu settlements do not appear on the maps (Merensky and Jeppe 1868; Raddatz 1886; Troye 1892).

Nyadembe's son Tshitakani Tshirundu was born around 1860 at Tshirundu's Kraal (Fouché 1937). He moved his family away from this site north into the plains, possibly to what is today TSH 29. His descendants say that this was because his son drowned in a nearby waterhole and he believed that Tshirundu's Kraal was cursed. He subsequently moved about 2 km west to Kremetartkop (the site TSH 11), where he built stone structures. After his death in approximately 1940 he was buried at Kremetartkop. One of Tshitakani's sons, Matenzhe Tshirundu, was born around 1920 on what became the farm, Framton. His kraal was situated approximately 600 m northeast of Kremetartkop, at TSH 10. After his death he was buried next to his father. His successor, Mavhusha Tshikale, was the last ruler of the Tshirundu people before they were dispersed by the exigencies of apartheid. He died in 1974 and is thought to be buried on the farm, Framton, but the site has not yet been identified.

The first recorded contact between the Venda and white settlers occurred during 1836 when Louis Trichardt's trek entered the Soutpansberg (Eloff ca. 1960). The town of Schoemansdal was founded in 1850, and European traders became more common in the region (Fouché 1937). The Boshoff family were the first European farmers to settle near the Ha-Tshirundu Mountains around 1860. These settlers were known for poaching game from what was then meant to be Crown land and lived largely independent of any state or colonial authority. In fact, farms in the Soutpansberg and Limpopo Valley were only officially mapped at the beginning of the twentieth century.[5] After World War I the Governor-General of the Union of South Africa granted large portions of the Limpopo Valley to returning South African soldiers. These included the farms of Framton, N'jelele's Drift, and Skirbeek within the Tshirundu's territory.[6] The Tshirundu people moved or were made to move from their villages to laborers' quarters on these farms or north into Zimbabwe.

In the mid-1990s a foreign consortium started to buy up the farms in this area and set out to create a particular vision of an African landscape. Their goal was to conserve an area of Africa in a so-called pristine or original state for generations to come. This process took land that had been occupied for millennia, and farmed for generations by a varied stream of people, and turned it into a particularly western image of what Africa is supposed to look like. This image draws on western perceptions of Africa that evoke the earliest travel writers and explorers who drew pictures and maps of Africa that elided the presence of people. This imaginary geography of Africa is, like the Orient, one of a single entity undifferentiated either by topography, society, culture, language, economy, politics, or religion (Said 1979). It is no accident, for example, that Africa is represented at Disney World in its "Animal Kingdom," which focuses on an imitation safari (Mathers 2004). This transformation of the land by the reserve evokes the heyday of the safari, which was defined by the possibility of traveling through an Africa that had no people, a country that was nothing but wilderness and game (Brantlinger 1985; Hibbert 1982). Africans did accompany safaris, but they were either the hidden porters or limited to the loyal gun bearer or gifted tracker (an honor most often given to bushmen, the indigenous inhabitants of this entire region). Safaris were always about hunting animals, either with gun or, more recently, with camera. These close-to-nature journeys have become in the West's imagination a representation of what is good about Africa. Contemporary safaris consciously evoke this era of travel to Africa, offering luxury campsites, wall-to-wall (bush-to-bush) servants, lots of alcohol and excellent food, along with a more often than not "great-white-hunter" guide (Harden 2000; Jones 1999:51). Even when safaris, both then and now, are aimed at observing people, in Africa these people become part of the land, so naturalized that they do not disturb the vision of an empty landscape (Hubbard and Mathers 2004; Pratt 1985). This particular vision of a "real" African landscape, although very much in line with government policy and foreign desires, manages to elide while at the same time claiming what can plainly be seen on the present landscape, including Stone Age sites, rock art, and early and middle Iron Age sites, as well as the later sites. These sites are not understood as evidence that this land was exploited, struggled over, and changed by people for hundreds or thousands of years, but rather as more evidence of its failed modernity and, therefore, its "natural" state as being empty of human agency (Ferguson 2006).

In recent years huge portions of the Limpopo Province have been subject to land claims made through the Restitution of Land Rights Act No. 22 of 1994 and amendments,[7] which establish guidelines for returning land that was illegally taken from its owners through colonial and apartheid legislation since 1913. The descendants of the Tshirundu have made a claim for a large section of the reserve, but the management is fighting the claims. Yet ironically the farms belonging to the white settlers of this land during the twentieth century have already been destroyed in ways that no land redistribution process could ever have achieved (see Figure 4.1). To create the pristine nature reserves, farmhouses were bulldozed, making them part of the archaeological record almost overnight—just fragments on the landscape. Eighty years of history that had substantially changed the environment through cattle farming was simply wiped out. The farmers, some of whom now work for the reserve, appear to be largely unconcerned by this erasure.

Conservation here has little to do with the region's complex social and political past. The desire reflected in this discourse to return the land

Figure 4.1   Site of a twentieth-century farmhouse.

to how it supposedly looked before people shows the extent to which conservation in South Africa is primarily about conserving nature from people. This is seen across this country as the South African government has declared large tracts of land as reserves, often at the expense of land claimants. The claimants' stake, in spite of the South African National Parks Board's commitment to a concept of people's parks[8] is turned into the opportunity to sell crafts on the borders of a game park or into the corporatization of ethnic identities (Cook 2005; van Wyk 2003).

ARCHAEOLOGY: REWRITING DIVERGENT LANDSCAPES

The landscape, past and present, and therefore archaeology as well, form a focal point of much of the tension between the reserve and the people of Tshirundu. One solution imagined by the reserve to the problem of land claims is to offer land elsewhere for claimants to occupy. Although this acknowledges their entitlement to land as a sterile economic commodity, it ignores the connection that these people might have with the landscape, the meaning its past has for them, and their own lived experience on this land. What is the role of archaeology, if any, in establishing the meaning of this landscape?

An archaeological investigation of the reserve's late Iron Age landscape was initiated by the reserve's management, who were interested in possibly developing some sites as additional tourist attractions (Kruger, forthcoming). This interest may appear to contradict an argument based on a desire for an empty landscape but, as we suggest above, actually conforms to the perception that African people, as long as they stay in the past, make little inroads on an image of a wild landscape (Hubbard and Mathers 2004). The archaeological survey began by sampling areas where farmers were likely to have settled. Some sites were found, as expected, along the drainage systems of the Limpopo and Nzhelele rivers and on hills that offered natural fortification. This sampling system was, however, inadequate, so for much of the area an arbitrary total coverage survey was necessary. More than 30 individual sites containing elaborate stonewalls, monoliths and wooden palisades, grinding stones, hut remains, potsherds, and beads were found on small hilltops in the Ha-Tshirundu Mountains (see Figure 4.2).

These elaborate stonewall structures are reminiscent of the Dzata ruins in the upper Nzhelele River and the Great Zimbabwe ruins near Masvingo in Zimbabwe. Most of the sites are built on the more prominent kopjes in the area. Radiocarbon dating[9] and surface ceramics indicate that the sites date to the nineteenth century. The characteristics of the walled sites, especially the presence of defensive structures such as palisades and loopholes, and their positions far from water sources suggest that defense was an important factor in their distribution (see Figure 4.3).

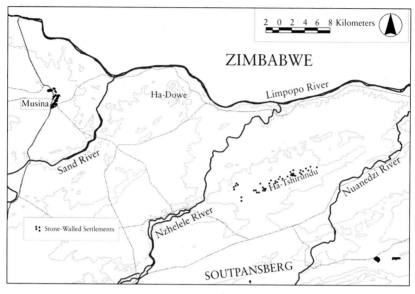

Figure 4.2 Distribution of the archaeological sites identified by the survey.

Figure 4.3 Characteristic palisade walls at Tshirundu's Kraal.

A typical interpretation of such a landscape is that the settlement pattern reflects a need for defense and security in a time of conflict. This is supported by much of the archaeology and history of this area and of Southern Africa during this period (Boeyens 2000; Hall 1987; Huffman 1987; Pikirayi 1993). This archaeological and historical research suggests a past dominated by movement and displacement. It is a past that could support the reserve's claim that the landscape could have little meaning to the people now living in the area and even those that might have passed through it during these times of stress. However, local histories do not understand the meaning of these sites in terms of conflict. The Tshirundu's perception of the landscape is very different, showing a history that is not limited by the exigencies of an archaeological survey and thus ranges over a wider area, suggesting movement and return, space, time, and meaning. The Tshirundu identify themselves and their ancestors as skilled and renowned rainmakers, *nyangas* (doctors), and miracle workers. The name *Tshirundu*, in fact, refers to a woven straw basket associated with rainmaking that is believed to bring good fortune. These baskets were also ceremonially used to cover the top of grain storage bins prior to planting and harvesting in order to ensure good harvests. In about 1860 Mpephu, the leader of the western Venda, gave the Tshirundu this land so they would be free to practice their rainmaking and healing skills in the service of Mpephu's people. The location of their walled villages was, therefore, primarily related to the ceremonial power of the sites, sites that perhaps required greater defense but also gave people a sense of security in times of flux. The monoliths found at these sites are generally associated with ritual power during the South Africa Iron Age and, therefore, support this meaning (Huffman 1987; Stayt 1968).

This area has a history and archaeology that points to centuries of conflict, yet the oral histories suggest a landscape of ritual and power. This meaning does not require a map or settlement pattern to be made real, but depends on memory of space linked to genealogies, although it can, as we have tried to show, be represented by maps animated by oral histories (Green and Green 2004). The land is made to belong to people through their construction of a landscape of ritual. Even in times of conflict, life goes about its usual pace for most people, requires the usual rituals, relationships, and small economies necessary for survival but also for just living. In placing too much reliance on site distribution, archaeology risks not seeing the practices of everyday life that are equally present on the landscape. The fact of the conflict that beset this region and that caused dispersion and movement of people out of it and across it is not denied by their landscape. The fluidity and hybridization of borderlands do not prevent people from imbuing the landscape with memories, meanings, and imaginations (Anschuetz et al. 2001). Even while moving, people create a sense of self and belonging through an ambulatory vision (Bender 2001).

TELLING STORIES OF POSTCOLONIAL ARCHAEOLOGIES

> We can surely learn from the Western Apache, who insist that the stories
> they tell, far from putting meanings upon the landscape, are intended
> to allow listeners to place themselves in relation to specific features of
> the landscape, in such a way that their meanings may be revealed or
> disclosed. Stories help to open up the world, not to cloak it. (Ingold
> 1993:171)

Landscapes remain inextricably linked to representations whether we
think of them as chronotypes or as crafts. A landscape remains an artifact "woven, carved, lived through representations" (Lazzari 2003:
211). This makes it even more important to pay attention to the crafters
of these representations such as archaeologists, so that maps become
representations of everyday practice in the past rather than artifacts of
archaeological practices. We argue for the need to pay attention to ways
in which a landscape approach in archaeology produces images and
representations that fix a past within a single possible history, in this
case a history of conflict and movement. This is not, however, meant
to suggest that a landscape is merely an image or a representation that
stands in for an object. Ingold usefully contrasts the everyday project
of dwelling in the world that makes up a landscape with the rather
"peculiar and specialized project of the surveyor or cartographer whose
objective is to represent it" (Ingold 1993:154). By recognizing that the
representation of a landscape is in part an artifact, it is possible to see
the land. As Spiegel argues, it is essential to recognize the autonomy of
the landscape (Spiegel 2004). Landscapes can give the impression of
being objects, but they are living processes not objects. Yet they are so
powerful for archaeologists because, given the challenge of archaeology,
which can only really perceive not know autonomy in the past, they
offer "the most solid appearance in which history can declare itself"
(Ingold 1993:162).

The challenge of recognizing the autonomy of a landscape while doing
the work required of archaeologists to map and represent the landscape
is similar to the challenge articulated by Haraway for feminist scholar-
ship as "how to have simultaneously an account of radical historical
contingency for all knowledge claims and knowing subjects, a critical practice for recognizing our own semiotic technologies for making
meanings, and a no-nonsense commitment to faithful accounts of a real
world" (Haraway 1988:579). Haraway suggests here that social scien-
tists, amongst which we would certainly include archaeologists, face the
challenge of describing a "real" world while also being implicated in the
construction of representations that have ideological power. The power
of the gaze, so important to archaeologists mapping sites, lies in how it

empties a landscape of both its past and its present. The gaze/visualization operates to separate the viewer from the object—conquering by seemingly coming from nowhere. The eye needs to be resituated firmly into the body of the observer. Haraway suggests that this challenge can in part be met through acknowledging that we only have situated knowledges, which are by definition partial because they are rooted within the body of a particular and situated observer (Haraway 1988). Objectivity thus becomes possible through partial and embodied vision. Archaeology's advantage when paying attention to the way representations are made and how they are used is that, unlike an analysis of texts, it is or should be harder for archaeology to erase the voices of the "native" or to limit native resistance to devices that circumvent and interrogate authority (Parry 1987). Archaeology's focus on the material embodiment of the practices of everyday life within the context of particular landscapes helps to ensure, although does not guarantee, that archaeologists are situated.

Ingold argues for an approach to landscape studies that combines temporality and landscape, recognizing that human life is a process that involves the passage of time and that this same life process also forms the landscapes in which people have lived (Ingold 1993). This dwelling perspective that emphasizes the ways the landscape forms, not as a backdrop but as an enduring aspect of the actions of past and present generations, highlights how the actions of archaeologists themselves are a form of dwelling (Ingold 1993). The knowledge gained from the practices of anthropologists and archaeologists is on par with the knowledge that comes from the practical activities of the native dweller; for all of us "the landscape tells—or rather is—a story" (Ingold 1993:152). Joyce argues that archaeology begins with storytelling, and it is the stories that South Africans have to tell that can form the basis of a meaningful contribution to archaeological practice by African people (Joyce 2002). Storytelling is fundamental to the ways that South Africans shape their identities and, reclaimed as "robust narratives born out of a certain soil and people," suggest the possibility of a South African archaeological theory and practice that includes both folk and academic archaeologies (Ouzman 2005:218). In asking "how do we draw a map of the future," Shepherd suggests that any such map needs to process memories, culture, and identities that are linked to the tensions and traumas of the present (Shepherd 2002). Shepherd's call to archaeology in South Africa to "think deeply through the past" encourages archaeologists to tell stories that guide the attention of listeners or readers into the world, rather than weaving a tapestry to cover the world up (Ingold 1993; Shepherd 2003). These are the stories we have tried to tell here.

NOTES

1. L.P. Hartley, *The Go-Between* (New York Review of Books, New York, 2002).
2. Kopje is the South African vernacular for a small hill, derived from Afrikaans.
3. These histories were collected by N. Kruger in January and June 2004 in the Upper Nzelele Valley, in the former Venda homeland. The interviews were facilitated by a local Nyanga, Dr. P. Ramavoya. Some of the informants are involved in the Land Claim. Interviews were conducted in Venda and English, using an interpreter, Tshinanga. First interviews focused on the informants' lineages and their memories of where their ancestors had lived. Later, informants were asked to specifically connect these memories with sites on the landscape.
4. Site numbers refer to sites identified by archaeological surveys conducted in November through January 2003/2004 by Neels Kruger. "TSH" stands for "Tshirundu," referring to the historical and geographical context of the sites. See Figure 4.2.
5. 1910 Cartographer: Surveyor General South African Archives # E 196. South African National Archives, Pretoria.
6. Executive Council Minutes 944 and 2015.
7. http://www.info.gov.za/acts/1994/a22-94.pdf
8. http://www.sanparks.org/people/heritage/
9. AD 1860, Quaternary Dating Research Unit, Council for Scientific and International Research, Pretoria. PTA Number 1136.

REFERENCES

Andah, Bassey W. 1995. European Encumbrances to the Development of Relevant Theory in African Archaeology. In *Theory in Archaeology: A World Perspective*, ed. by Peter J. Ucko, pp. 96–109. Routledge, London.

Anderson, Benedict R. 1991. Imagined Communities: Reflections on the Origin and Spread of Nationalism. Rev. ed. Verso, London.

Anschuetz, Kurt F., Richard H. Wilshusen, and Cherie L. Scheik. 2001. An Archaeology of Landscapes: Perspectives and Direction. *Journal of Archaeological Research* 9(2):157–211.

Asad, Talal. 1973. *Anthropology & the Colonial Encounter*. Humanities Press, New York.

Ashmore, Wendy. 2004. Social Archaeologies of Landscape. In *A Companion to Social Archaeology*, ed. by Lynn Meskell and Robert W. Preucel, pp. 255–271. Blackwell Publishers, Oxford.

Bender, Barbara. 2001. Landscapes On-the-Move. *Journal of Social Archaeology* 1(1):75–89.

Boeyens, Jan C.A. 2000. In Search of Kaditshwene. *South African Archaeological Bulletin* 55:2–17.

Brantlinger, Patrick. 1985. Victorians and Africans: The Geneology of the Myth of the Dark Continent. *Critical Inquiry* 12(1):166–203.

Bruner, Edward M. 1995. The Ethnographer/Tourist in Indonesia. In *International Tourism Identity and Change*, ed. by Marie-Francoise Lanfant, John B. Alcock, and Edward M. Bruner, pp. 224–241. SAGE Publications, London.

Carruthers, Jane. 2003. Friedrich Jeppe: Mapping the Transvaal ca. 1850–1899. *Journal of Southern African Studies* 29(4):955–976.

Cook, Susan. 2005. Chiefs, Kings, Corporatization, and Democracy: A South African Case Study. *Brown Journal of World Affairs* 11(2):125–137.

Crick, Malcolm. 1985. "Tracing" the Anthropological Self: Quizzical Reflections on Field Work, Tourism, and the Ludic. *Social Analysis* 17:71–92.

Duncan, James, and Derek Gregory (editors). 1999. *Writes of Passage: Reading Travel Writing*. Routledge, London.

Eloff, Johannes Frederick ca. 1960. *Die Gevolge van die aanraking met die Blankes op die politieke organisasie en die gesagsbeginsel by die Venda: 'n verslag*. Department of Anthropology and Archaeology, University of Pretoria, Pretoria, South Africa.

Fabian, Johannes. 1983. *Time and the Other: How Anthropology Makes Its Object*. Columbia University Press, New York.

Ferguson, James. 2006. *Global Shadows: Africa in the Neoliberal World Order*. Duke University Press, Durham.

Fouché, Leo. 1937. *Mapungubwe, Ancient Bantu Civilization on the Limpopo*. Cambridge University Press, Cambridge.

Galani-Moutafi, Vasiliki. 2000. The Self and the Other: Traveler, Ethnographer, Tourist. *Annals of Tourism Research* 27(1):203–224.

Green, Lesley Fordred. 2004. Space and the Body: Rethinking the Division between Biological and Sociocultural Anthropology. *Anthropology Southern Africa* 27(1&2):1–3.

Green, Lesley Fordred, and David R. Green. 2004. From Chronological to Spatio-Temporal Histories: Mapping Heritage in Arukwa, Área Indígena do Uaçá, Brazil. *Anthropology Southern Africa* 27(1&2):19–26.

Hall, Martin. 1987. *The Changing Past: Farmers, Kings and Traders in Southern Africa, 200–1860*. David Philip, Johannesburg.

Hall, Martin, and Pia Bombardella. 2005. Las Vegas in Africa. *Journal of Social Archaeology* 5(1):5–24.

Haraway, Donna. 1988. Situated Knowledges: The Science Question in Feminisms and the Privilege of Partial Perspective. *Feminist Studies* 14(3):575–599.

Harden, Blaine. 2000. The Last Safari. *The New York Times* 4 June: Travel Section. New York.

Hibbert, Christopher. 1982. *Africa Explored: Europeans in the Dark Continent, 1769–1889*. A. Lane, London.

Hubbard, Laura, and Kathryn Mathers. 2004. Surviving American Empire in Africa: The Anthropology of Reality Television. *International Journal of Cultural Studies* 7(4):437–455.

Huffman, T.N. 1987. *Symbols in Stone*. Witwatersrand University Press, Johannesburg.

Ingold, Tim. 1993. The Temporality of the Landscape. *World Archaeology* 25(2):152–174.

Jones, Amanda. 1999. Africa, the Way It Was. Where the Gin and Tonics Flow Freely under the Baobab and One Never Lifts the Luggage. *San Francisco Examiner Magazine* March 14:16–51.

Joyce, Rosemary. 2002. *The Language of Archaeology: Dialogue, Narrative, and Writing*. Blackwell Publishing, Oxford.

Kaspin, Deborah. 1997. On Ethnographic Authority and the Tourist Trade: Anthropology in the House of Mirrors. *Anthropological Quarterly* 70(2):53–57.

Keesing, Roger M. 1994. Theories of Culture Revisted. In *Assessing Cultural Anthropology*, ed. by Robert Borofsky, pp. 302–312. McGraw Hill, New York.

Kinahan, John. 1995. Theory, Practice and Criticism in the History of Namibian Archaeology. In *Theory in Archaeology: A World Perspective*, ed. by Peter J. Ucko, pp. 77–95. Routledge, London.

Kruger, Neels. Forthcoming. *Interpretations of Conflict; Conflict of Interpretations: The Archaeology of the Lower Nzelele Valley, Limpopo Province*. Master's thesis, Department of Anthropology and Archaeology, University of Pretoria, Pretoria, South Africa.

Lazzari, Marisa. 2003. Archaeological Visions: Gender, Landscape and Optic Knowledge. *Journal of Social Archaeology* 3(2):194–222.

Lowe, Lisa. 1991. *Critical Terrains: French and British Orientalisms*. Cornell University Press, Ithaca.

Mack, Alexandra. 2004. One Landscape, Many Experiences: Differing Perspectives of the Temple Districts of Vijayanagara. *Journal of Archaeological Method and Theory* 11(1):59–81.

Mathers, Kathryn. 2004. Re-imagining Africa: What American Students Learn in South Africa. *Tourism Review International* 8(2):127–141.

Merensky, Alexander, and Fredrich Jeppe. 1868. Original Map of the Transvaal or South African Republic. In The Jeppe-Merensky Map of the Transvaal 1:1,850,000, by W.C. Watson. *The South African Survey Journal* 11(5):13. 1968.

Mitchell, Timothy. 1988. *Colonizing Egypt*. University of California Press, Berkeley.

Ntarangwi, Mwenda. 2000. Education, Tourism, or Just a Visit to the Wild. *African Issues* 28(1&2):54–60.

Olwig, Kenneth. 2003. Landscape: The Lowenthal Legacy. *Annals of the Association of American Geographers* 93(4):871–877.

Ouzman, Sven. 2005. Silencing and Sharing Southern African Indigenous and Embedded Knowledge. In *Indigenous Archaeologies: Decolonizing Theory and Practice*, ed. by Claire Smith and H. Martin Wobst, pp. 208–225. One World Archaeology No. 47. Routledge, London.

Parry, Benita. 1987. Problems in Current Theories of Colonial Discourse. *The Oxford Literary Review* 9(1–2):27–58.

Pikirayi, Innocent. 1993. *The Archaeological Identity of the Mutapa State: Towards an Historical Archaeology of Northern Zimbabwe*. Societas Archaeologica Upsaliensis. Distributed by Department of Archaeology, Uppsala University, Uppsala.

Pratt, Mary Louise. 1985. Scratches on the Face of the Country; or, What Mr. Barrow Saw in the Land of the Bushmen. *Critical Inquiry* 12(1):119–143.

———. 1992. *Imperial Eyes: Travel Writing and Transculturation*. Routledge, London.

Raddatz, H. 1886. Das Untere Olifantbecken (Süd-Afrikanische Republik). *Petermanns Geographische Mitteilungen* 32: Plate 4. Gotha.

Said, Edward W. 1979. *Orientalism*. Vintage Books, New York.

Shepherd, Nick. 2002. Heading South, Looking North: Why We Need a Post-colonial Archaeology. *Archaeological Dialogues* 9(2):74–82.

———. 2003. State of the Discipline: Science, Culture and Identity in South African Archaeology, 1870–2003. *Journal of Southern African Studies* 29(4):823–844.

Sluyter, Andrew. 2001. Colonialism and Landscapes in the Americas: Material/Conceptual Transformations and Continuing Consequences. *Annals of the Association of American Geographers* 91(2):410–428.

Spiegel, Andrew D. 2004. Walking Memories and Growing Amnesia in the Land Claims Process: Lake St. Lucia, South Africa. *Anthropology Southern Africa* 27(1&2):3–10.

Stayt, H.A. 1968. *The Bavenda*. Cass, London.

Trigger, Bruce G. 1989. *A History of Archaeological Thought*. Cambridge University Press, Cambridge.

Trouillot, Michel-Rolph. 1991. Anthropology and the Savage Slot: The Poetics and Politics of Otherness. In *Recapturing Anthropology: Working in the Present*, ed. by Richard G. Fox, pp. 17–44. School of American Research Press, Sante Fe.

Troye, Gustav. 1892. Troye's New Map of the Transvaal Colony. In *New Map of the Transvaal Colony*, by G. Troye. Grocott and Sherry, Grahamstown, South Africa.

Urry, John. 1990. *The Tourist Gaze: Leisure and Travel in Contemporary Societies*. SAGE Publications, London.

Van den Abbeele, G. 1980. Sightseers: The Tourist as Theorist. *Diacritics* 10:3–14.

Van Wyk, Ilana. 2003. Land Claims and Corporate Imitation: Brokering Development in Maputoland, Kwazulu-Natal. *Anthropology Southern Africa* 26(1&2):63–71.

Wheeler, Roxann. 1999. Limited Visions of Africa: Geographies of Savagery and Civility in Early Eighteenth-Century Narratives. In *Writes of Passage: Reading Travel Writing*, ed. by James Duncan and Derek Gregory, pp. 14–48. Routledge, London.

CHAPTER 5

Driekopseiland Rock Engraving Site, South Africa: A Precolonial Landscape Lost and Re-membered

David Morris

INTRODUCTION

Uniquely in the historiography of South African rock art sites, the engravings at Driekopseiland near Kimberley (see Figure 5.1) entered the written record as part of a fervent exposé on land loss by indigenous people in the nineteenth century. In the 1870s the engravings remained as one of the few tangible traces—indeed, as George Stow (1905:397) would have it, as the *title deeds*—of previous occupancy by "Bushmen." Some decades before this, Khoe-San[1] groups in the region were losing their independence, with land and access to water being seized by encroaching colonial pastoralists as the frontier shifted inland (Penn 2005; Stow 1905:394–395). From the 1870s the discovery of diamonds led to the rapid extension of colonial hegemony here and the beginning of the industrialization of South Africa's economy.

Stow was blunt about what he characterized as the fraudulent transaction by which white Trekboers first gained ownership of the tracts between the Riet and Vaal Rivers in 1839. Official records (Arnot and Orpen 1875:252–253) show that the transfer of land was entered into at Van Wyksvalley (now Boshof) on 18 May of that year. One David Dantsie, "Corander Boesman" (Korana Bushman) by birth, with "Corander name" De Goep, asserted that he, as a leader, had inherited from his father, Horingkap, son of Tgontgoup, all the country between the Modder River and the Vaal River, to its junction with the Sand River. Field-cornet D.S. Fourie and other white farmers would pay to Dantsie one riding horse and 70 fat-tailed sheep. Placing his mark on the document, the illiterate Dantsie undertook "never to reclaim this tract of land ... [and] never again to ask for payment," and that he would take his abode and his people "over the Vaal River, all my people being satisfied therewith."

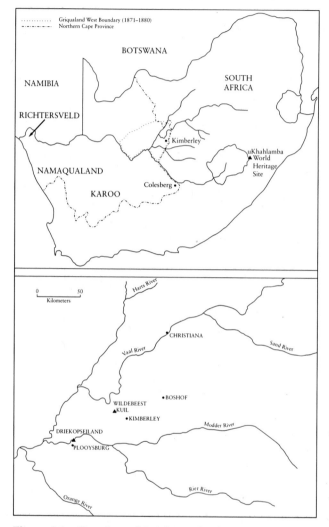

Figure 5.1 Situation of Driekopseiland on the Riet River relative to other places and regions mentioned in the text.

"We can imagine this unfortunate Bushman," Stow would write, "surrounded by armed men, signing away *of his own free will* the birthright of his tribe for a riding horse and some three score sheep!" (his emphasis). "What," asked Stow, "did the unfortunate who put his hand to the cross know of the actual contents of the paper in front of him, or the extent of the land which it purposed to alienate?" The sheep, Stow added, were "valued in those days at some four shillings and sixpence each, [in exchange] for upwards of two and a quarter millions of acres of land!" (The indigenous fat-tailed variety of sheep would have been far inferior, in the eyes of commercial colonial farmers, to the imported wool-producing merinos.)

The matter was not to go unchallenged. Although in 1841 Jan Bloem, Korana leader, went on record confirming Dantsie's claim and hence his right to dispose of the land (Arnot and Orpen 1875), a contender, a Bushman named Kousop and a grandson of the above Tgontgoup, began agitating in 1850. He commenced by having letters sent by an agent to white farmers in the area "desiring them immediately to quit their farms." Kousop would be neither cowed nor placated and in 1858 instigated a rising in which farms were attacked across a broad front in the vicinity of modern Christiana, Boshof, and Kimberley. A commando was raised in retaliation and Kousop and other leaders and raiders were killed, while 43 prisoners were subsequently murdered (Morris 2000).

The rock engravings of Driekopseiland (then known as Blauwbank) feature in Stow's narration of these events (see Figure 5.2) as "the ancient title deeds of [the Bushman] race to the widespread plains around them" (1905:397). The site (which Stow was also the first person to record) constituted solid evidence of an ancient and aboriginal Bushman presence.

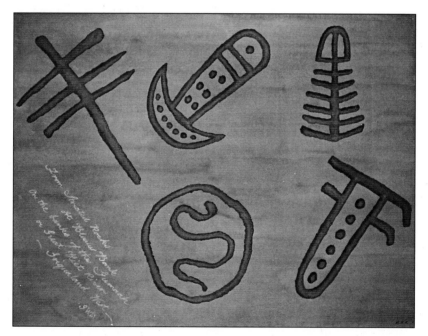

Figure 5.2 One of George Stow's Driekopseiland copies. The text reads, "From striated rocks at Blauwbank on the banks of the Gumaap or Great Riet River, Griqualand West. GWS." (McGregor Museum Rock Art Collection).

As "the grand testimonials of the great antiquity of their occupation," he wrote, the spot "must have been, during the time of their undisturbed sovereignty, a place memorable to their race, where thousands of square feet of ... rock surface are covered with innumerable mystic devices, intermingled with comparatively few animal figures" (1905:398).[2]

Driekopseiland is just one of many rock engraving sites that populate the broader landscape, and which might have been construed (in Stow's terms) as the ubiquitous "title deeds" of a former Khoe-San "sovereignty." But already, as early as the later nineteenth century, the near invisibility of the Khoe-San here made this effectively a "cleared landscape." A second generation of colonial mapmaking and place-naming had, in the 1860s, erased part of an earlier overlay of colonial-era names, as British settlers replaced Dutch-speaking Griqua frontiersmen who had already been obliterating the presence and toponymy of the indigenous inhabitants. In the 1860s the Griqua farms Courasie's Pan, Uithaaldersfontein, Jantjes Dam, and Slypsteen—to mention but a few—became Leinster, Belmont, Ottawa, and Summerhill respectively (Kurtz 1988). Only here and there did an echo of autochthonous naming survive, for example in the farm name *Schutsekamma*, which derives from the !Ora *Khoese //ganadi*, meaning "nine camelthorn trees" (Levi Namaseb, personal communication 18 July 2000; van Vreeden 1961). Bushmen, gone from the land, were occasionally hailed anachronistically in such farm names as *Boschmans Pan*.

This chapter touches upon this history of clearance, of eviction and exclusion, and the way the landscape has been rewritten, remapped, and subjected to new uses and forms of economic exploitation. The rock engraving sites have remained as perhaps the most tangible traces of the Later Stone Age precolonial past here. But just as the original inhabitants became largely invisible, so other actors upon the landscape came to be invoked to explain the presence of the engravings at sites such as Driekopseiland. Mainstream archaeology did not sink to such depths of mythmaking but, even so, it failed (by and large and until recently) to pursue indigenous insights that would enhance an appreciation of the site and its contexts, and to acknowledge and provide means for descendants to reconnect with a heritage from which they had been excluded. Today, it would be well for archaeology as a discipline to consider its role vis-à-vis heritage representation, a matter taken up in the final section of this chapter.

CLEARANCE: A MUTE SHIFT TO INVISIBILITY

Later strata of social and political history in South Africa have been marked by notorious and well-documented evictions and forced removals as people were resettled in designated Homelands and Group Areas

(Hallett 1984).[3] By contrast, the earlier "disappearances" of Khoe-San people from landscapes such as Driekopseiland are reflected by a comparatively mute shift from archaeological evidence of presence to that of "absence" and cultural transformation. Contemporary commentary was minimal—though the missionary John Philip stirred up debate in the 1820s-30s (Ross 1993),[4] with Stow being a somewhat lone voice of conscience later in the century and largely after the fact (his manuscript of the 1870s-80s was published posthumously in 1905).

Historical records (e.g., Lye 1975:146–147) show that even before the 1839 "agreement" (about which Stow had written), Bushmen occupied the area precariously. In January 1835 Andrew Smith, traveling near Driekopseiland, told of how Bush women visited his camp to obtain tobacco, but that "by no means could we succeed in getting a glimpse of their countrymen. The men ... are always extremely shy of strangers ... the men were in the hills, but afraid to come near us" (Lye 1975).There was a strong Griqua presence already, transhumant colonial farmers were moving into the area, and there were, in addition, in this frontier mix groups of resident Tswana and Xhosa. Sundry travelers, from the Cape or trekking between mission centers, passed along the valley of the Riet River (Humphreys 1972, 1997). In the decades preceding this, moreover, earlier social configurations had probably been severely disrupted in the disturbances known as the *Difaqane* (Hamilton 1995). In parts of the Karoo, punitive commando raids smashed Khoekhoen and San resistance to Trekboer encroachment from the late eighteenth century (Penn 2005), when women and children were taken as "tame Bushmen" to labor on colonial farms (Eldredge 1994). As the relationship between colonists and indigenous people declined, so the choice for many Khoe-San had been famine, retreat to the mountains, or—as Philip would characterize it—to sink "into servitude as the herdsmen and domestics of the boors [sic]." With the frontier expanding, Philip noted, "colonists, after having deprived the poor natives of their springs of water, now penetrated into the deserts and mountains to seize their women and children, and to reduce them to slavery on the lands which their husbands and fathers had occupied as a free and independent people" (cited in Ross 1993:199). Spiraling conflict reached a point in the 1770s, when, as Philip put it, "the whole race of Bushmen or Hottentots, who had not submitted to servitude, was ordered to be seized or extirpated; the privilege of slavery was designed exclusively for the women and children; the men, whose habits disqualified them for the purposes of the colonists, and whose revenge was probably dreaded, were destined for death."

Having described the Khoe-San as the "wretched victims of European avarice and cruelty," Philip himself then drew on the conventional imagery of barbarism to contrast those Khoe-San who were mission converts against those who were not. This was symptomatic of a widespread ambivalence in Cape liberalism which, as Keegan (1996) argues, led to the ultimate failure of the humanitarian challenge here in the nineteenth century.[5]

Later, land immediately to the south of Driekopseiland was granted to British "Albania Settlers" in the 1860s, ostensibly as a protective buffer between the Griqua and encroaching Trekboers, but with the protection of British interests clearly as an ulterior motive (Kurtz 1988). In the following decade the transfer of land into white ownership accelerated rapidly after the discovery of diamonds in the region.

Cadastral mapping, which defined legal title, also anticipated the development and spread of colonial farming—sometimes literally ahead of the fact. One map (Ford, McGregor Museum collection), overtaking the historical events of the day, laid out a grid of properties well beyond what would be the agreed northern boundary of Griqualand West—a spread of hoped-for white ownership that was stalled until much later Homeland consolidation and forced clearances made way for it in the twentieth century. Beginning in the 1870s, wire fencing traced out the charted polygons across the veld. The Tswana remained independent (until 1885) to the north of the Crown Colony of Griqualand West (which was proclaimed after the discovery of diamonds) but, within the colony, Locations were set up by 1877 to contain local Tswana farming communities—these being the forerunners of the Homelands under Apartheid (Shillington 1985). Those people who were not white, did not slot into the new Tswana Locations, or who failed to find niches in the young towns that sprang up—people who were often largely, though not exclusively, of Khoe-San background—found themselves, well before the end of the nineteenth century, either living lives of servitude on farmland that was no longer their own or eking out an existence foraging for seasonal labor, or any other means of survival, as a floating rural underclass literally "on the move."[6] These latter were the so-called *los Hotnots* (loose Hottentots) of no fixed abode, a category of persons who have persisted (known today as *Karretjiemense* "donkey-cart people"), and whose numbers grow owing to rising unemployment in the 1990s and early 2000s (de Jongh 2002).

For surviving descendants of the Khoe-San makers of rock engravings, then, it was by these processes of dispossession that links with the land and with rock engraving sites such as Driekopseiland were constrained, or severed entirely.

In the archaeological record of the period the Khoe-San voice appears to go silent. Stone tool making and other aspects of "terminal" Later Stone Age material culture cease to be practised (on one possible aspect of this final phase, see Henderson 2002; Morris 2002b, 2005). The visible heritage traces of the nineteenth century are "fabric-heavy" ones, mainly of white farmers and, later, diamond diggers (citing Byrne's useful term for comparable traces in Australia—"think homesteads and court houses"), whereas those traces reflecting the post-contact colonial underclass—especially the *los Hotnots*—are "fabric-light" and ephemeral, with the odds stacked against their survival as part of the material record (Byrne 2003:172). This relative invisibility is compounded by the fact that the scant material resources of the colonial underclass would increasingly have been a borrowing of elements from colonial society: beads, clay pipes, cheap English earthenwares, glassware, bottles, cutlery, and so on. Also included would be food, part of payment in kind to shepherds (Sampson 1992), the remains of which would show up archaeologically as sheep bones and dentition, and domestic grain, pumpkin, and fruit pips. While the material objects themselves may not be distinctive, their distribution and density, and the behavior patterns and economic status they bespeak, are. These spatial and economic indices would certainly underscore the fact and extent of dispossession and "clearance."

Language death occurred in tandem with these processes of social disintegration and subjugation (Traill 1996). Khoe-San personal names were lost and replaced by Dutch/Afrikaans ones. Despite this, it is remarkable how aspects of local idiom and lore, with roots in the precolonial past, live on amongst Afrikaans-speaking "Coloured" descendants of Northern Cape Khoe-San people. Myths and even rites, for example, concerning the "watersnake" (e.g., Hoff 1997; Lange et al. 2007; Waldman 2007) are still widely current, while in rural areas farmworkers descended from Khoe-San are the de facto "owners and custodians" of knowledge of /Khoba (*Hoodia* spp.) and other faunal/floral lore (de Jongh 2002). They are not, however, party *de jure* to the recent benefit-sharing agreement between the Council for Scientific and Industrial Research (CSIR) and the San (Wynberg 2004)—an issue that may yet come to be contested. Willerslev (2004), working in another continent, has indicated a comparable instance of indigenous knowledge survival despite language loss. Not that there is any direct historical continuity linking, for instance, the present-day *Karretjiemense* with the foragers of the precolonial era: the contemporary Karoo "foragers" are, as de Jongh shows, "a product of the modern era" (2002:446). Accommodated officially within the imposed "Coloured" racial identity, some individuals and cultural groups nevertheless begin, tentatively or more forcefully, to assert such links and autochthonous self-definitions. A woman in the Karoo quoted by de Jongh (2002:459) articulated identity thus: "*Ons is te arm om bruin te wees. Ons is die geel mense*" (We are too poor to be brown ["Coloured"] people. We are the yellow [San] people). Traill (1996:165) cites the ironic remark of Emma Sors, a member of a *Karretjiemense* group near Colesberg, that the only language she knew was "*hierdie Boesmantaal van ons*" (this Bushman language of ours), that is, Afrikaans! Brody (2002) refers to "men and women who looked like Bushmen, said they were Bushmen, but whose everyday reality appeared to lie somewhere between migrant farm worker and rural *lumpenproletarian*." The extent of culture loss is not small.

The unfolding spatial aspects of the history of these people in relation to power and identity had rendered their "Colouredness" in effect a nonidentity, lacking potential for any territorial claims (cf. Seirlis 2004). In contrast to Bantu-speaking groups (as de Jongh 2002 points out), "Coloured" Khoe-San descendants found themselves, at the outset of the twentieth century, with none of their land left and without an existence independent of colonial society. They were thereby also automatically disqualified from the post-1994 land restitution program, since the historical cut-off date was 1913, the year in which the colonial government formally restricted African land ownership in the Natives Land Act.[7]

Engelbrecht (2002:244), a Kimberley-based Khoe-San activist, expresses the situation eloquently when he states, "As Coloureds we feel out of Africa, while everyone around us is either African or Afrikaner. As Coloureds we were made to feel that we were only a mixed and bastard breed of people with no real ties to Africa, while the so-called Bantu people connect to Africa as Africans and the South African Europeans connect to Africa as Afrikaners. As Coloureds our history is overlooked and our children are effectively alienated from the reality of our proud heritage and first nation past."

Many of the descendants of the makers of rock art in the Karoo and adjoining areas—those who are itinerant seasonal workers in particular—are today "not only amongst the poorest of the poor in South Africa, but they are virtually unknown and socially invisible to other South Africans" (de Jongh 2002:446; cf. Sylvain 2005 on related current processes of marginalization in the Kalahari). The ranks of these poorest of rural people are currently on the increase as they suffer evictions or loss of employment because of farming restructuring, including "casualization" of labor (short-term contracts as opposed to permanent employment), conversion from livestock to game farming (which is less labor intensive), and retrenchments as farmers resist new post-Apartheid laws on workers' land, employment, and human rights (McLay 2003—who points out that in deep rural areas law-enforcers are often also farmers).

CHANGING PLACE AT DRIEKOPSEILAND IN THE TWENTIETH CENTURY

Under white ownership since the late nineteenth century, a "fabric-heavy" impact and the knock-on effects of twentieth-century agricultural development are today very much in evidence on the rock engraving site of Driekopseiland itself (Morris 2002a). It was one such impact—the proposal of a weir[8]—which provoked South Africa's Historical Monuments Commission to declare the site a national monument in 1944.

Clearly a major locale in the precolonial landscape, with more than 3,500 engravings spread across sheets of glaciated rock at this point in the bed of the Riet River, it is one of the biggest and most spectacular rock art sites in the region (see Figures 5.3 and 5.4). From being a "center" of evident significance, the site today straddles not only farm but also magisterial district boundaries—a circumstance that has bedeviled the legal definition of its extent by the Monuments Commission and successor heritage authorities since the mid-twentieth century. Its declaration as a heritage site was twice revised, yet to this day only half the site enjoys full legal protection. In effect, the engraving site remains a chunk of precolonial spatiality still challenging the cadastral logic of the colonial order.

Figure 5.3 The site of Driekopseiland, early twenty-first century.

Figure 5.4 A profusion of engravings spread across the glaciated surface at Driekopseiland.

The rock art site has not escaped the abuses of twentieth-century agricultural practice. Construction of the weir, as proposed in the early 1940s, went ahead (albeit just upstream of the site instead of submerging it—thanks to the timely intervention of McGregor Museum director Maria Wilman, who enlisted General Smuts's support in spurring the Monuments Commission to action [Morris 2002a]). About 150 engravings lie behind the weir. Building operations involved the mixing of cement and carting of materials across the site. In the 1970s the weir was increased in height, altering river dynamics so that flood-borne debris is dumped with force onto parts of the adjacent engraved surface. Engravings at that point have deteriorated markedly since the 1930s (Morris 1994). Today the weir irrigates adjacent farmlands as well as supplying water to Plooysburg, a small town nearby.

Alien vegetation invades the vicinity; *Phragmites communis* (reed) has taken root in flood-borne silt, while, more seriously, *Eucalyptus* saplings (a nineteenth-century import from Australia), previously having infested the north bank of the river, have been springing up ever closer to the engravings. Changes in plant and animal life consequent to the building of dams and canals along the Riet include water-weed settlement and encroachment, and increases in populations of blackfly and red-billed

Quelea (a common African bird regarded as a pest since the 1940s). The *Quelea* are now also having an increased impact in terms of agricultural losses. Large areas alongside the river, including the banks adjacent to Driekopseiland, have been stripped of their natural vegetation and put to the plough, with center-pivot irrigation fed from the river. The impact of this on archaeological resources cannot be overestimated (Morris 2002a).

A new threat is the encroachment of alluvial diamond mining, now getting under way within a kilometer upstream. Engraving sites further up the river at Schutsekamma have already been destroyed because of exemptions for mining under older legislation and inadequate adherence to, and policing of, current environmental and heritage laws (Morris 2004b).

The idyllic setting of the glaciated rocks on which the engravings occur is a favored swimming and *braai* (barbecue) spot for farmers and their friends or weekend visitors, and fishermen also frequent it. These activities, too, have been detrimental to the engravings. Vehicles are sometimes driven down onto the site and over the art. (On a leisurely Sunday afternoon in the 1980s, policemen from Plooysburg were found with their truck parked on top of the engravings beside the river and, with buckets and brushes, were washing down their vehicle. Given their role to uphold legal provisions for the protection of heritage, the police might themselves have been expected to treat the site with respect).

ACCESS AND INTERPRETATION

Public access to Driekopseiland has been permitted, on private land, since the site became a national monument in 1944, and at least one of the landowners has been especially accommodating in this respect. In practice, the privilege would have been reserved for and/or taken up mainly by white visitors, and descendants of Khoe-San who have ventured there specifically to see the engravings in recent years (alienated from their heritage, few would even know of such sites in the first place) have done so mainly on excursions organized by the McGregor Museum or the Wildebeest Kuil Rock Art Center.[9]

Interpretation of the site also became the preserve of the few, with the debate about the significance and meaning of the engravings becoming one in which descendants of the makers of the art had little power or opportunity to play a part. Indeed, in the elaboration of settler myths, a Khoe-San context was sometimes not even entertained, and the enigmatic geometric designs festooned across the site came to be attributed to non-African colonizers.

From the end of the nineteenth century the influential historian George Theal (1919:19) was articulating the view that Bushmen, "though gifted with artistic tastes," were "an almost unimprovable race ... [who] had become inert and stagnant"; a condition "not sufficient to satisfy God's law of progress." In an evolutionary sense they had come to represent the lowest stage of humanity, quite simply, as "pure savages." Evidence of sophistication in the rock art had some writers arguing, as did Péringuey (1909:418), that the Bushmen were responsible only for the most recent "decadent art," which was marked by "conspicuous retrogression." Some of the engravings, it was thought, belonged to an earlier, pre-Bushman stratum. In the first half of the twentieth century it was widely accepted that South Africa had been occupied by successive waves of migration of different races and peoples. In geographic terms it was an "ethnological cul-de-sac" (Schapera 1930:25) where earlier racial stock was either replaced or hybridized. Schapera (1930:27) could even state that "the stone industries associated in South Africa with the Bushmen were not indigenous to the country, but constitute an invading element which ... superseded the two pre-existing stone cultures."

Some writers envisaged long-distance cultural influences on a grand scale. Dart (1925:426) argued that the "pictorial art of the Bushmen ... has preserved through the lapse of centuries unassailable evidence of the impacts of ancient civilizations of the Eastern Mediterranean and Mesopotamian areas." As recently as 1952, even a prehistorian of the stature of van Riet Lowe was not reticent to speculate about such cross-continental links. At Driekopseiland he noted image types seen across the continent, and even beyond (1952:769), that appeared to be utilitarian rather than aesthetic and evinced "a 'feeling for writing,' an anxiety to convey a message in a symbol, i.e., an ideograph rather than a pictograph" (1952:770).

Slack (1962) used van Riet Lowe's paper as a springboard for her own more extravagant speculations about connections with "an Egyptian or even Mediterranean civilization." Media coverage, even to the present day (e.g., *Sunday Independent*, Johannesburg, 21 September 2003; *Noordkaap*, Kimberley, 7 June 2006), attests to the popular appeal of such off-beat accounts, which are sustained by books such as Hromnik's *Indo-Africa* (1981) and Fell's bizarre pursuance of, in his case, Libyan explorers using Ogham script (Willcox 1984:210). Sullivan's *Spirit of the Rocks* (1995) refers to the Driekopseiland engravings as "notations, perhaps calculations related to the moon, and/or trader tallies," including "rune-like symbols" and "Celtic crosses," "diligently scratched ... on the rocks" by "scribes" of literate traders, perhaps merchants of the Khazar Empire. Credo Mutwa (1996:191–194), who projects himself as a "Zulu shaman," rejects the association of rock engravings with Bushmen as the misguided opinion of white farmers and "many in the scientific establishment in South Africa" (for a critique of various aspects of these claims, see Morris 2004b; Morris et al. 2006).

Many of the more "mainstream" accounts of Driekopseiland have been hardly less denigrating. Willcox, who once remarked that "Palaeolithic man and his modern representative the Bushman remained, in their capacity for abstract thinking, always young children" (1956:85)—thus echoing Frobenius's (1909:132) famous observation that Bushmen represented "the last lisping utterance that reaches us from the childhood of mankind"—was later to draw on the work of Kellogg to argue that there was a resemblance between the Driekopseiland engravings and the prerepresentational drawings of children (Willcox 1963:59). The art was that of a people "still in the 'young child' stage of artistic development" (1964:58).

But the more significant archaeological arguments have turned on the question of ethnicity. The massive preponderance of geometric engravings at Driekopseiland, with few animal images and hardly any human figures, stands in striking contrast to other sites in the region, for example Wildebeest Kuil, where animal images and human figures predominate. A repeated and often persuasive response to this variability has been to invoke ethnicity as explanation; the principal debate has been over precisely which ethnic group was responsible for which forms of engravings. Cooke (1969:100) sums up the view of several commentators with his remark that the geometric engravings at Driekopseiland bear "little or no resemblance to the true art of the Stone Age Bush people." The animal images at sites such as Wildebeest Kuil are generally accepted as San tradition, while many of the rock art specialists pronouncing on the contrasting site of Driekopseiland have felt that the engravers of the geometric art there were Korana or perhaps some "hybrid" population (Battiss 1948; Broom cited by Wilman 1933; Cooke 1969; Willcox 1963). Most recently, Smith and Ouzman (2004) have seen Driekopseiland as conforming to what they define as a distinct Khoekhoe herder rock art tradition. The distribution of sites with geometric rock art does appear to match the hypothesized migration routes by which herders are thought to have spread through South Africa about 2000 years ago, lending this approach credence (but on the advent of herding, see Sadr 2003).

An alternative perspective on the site (Morris 2002a, 2004c) takes its cue partly from Inskeep's (1971:101) misgivings concerning an "either/ or" approach to the authorship issue that "it tends to condition the mind to a narrow field of possibilities, whereas the truth may be very complex." There is in fact little clear-cut evidence, as yet, for distinct ethnic and/or economic contexts relative to the various sites in question, no convincing indication of population replacement, nor for the appearance of a distinctively different material culture concomitant with the geometric engravings at Driekopseiland. This alternative perspective does not discount the possibility that identity/authorship issues relative to a dynamic social landscape had a bearing, and it notes that regional differences in rock art repertoires of the last two millennia elsewhere in southern Africa may reflect different trajectories of change and forms of interaction between hunter-gatherers and other social groups in their respective areas (e.g., Blundell 2004; Jolly 1998; Parkington 1996). Referring to such interaction, Wilmsen has pointed to the way the content of mythology "transcends time and tribe and ethnicity," indicating a complex history of social relations where elements of cosmologies "were constructed and transmitted in a less segmented social environment than presently exists" (Wilmsen 1986:358). In their relations with others, foragers may have been particularly receptive to outside ideas, suggests Guenther (1999:87), who also believes it is nearly impossible, in the Khoe-San context, to sift imported beliefs and rituals from those that are not. "The 'Common Bushman' core of beliefs that constitutes the benchmark for differentiating indigenous from derived items," he adds, "is too varied and fluid to serve as a standard for evaluation." Schapera (1930) and Barnard (1992) have both noted "striking resemblances" in religion across the Khoe-San spectrum, while Biesele (1993:34–37) finds San and Khoekhoe "traditions" to be "practically indistinguishable." In his study *Tricksters and Trancers: Bushman Religion and Society*, Guenther (1999:87–88, 128–129) cites both San and Khoekhoe sources, noting how histories of contact will have resulted in myths permeating and blending across boundaries. One particular example is the story of the moon and the hare, which Bleek characterized as a "veritable Hottentot myth" because of its apparent preponderance in Namaqualand—notwithstanding his having collected nine versions of the same myth from the /Xam San of the Karoo. Lewis-Williams has similarly drawn attention to the close correspondences between Korana rituals and beliefs and those of the /Xam (Lewis-Williams 1981:105–106).

Instead, then, of invoking ethnicity or cultural diversity as the inevitable mechanism explaining variation in rock art, this perspective (Morris 2002a) foregrounds a metaphorical understanding of landscape, and of different features within it, grounded in a rich corpus of ethnography and contemporary indigenous knowledge, in an attempt to understand variability here relative to archaeological and paleoenvironmental evidence of historical change in the region. In this view ethnicity and culture, as phenomena, are taken to be situated and dynamic rather than primordial or ulterior features of bounded cognitive systems (cf. Parkington 1993).

Specifically, it is suggested that landscape processes, long overlooked as being analytically significant, are all-important to our understating of Driekopseiland and its engravings (Morris 2002a). Central to the interpretation is the observation that when the river rises in the wet season the engravings are submerged. By virtue of water, that most potent of symbolic elements, the environmental setting of the site becomes a locus of particular cultural and social significance.

When Stow wrote about Driekopseiland in the 1870s, he cited San informants on the apparent ritual significance of the place, but what appears in print reads like a parody; it seems clear that detail was lost in transmission, and his account provides little that could be used reliably for an indigenous insight. However, when read in conjunction with other nineteenth- and twentieth-century ethnographic accounts, including those with reference to the social significance of water, several strands of evidence may be discerned. These indicate, firstly, the way that special features in the landscape have been imbued historically with meaning. A key instance in /Xam folklore is the legend "The Death of the Lizard," given by /Han≠kass'o in the 1870s (Bleek and Lloyd 1911; Deacon 1986; Deacon and Foster 2005), in which the broken lizard, probably a metaphor relating to rain, becomes a cluster of hills in the landscape. Surviving precolonial place-names are replete with hints of physical features having been similarly infused with significance. Consonant with this relational way of knowing the world (Bird-David 1999) is the idea that places and rock faces were meaningful supports (Heyd 1999), mediating spirit worlds (Lewis-Williams and Dowson 1990), the surfaces bearing the images are a "most fundamental part of the context."

Secondly, the ethnography of the last century and a half refers to ritual practices, specifically the female puberty rites, which have (or had) a specific geographical focus at the water source. Facial or body marking (and sometimes the daubing of objects) with ochre, scarification, and other modes were a widely consistent feature of the ceremonies of reintroduction that concluded the rites (the literature is vast, with instances of marking in relation to the "new maiden" and the water source from across the Khoe-San spectrum [Bleek 1933; Hewitt 1986 from a /Xam [San] context; Hoernlé 1918 for a Nama [Khoekhoe] example]). A third strand is the biaxial cosmology that is evident in /Xam and other legends and lore, namely a horizontal axis between camp and hunting ground and a vertical one between spirit worlds over and under the earth, both of which are mediated by water in the form of rain and the waterhole (Lewis-Williams 1996). The nearly palpable power of place at Driekopseiland, the hypothesized ritual practices, and the rich field of social meanings in Khoe-San beliefs in relation to !Khwa, the rain/water (or its manifestation as the "watersnake"), and the "new maiden" appear to converge at precisely the symbolically potent intersection of these schematic axes.

Lastly, the objective geography of Driekopseiland is a unique sequence of events that led to the exposure here, probably in late Holocene times, of glacially smoothed basement rock aligned with the flow of the river, which bulges and dips above or below the water according to the season. As such the site resonates with environmental rhythms, and these, in turn, were very likely resources for cultural construal—the natural becoming supernatural (Tilley and Bennett 2001)—in ways that are consistent with the ethnography. Upon this great, smooth, undulating surface (itself perhaps construed as a giant, fecund "watersnake," which are associated with rivers in many tales), more than 3,500 rock engravings are densely placed, such that they become submerged when the rains come in the wet season, but equally are left high and dry when river flow dwindles, or ceases altogether.

As a powerful place, it is possible that Driekopseiland became a focus in rites, perhaps specifically those associated with the "new maiden," who represented "the rain's magic power" (according to ≠Kamme-an, Dia!kwain's mother [Lewis-Williams 2000]). The place itself may also have been an active element in these rites in the redefinition of social personhood (cf. Houseman 1998), and the power of the place may have been enhanced in particular periods in its history (perhaps periods of ritual intensification in response to environmental and/or social stress) by marking with engravings, which themselves may be a residue of ritual sequence. Waldman (1989) and Guenther (1999:174) have shown that these rituals are or were practised with great emotional and symbolic intensity.

A metaphorical understanding of place—and the possibility that different parts of the landscape might vary in ritual significance (hilltops very likely being associated with rain-making rites)—may be factors more germane to the questions of variability in the rock art of the region than appeals to ethnicity and cultural difference. If Stow's version of the emic significance of Driekopseiland was at least a second—and possibly a third-hand—narration, it has been possible to construct, to re-member,[10] as it were, a fuller version more solidly grounded in relevant ethnographic and indigenous knowledge accounts. In drawing upon these insights, there are better chances today for people to reconnect with their heritage in a meaningful way; if not to mend the "broken string" (the metaphor that Dia!kwain used to describe his separation from his place in the Karoo [Bleek and Lloyd 1911:236-7]),[11] at least to trace the events and understand more fully the significance of places such as Driekopseiland.

RECLAIMING THE CLEARED LANDSCAPE

Rock art sites have, indeed, been a vehicle by which Khoe-San people and their descendants have reasserted a link with "cleared landscapes" in recent years (Chennells and /Useb 2004; Kora-Na-San 1999). Thus, archaeology plays a role in the politics of identity and cultural reclamation. Speaking for "Coloured" Khoe-San descendants, Engelbrecht has stated that "archaeologists must understand that within South Africa everything they excavate will bring us closer to our past, a past which has until now been denied to us as we have been forcibly divorced from our heritage" (2002:242). The development of the Wildebeest Kuil Rock Art Center outside Kimberley (Morris 2006) is an example of a place where public recognition is given to some of the history outlined above in a heritage site which happens also to be on land now owned by the !Xun and Khwe, refugee San language speakers from Angola and Namibia. As do other Khoe-San descendants in the area, the !Xun and Khwe see in the art a connection to a broad Khoe-San cultural inheritance in southern Africa (Morris 2003; Weiss 2005). The politics around the site revolve in part upon the way that these links are articulated, and one of the greater challenges at Wildebeest Kuil has been, and will be, negotiating the way that the "Coloured" Afrikaans-speaking Khoe-San constituency is involved (a representative serves on the Trust that manages the site). For reasons that will be apparent from the above, they are, as a community, relatively less able than the !Xun and Khwe to demonstrate Khoe-San "authenticity," let alone coherence, and hence are more marginalized, more invisible (de Jongh 2002; cf. Sylvain 2005) than some others relative to their Khoe-San cultural heritage. They are at the same time more likely to include descendants of the makers of the engravings here, whereas the !Xun and Khwe originate in Angola, more than 2,000 km to the north.

The Wildebeest Kuil Rock Art Center, as a space manifestly set aside as "Khoe-San," represents in a sense a reinhabiting of a small part of this vast "cleared landscape." Unwittingly, though, it perpetuates a kind of cadastral containment and segregation through what Byrne refers to as the "continued hegemony of the 'site' concept" (2003:188). Relative to the total "cultural landscape" that stretches from horizon to horizon, with "off-site" scatters of artifacts stretching in variable densities over kilometers, heritage practice generally favors the neatly circumscribed site—legally defined and easily managed. The behavioral context of the artifacts is compromised, Byrne notes, and "a continuous pattern of activity is made to look like discontinuous pods of activity: highly mobile precontact hunter-gatherers are retrospectively 'settled down' into sites." Broader cultural landscapes are being defined in South Africa, for example in national parks, including the uKhahlamba World Heritage Site. But in the west central interior the potential for this is limited, with almost all land under private ownership. Wildebeest Kuil is unique in this context as a servitude defined explicitly for rock art preservation. Virtually all other rock art sites and related heritage resources, including those that characterize a "/Xam Heartland" in the Karoo and of course Driekopseiland, are isolated on (sometimes straddling boundaries between) private farms. Landowners in some areas are increasingly nervous of land claims based on the presence of such precolonial heritage resources.

If sites have been segregated owing to their cadastral and heritage management status, another segregating tendency stems from the elaboration of a "literary lattice" (Humphreys 1998), the operation of which is perpetuated in the post-1994 era in South Africa by discourse on multicultural diversity (Rassool 2000) and ethnic politics (Crais 2006). It was in terms of a literary lattice in the colonial era that people and phenomena were typed and ordered in space and time. One of the most influential and enduring of such templates was Theal's (1919) fixing of "Bushman," "Hottentot," and "Bantu" as fundamental racial categories. As a classificatory device, Humphreys notes, such a scheme has required "filling up" and hence has tended to induce elements of identity, or distinction, which need not have existed before. "Rainbow nation" discourse since 1994, ironically, has in some senses encouraged the reification of ethnicity beyond its sell-by date, and nowhere have claims over idealized indigenous identities and leadership positions been more actively asserted than amongst descendants of the Khoe-San. Numerous groups, the Kora-Na-San Assemblies First Nation, the San Diaspora of South Africa, the Korana Royal House—to name but a few—emerged in the late 1990s, each with its own Paramount Chief (the possibility of a salaried position in a House of Traditional Leaders was a strong imperative for the invention of new chieftaincies), each eager to assert its own (often territorial and invariably overlapping) jurisdiction in the heritage and diversity stakes. Many of these organizations operated outside of the more widely recognized San structures such as the Working Group for Indigenous Minorities in Southern Africa (WIMSA), the South African San Institute (SASI), and the National Khoisan Consultative Conference. Some heritage claims by such groups began to be made on the basis of obsolete ideas from writings of the earlier twentieth century (notably Theal) ingested by community researchers at the local library. These came to be cited, not as somewhat dated speculations, but as the definitive "indigenous knowledge" of specific identity-conscious groups, which archaeologists (some might suggest) had no business to gainsay (cf. Smith 2004 on the reappearance of older "authoritative utterances").

Whether or not archaeology could or should have a role in adjudicating such claims, it is responsible today perhaps more than ever for generating meanings either for, or which percolate out into, the public domain, and which serve as resources drawn upon by communities and by the heritage, tourism, and education sectors (Morris 2003). A proactive approach is advocated by Joyce (2002; cf. Leone 1983), namely to engage with stakeholders, sharing knowledge not only about the past but, just as critically, on how archaeology knows the past and on the methods used to produce this knowledge. This has been an important consideration in the development of the Wildebeest Kuil Rock Art Center (Morris 2003, 2006; see also Parkington and Rusch 2002 on returning the rock art archive by way of the Clanwilliam Living Landscape Project in the Western Cape). Here space—physical as well as conceptual—is also allowed for alternative voices and self-representation. Crucially, as the history of investigation at Driekopseiland reviewed above would suggest, and relative to the prevailing "diversity" tropes, archaeologists need to be attentive and discerning in their own representations of, and debates concerning, such concepts as culture and identity (cf. Cooper 2005; Fox and King 2002). Essentialist and ahistoric conceptions of the past have all too readily been appropriated, in other times and places, to questionable ends (Arnold 2006). Today ideas about the past are susceptible to being drawn into perhaps more subtle but no less troubling complicities relative to contemporary material and ideological interests (Rassool 2000; Sewell 2005:62; Shepherd 2003; Sylvain 2005; West and Carrier 2004).

Driekopseiland entered the written record in the highly charged context of land loss. The engravings remained, as Stow put it, as the "title deeds" of people who had disappeared from the surrounding landscape. Today their descendants are saying, "We want to return to our roots and to retrieve our Khoisan identity" (Engelbrecht 2002:244). To the extent that archaeology might play a role in these politics of identity and cultural reclamation—a role it will not in fact be able to avoid—the sharing of insights and methods, with the epistemological concerns raised here, will be its most important contribution.

NOTES

1. Khoe-San is a collective term used here for various precolonial groups of foragers, hunters with sheep, and herders (see Crawhall 2006:110 on the acceptability of *Khoe-San* over *Khoisan*). Identities, particularly at this period, were fluid, and new alliances between groups were often formed and reformed in the face of advancing colonial interests. Contemporary references to "Bushmen" and "Hottentots" or "Koranas" would have implied San foragers or Khoe herders respectively, although these distinctions were not always clear-cut. Currently, the exact authorship of the Driekopseiland engravings relative to these categories is subject to debate (see Morris 2002a).

2. More than a century after Stow's visit to Driekopseiland, this episode in local history would feature in an Afrikaans novel by Dolf van Niekerk called *Koms van die Hyreën* [The coming of the He-Rain] (1994). In a tale set in the late twentieth century, rock engravings become a key factor in a bid to claim back ancestral land.

3. The archaeological traces of bulldozed settlements would doubtless be a focus of future research.

4. Philip prefigured a viewpoint that would be entertained in some of the arguments of Elphick (1977) and of the Kalahari revisionists (Ross 1993:201, 207) when he posited that the *bosjesmans* ("Bushmen") were in fact a colonial creation and that "Hottentots" (Khoekhoe), once deprived of their stock, retreated to the mountains to live by the hunt.

5. Stow's own position relative to the "Janus face" of Cape liberalism is said to be evident in his very championing of Bushmen as the oldest of South Africa's inhabitants. By pointing to the likelihood of a San presence antedating that of Bantu-speaking Africans, Stow had "reinforced—from a novel perspective—settler views that Africans had no prior rights to the country" (Dubow 2004:129).

6. Incipient reserves for Khoekhoen and San at the early nineteenth-century mission stations of Toverberg and Hephzibah near Colesberg, and others in the region, had provided opportunities for communal land tenure and relative independence from colonial farmers. But the early collapse of these mission ventures spelt final dispossession and the incorporation of these people as an underclass in colonial society (Schoeman 1993, in de Jongh 2002).

7. An historic exception to this was the 1998 land claim by the Richtersveld Community, which was based on an argument that until after 1913 the community held aboriginal title to land of which they were subsequently dispossessed. Despite efforts by government to exclude such claims, the South African courts were forced for the first time to confront the issue of aboriginal title (Patterson 2004).

8. Coincidentally, about a century previously and in the very vicinity of Driekopseiland (then referred to as *Blue-bank*), Andrew Smith (Lye 1975:144-145) remarked upon the "good soil" thereabouts and ventured that "if it ever prove profitable for the natives to raise the water in any quantity from the bed of the stream, rich crops of grain might be procured sufficient for the supply of a large population." He envisaged the Cape government setting the example by encouraging "wealthy speculators to change the course of rivers ... or do it themselves."

9. On the development of public access to rock art, in particular at Wildebeest Kuil, see Morris 2003, 2006.

10. I intend the word "re-member" as a nonce word meaning "to reconstruct" (as in Schwartz 1988:118), "to bring together anew" (as in Weiner 2005:86), and "to put together again" (Oxford English Dictionary). Schwartz, in her 1988 article "Joseph's Bones and the Resurrection of the Text: Remembering in the Bible," refers to how "the object we long to recover is forever receding behind us ... All we have, all we *can* have, are reconstructions, re-, and we must include that hyphen, -memberings." Brian A. Weiner, in chapter 3 of his book *Sins of the Parents* (2005), "The Birth and Death of Political Memories," suggests that "to re-member seems to presuppose an earlier *dis-membering*... Re-membering may be defined, then, as bringing together anew that which has become dismembered, disunited, or forgotten" (2005:86). It is used with similar connotations by G. Terán in a chapter "Vernacular Education for Cultural Regeneration" in C.A. Bowers and F. Apffel-Marglin *Rethinking Freire* (2005).

11. "The place does not feel to me, as the place used to feel to me ... because the string has broken for me." Dia!kwain 1875, quoted in Bleek and Lloyd 1911.

REFERENCES

Arnold, Bettina. 2006. Pseudoarchaeology and Nationalism. In *Archaeological Fantasies: How Pseudoarchaeology Misrepresents the Past and Misleads the Public*, ed. by G.G. Fagan, pp. 154–179. Routledge, London.

Arnot, David, and Francis H.S. Orpen. 1875. *The Land Question of Griqualand West: An Enquiry into the Various Claims to Land in That Territory; Together with a Brief History of the Griqua Nation*. Saul Solomon, Cape Town.

Barnard, Alan. 1992. *Hunters and Herders of Southern Africa: A Comparative Ethnography of the Khoisan Peoples*. Cambridge University Press, Cambridge.

Battiss, Walter W. 1948. *The Artists of the Rocks*. Red Fawn Press, Pretoria.

Biesele, Megan. 1993. *Women Like Meat: The Folklore and Foraging Ideology of the Kalahari Ju/'hoan*. Witwatersrand University Press, Johannesburg.

Bird-David, Nurit. 1999. "Animism" Revisited: Personhood, Environment and Relational Epistemology. *Supplement to Current Anthropology* 40:S67–91.

Bleek, Dorothea F. 1933. Beliefs and Customs of the /Xam Bushmen. Part V. The Rain. *Bantu Studies* 7:297–312.

Bleek, Wilhelm H.I., and Lucy C. Lloyd. 1911. *Specimens of Bushman Folklore*. George Allen, London.

Blundell, Geoffrey. 2004. *Nqabayo's Nomansland: San Rock Art and the Somatic Past*. Studies in Global Archaeology 2, Uppsala.

Brody, Hugh. 2002. In Memory of Elsie Vaalbooi. *Open Democracy* 16 December 2002.

Byrne, Denis R. 2003. Nervous Landscapes: Race and Space in Australia. *Journal of Social Archaeology* 3:169–193.

Chennells, Roger, and Joram /Useb. 2004. Indigenous Knowledge Systems Protection of San Intellectual Property: Media and Research Contracts. Paper presented at the Southern African Association of Archaeologists Conference. South African San Institute (SASI) and Working Group of Indigenous Minorities in Southern Africa (WIMSA), McGregor Museum, Kimberley, South Africa.

Cooke, Cranmer K. 1969. *Rock Art of Southern Africa*. Books of Africa, Cape Town.

Cooper, Frederick. 2005. *Colonialism in Question: Theory, Knowledge, History*. University of California Press, Berkeley.

Crais, Clifton. 2006. Custom and the Politics of Sovereignty in South Africa. *Journal of Social History* 39:721–740.

Crawhall, Nigel. 2006. Languages, Genetics and Archaeology: Problems and the Possibilities in Africa. In *The Prehistory of Africa: Tracing the Lineage of Modern Man*, ed. by H. Soodyall, pp. 109–124. Jonathan Ball Publishers, Jeppestown.

Dart, Raymond A. 1925. The Historic Succession of Cultural Impacts upon South Africa. *Nature* 115 (2890):425–429.

Deacon, Janette. 1986. "My place is the Bitterpits." The Home Territory of the Bleek and Lloyd's /Xam San Informants. *African Studies* 45:135–155.

Deacon, Janette and Craig Foster. 2005. *My Heart Stands in the Hill*. Struik Publishers, Cape Town.

de Jongh, Michael. 2002. No Fixed Abode: The Poorest of the Poor and Elusive Identities in Rural South Africa. *Journal of Southern African Studies* 28:441–460.

Dubow, Saul. 2004. Earth History, Natural History, and Prehistory at the Cape, 1860–1875. *Comparative Studies in Society and History* 46:103–133.

Eldredge, Elizabeth A. 1994. Slave Raiding across the Cape Frontier. In *Slavery in South Africa: Captive Labor on the Dutch Frontier*, ed. by E.A. Eldredge and F. Morton, pp. 93–126. University of Natal Press, Pietermaritzburg.

Elphick, Richard. 1977. *Kraal and Castle: Khoikhoi and the Founding of White South Africa*. Yale University Press, New Haven.

Engelbrecht, Martin L. 2002. The Connection between Archaeological Treasures and the Khoisan people. In *The Dead and their Possessions: Repatriation in Principles, Policy and Practice*, ed. by C. Fforde, J. Hubert, and P. Turnbull, pp. 242–244. Routledge, London.

Fox, Richard G., and Barbara J. King. 2002. Introduction: Beyond Culture Worry. In *Anthropology Beyond Culture*, ed. by R. Fox and B. King, pp. 1–22. Berg, London.

Frobenius, Leo. 1909. *The Childhood of Man: A Popular Account of the Lives, Customs and Thoughts of Primitive Races*. Translated by A.H. Keane. Sealey, London.

Guenther, Mathias. 1999. *Tricksters and Trancers: Bushman Religion and Society*. Indiana University Press, Bloomington.

Hallett, Robin. 1984. Desolation on the Veld: Forced Removals in South Africa. *African Affairs* 83 (332):301–320.

Hamilton, Carolyn (editor). 1995. *The Mfecane Aftermath: Reconstructive Debates in Southern African History*. University of the Witwatersrand Press, Johannesburg.

Henderson, Zoe. 2002. A Dated Cache of Ostrich Eggshell Flasks from Thomas' Farm, Northern Cape Province, South Africa. *South African Archaeological Bulletin* 57:38–40.

Hewitt, Roger L. 1986. *Structure, Meaning and Ritual in the Narratives of the Southern San*. Quellen zur Khoisan Forschung 2. Helmut Buske Verlag, Hamburg.

Heyd, Thomas. 1999. Rock Art Aesthetics: Trace on Rock, Mark of Spirit, Window on Land. *Journal of Aesthetics and Art Criticism* 57:451–458.

Hoernlé, A.Winifred. 1918. Certain Rites of Transition and the Conception of !nau among the Hottentots. *Harvard African Studies* 2:65–82.

Hoff, Ansie. 1997. The Water Snake of the Khoekhoen and /Xam. *South African Archaeological Bulletin* 52:21–37.

Houseman, Michael. 1998. Painful Places: Ritual Encounters with One's Homelands. *Journal of the Royal Anthropological Institute* n.s. 4:447–467.

Hromnik, Cyral A. 1981. *Indo-Africa: Towards a New Understanding of the History of sub-Saharan Africa*. Juta, Cape Town.

Humphreys, Anthony J.B. 1972. The Type R Settlements in the Context of the Later Prehistory and Early History of the Riet River Valley. Master's thesis, Department of Archaeology, University of Cape Town.

———. 1997. Riet River Revisited: Comments on Recent Findings at Pramberg. *Southern African Field Archaeology* 6:78–81.

———. 1998. Populations, Prehistory, Pens and Politics: Some Reflections from North of the Orange River. *Southern African Field Archaeology* 7:20–25.

Inskeep, Raymond R. 1971. The Future of Rock Art Studies in Southern Africa. In *Rock Paintings of Southern Africa*, ed. by M. Schoonraad. Supplement to the *South African Journal of Science*, Special Issue.

Jolly, Pieter. 1998. Modelling Change in the Contact Art of South Eastern San, Southern Africa. In *The Archaeology of Rock Art*, ed. by C. Chippindale and P.S.C. Taçon, pp. 247–267. Cambridge University Press, Cambridge.

Joyce, Rosemary A. 2002. Academic Freedom, Stewardship and Cultural Heritage: Weighing the Interests of Stakeholders in Crafting Repatriation Approaches. In *The Dead and their Possessions: Repatriation in Principles, Policy and Practice*, ed. by C. Fforde, J. Hubert, and P. Turnbull, pp. 99–107. Routledge, London.

Keegan, Timothy. 1996. *Colonial South Africa and the Origins of the Racial Order*. David Philip, Cape Town.

Kora-Na-San. 1999. Business Plan for San Diaspora of South Africa. Manuscript on file, McGregor Museum Collection, Kimberley, South Africa.

Kurtz, June M. 1988. The Albania Settlement of Griqualand West, 1866–1878. Master's thesis, Department of History, Rhodes University.

Lange, Mary Elizabeth, and Johanna de Wee, Martha van Rooi, Maria Malo, Elizabeth Sixaxa, Maku Hlopezulu, and Noxolo P. Saaiman. 2007. *Water Stories*. MEL, Durban.

Leone, Mark P. 1983. Method as Message: Interpreting the Past with the Public. *Museum News* 62:34–41.

Lewis-Williams, J. David. 1981. *Believing and Seeing: Symbolic Meanings in Southern San Rock Paintings*. Academic Press, London.

———. 1996. "A Visit to the Lion's House": The Structures, Metaphors and Sociopolitical Significance of a Nineteenth Century Bushman Myth. In *Voices from the Past: /Xam Bushman and the Bleek and Lloyd Collection*, ed. by J. Deacon and T.A. Dowson, pp. 122–141. Witwatersrand University Press, Johannesburg.

Lewis-Williams, J. David (editor). 2000. *Stories that Float from Afar: Ancestral Folklore of the San of Southern Africa.* David Philip, Cape Town.

Lewis-Williams, J. David and Thomas A. Dowson. 1990. Through the Veil: San Rock Paintings and the Rock Face. *South African Archaeological Bulletin* 45:5–16.

Lye, William F. (editor). 1975. *Andrew Smith's Journal of His Expedition into the Interior of South Africa, 1834–36: An Authentic Narrative of Travels and Discoveries, the Manners and Customs of the Native Tribes, and the Physical Nature of the Country.* A.A. Balkema, Cape Town.

McLay, Karin. 2003. Farm Workers in the Karoo: Isolation = Exploitation. http://www.zsa.ca/En/Articles/article.php?aid = 307, accessed June 12, 2005.

Morris, David. 1994. Deterioration of Rock Engravings. *The Digging Stick* 11(3):10.

———. 2000. A Horse and Seventy Sheep for Your Land! *Now and Then: Newsletter of the Historical Society of Kimberley and the Northern Cape* 7(2):6–7.

———. 2002a. Driekopseiland and "The Rain's Magic Power": History and Landscape in a New Interpretation of a Northern Cape Rock Engraving Site. Master's thesis, Department of Anthropology and Sociology, University of the Western Cape, Cape Town.

———. 2002b. Another Spouted Ostrich Eggshell Container from the Northern Cape. *South African Archaeological Bulletin* 57:41.

———. 2003. Rock Art as Source and Resource: Research and Responsibility towards Education, Heritage and Tourism. *South African Historical Journal* 49:193–206.

———. 2004a. Between a Rock and a Hard Place. *Earthyear*, supplement to the *Mail and Guardian, Johannesburg,* December 2004.

———. 2004b. Preserving the Archives of Ancient Africa? Loony Claims at the Fringes of Archaeology. *The Digging Stick* 21(2):9–12.

———. 2004c. Comment on Taking Stock: Identifying Khoekhoen Herder Rock Art in Southern Africa (Smith and Ouzman). *Current Anthropology* 45:518–519.

———. 2005. Further Evidence of Spouts on Ostrich Eggshell. Containers from the Northern Cape; and a Footnote to the History of Anthropology and Archaeology at the McGregor Museum, Kimberley. *South African Archaeological Bulletin* 60:112–114.

———. 2006. The Importance of Wildebeest Kuil: "A Hill with a Future, a Hill with a Past." Paper presented at SACRA Conference, Kimberley, February 2006. (also in press, SACRA Conference Proceedings.)

Morris, David, Maryna Steyn, and Isabelle Ribot. 2006. A Burial from Driekopseiland, Northern Cape. *South African Archaeological Bulletin* 61:133–141.

Mutwa, Credo. 1996. *Song of the Stars: The Lore of a Zulu Shaman,* ed. by S. Larsen. Station Hill Openings, Barrytown, New York.

Parkington, John E. 1993. The Neglected Alternative: Historical Narrative Rather Than Cultural Labelling. *South African Archaeological Bulletin* 48:94–97.

———. 1996. What is an Eland? N!ao and the Politics of Age and Sex in the Paintings of the Western Cape. In *Miscast: Negotiating the Presence of the Bushmen,* ed. by P. Skotnes, pp. 281–289. University of Cape Town Press, Cape Town.

Parkington, John E., and Neil Rusch. 2002. *The Mantis, the Eland and the Hunter. Follow the San...* Clanwillian Living Landscape Project, Cape Town.

Patterson, Stephanie. 2004. The Foundations of Aboriginal Title in South Africa? The *Richtersveld Community v. Alexkor Ltd* Decisions. *Indigenous Law Bulletin* 18. http://www.austlii.edu.au/au/journals/ILB/2004/18.html, accessed August 9, 2006.

Penn, Nigel G. 2005. *The Forgotten Frontier: Colonist and Khoisan on the Cape's Northern Frontier in the 18th Century.* Ohio University Press and Double Storey Books, Athens, Ohio and Cape Town.

Péringuey, Louis. 1909. On Rock Engravings of Animals and the Human Figure Found in South Africa. *Transactions of the South African Philosophical Society of South Africa* 18:401–420.

Rassool, Ciraj. 2000. The Rise of Heritage and the Reconstitution of History in South Africa. *Kronos: Journal of Cape History* 26:1–21.

Ross, Robert. 1993. Donald Moodie and the Origins of South African Historiography. In *Beyond the Pale: Essays on the History of Colonial South Africa*, ed. by R. Ross, pp. 192–212. Witwatersrand University Press, Johannesburg.

Sadr, Karim. 2003. The Neolithic of Southern Africa. *Journal of African History* 44:195–209.

Sampson, C. Garth. 1992. Bushman (Oesjwana) Survival and Acculturation on the Northeast Frontier 1770–1890: Some Archaeological Implications. *Abstracts of the Southern African Association of Archaeologists Biennial Conference* 1992:13–14.

Schapera, Isaac. 1930. *The Khoisan Peoples of South Africa: Bushmen and Hottentots*. Routledge and Kegan Paul, London.

Schoeman, Karel. 1993. Die Londense Sendinggenootskap en die San: die Stasies Toornberg and Hephzibah, 1814–1818. *South African Historical Journal* 28.

Schwartz, Regina M. 1988. Joseph's Bones and the Resurrection of the Text: Remembering in the Bible. *PMLA* 103(2):114–124.

Seirlis, Julia K. 2004. Islands and Autochthons: Coloureds, Space and Belonging in Rhodesia and Zimbabwe. *Journal of Social Archaeology* 4:405–427.

Sewell, William H. 2005. *Logics of History: Social Theory and Social Transformation*. University of Chicago Press, Chicago.

Shepherd, Nick. 2003. State of the Discipline: Science, Culture and Identity in South African Archaeology, 1870–2003. *Journal of Southern African Studies* 29:823–844.

Shillington, Kevin. 1985. *The Colonisation of the Southern Tswana, 1870–1900*. Ravan Press, Johannesburg.

Slack, Lina M. 1962. *Rock Engravings from Driekopseiland and Other Sites Southwest of Johannesburg*. Centaur Press, London.

Smith, Andrea L. 2004. Heteroglossia, "Common Sense," Social Memory. *American Ethnologist* 31:251–269.

Smith, Benjamin W., and Sven Ouzman. 2004. Taking Stock: Identifying Khoekhoen Herder Rock Art in Southern Africa. *Current Anthropology* 45:499–526.

Stow, George W. 1905. *The Native Races of South Africa*. Swan, Sonnenschein, London.

Sullivan, Brenda. 1995. *Spirit of the Rocks*. Human and Rousseau, Cape Town.

Sylvain, Renée. 2005. Disorderly Development: Globalization and the Idea of "Culture" in the Kalahari. *American Ethnologist* 32:354–370.

Terán, Gustavo. 2005. Vernacular Education for Cultural Regeneration: An Alternative to Paulo Freire's Vision of Emancipation. In *Rethinking Freire: Globalization and the Environmental Crisis,* ed. by C.A. Bowers and F. Apffel-Marglin, pp. 69–82. Lawrence Erlbaum Associates, Mahwah, New Jersey.

Theal, George M. 1919. *History of South Africa: Volume 1. Ethnography and Condition of South Africa before A.D. 1505*. Facsimile edition, 1964. C. Struik, Cape Town.

Tilley, Christopher, and Wayne Bennett. 2001. An Archaeology of Supernatural Places: The Case of West Penwith. *Journal of the Royal Anthropological Institute* n.s. 7:335–362.

Traill, Anthony. 1996. !Khwa-Ka Hhouiten Hhouiten, "The Rush of the Storm": The Linguistic Death of /Xam. In *Miscast: Negotiating the Presence of the Bushmen*, ed. by P. Skotnes, pp. 161–184. University of Cape Town Press, Cape Town.

Van Niekerk, Dolf. 1994. *Koms van die Hyreën* [The coming of the He-Rain]. Tafelberg, Cape Town.

Van Riet Lowe, Clarence. 1952. The Rock Engravings of Driekops Eiland. In *Congrés Panafricain de Préhistoire: Actes de la IIe Session, Alger* 1952:769–776. Paris.

Van Vreeden, Barend F. 1961. Die oorsprong en geskiedenis van pleknames in Noord-Kaapland en die aangrensende gebiede. Ph.D. dissertation, University of the Witwatersrand, Johannesburg.

Waldman, P. Linda. 1989. Watersnakes and Women: A Study of Ritual and Ethnicity in Griquatown. Honors thesis, Department of Social Anthropology, University of the Witwatersrand, Johannesburg.

Waldman, P. Linda. 2007. *The Griqua Conundrum: Political and Socio-Cultural Identity in the Northern Cape, South Africa*. Peter Lang AG, Bern.

Weiner, Brian A. 2005. *Sins of the Parents: The Politics of National Apologies in the United States*. Temple University, Philadelphia.

Weiss, Lindsay M. 2005. The Social Life of Rock Art: Materiality, Consumption, and Power in South African Heritage. In *Archaeologies of Materiality*, ed. by L. Meskell, pp. 46–70. Blackwell, London.

West, Paige, and James G. Carrier. 2004. Ecotourism and Authenticity: Getting Away from It All? *Current Anthropology* 45:483–498.

Willcox, Alex R. 1956. *Rock Paintings of the Drakensberg*. Parrish, London.

———. 1963. *The Rock Art of South Africa*. Nelson, London.

———. 1964. The Non Representational Petroglyphs of South Africa. *South African Journal of Science* 60:55–58.

———. 1984. *The Rock Art of Africa*. MacMillan South Africa, Johannesburg.

Willerslev, Rane. 2004. Spirits as "Ready to Hand": A Phenomenological Analysis of Yukaghir Spiritual Knowledge and Dreaming. *Anthropological Theory* 4:395–418.

Wilman, Maria. 1933. *The Rock Engravings of Griqualand West and Bechuanaland, South Africa*. Deighton Bell, Cambridge.

Wilmsen, Edwin N. 1986. Of Paintings and Painters, in Terms of Zu/'hoasi Interpretations. In *Contemporary Studies on Khoisan 2*, ed. by R.F.K. Keuthmann, pp. 347–372. Helmut Buske Verlag, Hamburg.

Wynberg, Rachel. 2004. Rhetoric, Realism and Benefit Sharing: Use of Traditional Knowledge of the *Hoodia* Species in the Development of an Appetite Suppressant. *Journal of World Intellectual Property* 7:851–876.

CHAPTER 6

Constructing the Wilderness and Clearing the Landscape: A Legacy of Colonialism in Northern British Columbia

Brenda Guernsey

In the northern region of the Canadian province of British Columbia, the dominant way that society portrays the forested landscapes is as "wilderness." The interpretation and labeling of the land in this way represents an ongoing legacy of colonialism that has its roots in a particular perception of the landscape held by early European newcomers. A contradiction lies between this dominant ideology of wilderness and the reality that First Nations[1] inhabitants of the same area continue to engage in a dynamic interaction with the land. Thus, seeing this region only as a wilderness dismisses other ways of reading these same landscapes. In this chapter, I explore how the colonial metanarrative of wilderness is a cultural and social construction that conceptually and physically erases First Nations and their ideologies from the landscape. This investigation will show that wilderness is only one of several possible layers of understanding the landscape.

CONTEXTUALIZING THE ISSUE

In British Columbia, the conceptualization of much of the land as a wilderness creates land-use tensions. These tensions are especially evident in the north, which has a sparse population and larger areas of forested land when compared to the southern regions of the province. Industrial and environmental interests often designate the northern areas as spaces for either resource extraction or conservation/preservation, both predicated upon and justified through a westernized notion of a wilderness. The understanding of the land as wilderness is a well-known, dominant perspective that is based on an underlying assumption that the land is devoid of any human cultural activity and that its fate is open for negotiation. For indigenous peoples, this is not the case, and the focus of my larger research is to make a First Nations perspective of the land more visible. Specifically, I am working with members of Kitsumkalum, a Tsimshian First Nation community in northern British Columbia, to explore and present their perspectives of the land that have been silenced by the dominant colonial ideology of the wilderness. However, for the purposes of this chapter I will examine how the concept of wilderness was first introduced and then became embedded in the ideology of northern British Columbia.

Contestations over the land are part of political and social life in British Columbia. At the forefront are talks between First Nations and the government that center on defining territorial rights, making the land question the fundamental issue at the treaty negotiation table. The settling of treaties is a complex and controversial process that involves the key stakeholders of the federal and provincial governments and individual First Nations governments, as well as many other "interest groups" who may have a stake in the outcome of the negotiations. These negotiations can change the political and social boundaries that define relations between First Nations and other sectors of society. The range of interest groups includes local non-First Nations communities, environmental groups, and industry, each with their own perception of how the land is valued (Coates 1992; McKee 1996). Although each of their perceptions may differ, they are all grounded in the portrayal of land as uninhabited wilderness. On the other hand, the First Nations are fighting for recognition of their title to the land.

The evolution of First Nations land claims issues in the province is based on conflicting contestations over the lands and the ideology of the land as wilderness. Was it or was it not owned and managed by First Nations? Land claims have been a part of the colonial history of British Columbia since the earliest times. Government policies that legislated against the settlement of land claims in the 1920s pre-empted the resolutions of the issue and prevented the signing of treaties in British Columbia. This refusal to acknowledge First Nations relationships to the land has its roots in the 1871 Act of Union that brought British Columbia into Confederation, and continues today. There was no provincial recognition of continued Aboriginal title to the land (Nichols and Rakai 2001:97). That failure led to a series of government policies that resulted in the current approach to making treaties under the coordination of the British Columbia Treaty Commission.

British Columbia is an extreme case because of the lack of treaties signed in the province, but it is not unique in its attitude towards First Nations land and land ownership. The Aboriginal land question has been marginalized socially and politically throughout Canada. Coates (1992:3) has argued that the reason the land question has been pushed aside is because of "a compelling lack of interest on the part of the non-native population." This disinterest has been normalized within the dominant society and, in the process, the importance of the land to Aboriginal peoples has been further marginalized and ignored. To explore how this normalization occurred, we need to look at colonial mechanisms that allowed for the representation of lands in a particular way and the effect that this representation had on the Aboriginal peoples.

As Peters (2001:143) states, "We cannot understand the position of either Aboriginal people or non-Aboriginal people in Canada if we fail to acknowledge the ways in which the colonial legacy permeates present conditions." In particular, the perception of the landscape as a wilderness perpetuates a colonial interpretation of land use and value while masking First Nations perceptions. Exploring why and how a dominating perception of land use and value is maintained requires a reflexive view that acknowledges the existence of other ways to understand the world. Any one perception of the world does not occur "just because," it occurs as a human construction. Understanding how wilderness is a constructed landscape can provide a good context for exploring alternatives to dominant colonial ideologies and for understanding the contemporary land conflicts involving First Nations and others.

Today, there are a diversity of landscape values in British Columbia that are specifically attributed to wilderness areas, and particularly those wilderness areas that are in the north or other regions remote from urban centers. These are regions comprised of communities based around primary industries, such as logging and mining, that necessarily involve extraction from, and manipulation of, the physical landscape. Bruce Willems-Braun (1997) explored some of the reasons for these differing values in his work with the Nuu-chah-nulth peoples of Vancouver Island. He found that this First Nations people were denied a voice during talks regarding the fate of Clayquot Sound in the early 1990s and were subsequently marginalized. His explanation lay in the "current and historical representational practices through which 'nature' is made to appear as an empty space of economic and political calculation and particular actors are authorized to speak for it" (ibid.:7). Willems-Braun (ibid.:7–11) provided evidence from recent promotional literature by the forest industry that embeds a colonial understanding of the landscape in the rhetoric of "nature." The ideology in that literature presents a road map for the way landscapes are understood and valued, as well as ideals that support economic gain that are considered "legitimate." Other authors have engaged in this analysis: "North American attitudes toward wilderness have changed over the centuries. Wilderness areas were initially regarded as places to be feared, then as domains to be exploited, and finally as regions to be saved" (Lutz et al. 1999:259).

Additionally, as primary resource towns experience the highs and lows that these economies typically go through, there has been an increasing interest in promoting the tourism qualities of northern British Columbia. Park boundaries were created as part of an ideological shift by the government in defining permitted uses of wilderness areas to include not only purely industrial interests but also preservation. This process began with the creation of federal and provincial parks in the nineteenth century and continues today, with ever-changing perceptions of how the preserved wilderness should be maintained. The changing view was that wild nature was no longer just a commodity or an obstacle to overcome, but was an endangered resource in need of protection. This became another perspective of wilderness held by the dominant society (Oelschlaeger 1991:4). This idea of the wilderness at risk has added another component to the ways that wilderness is perceived, yet it still relies on the underlying assumption that a "true wilderness" is a landscape devoid of humans. This type of thinking contributes to the complications First Nations experience in resolving their claims for Aboriginal ownership of land in the province, and for their place on that land.

Land claim issues are part of the political, economic, and cultural landscape of British Columbia because such a large amount of the land "remains the subject of unresolved claims" (Cassidy 1992:15). Many would argue that in order to settle land claims, there needs to be a change in the cultural landscape of Canada, not simply a rearrangement of territory. In order for this to take place, Manore suggests that viewing wilderness as a paradigm will encourage "interconnectedness, control, and ownership with balance and sharing, and homogenization with diversity" (1998:83). Manore does not explain how this view should be implemented, and it may be a premature idea. I argue that it would be more productive to gain an understanding of "other" landscapes thus far silenced and marginalized before creating new or alternative views. In the next two sections, I first offer suggestions on how the "wilderness" of northern British Columbia is a colonial construction of the landscape, followed by a discussion of how the settlement of the land cleared the landscape of Aboriginal peoples.

CONSTRUCTING THE WILDERNESS

Wilderness is a way of understanding a particular landscape. In the early seventeenth century, the concept of "landscape" resulted from the artistic movement of landscape paintings of the time. More particularly, landscape expressed how these paintings depicted a specific representation of the world as seen and interpreted by the artist (Duncan 2000:429). Cosgrove (in Duncan 2000:430) has more recently characterized landscape "as a way of seeing." Similarly, Wilson (in Taylor 1998:87) describes landscape as "a way of seeing the world ... It is something we think, do, and make as a social collective." Through these types of social interactions, landscapes are culturally constructed (Tilley 1994).

As a concept, "landscape" presents a way to understand the world as a representation of a particular worldview. This representation is propagated through the social transmission of culture, which allows landscapes to be read, interpreted, and written upon (Tilley 1994). Thus, landscapes are cultural constructions. We are taught how to read a landscape through our social and cultural experiences; we interpret them through that learned cultural lens and write upon them through how we, in turn, represent to others our particular understanding of a landscape. "Wilderness" is an example of one particular perception and understanding of a landscape that, through the exercise of colonial power, became the dominant way of interpreting the forested landscapes of British Columbia.

"Wilderness" was the way that early Europeans read the landscapes of North America. Missionaries conveyed images back to Europe through their correspondences. These communications shaped future colonists' understanding of the land prior to their arrival in the "new world" (Taylor 1998:91–93). While ministering to the Nisga'a Nation in northern British Columbia at the turn of the twentieth century, Reverend James McCullagh wrote a recurring article for the Church Missionary Society's *Aiyansh Notes* entitled "Autumn Leaves." In June 1908 he wrote, "[a] very beautiful parish it is too. Almost identical in size with the whole of Palestine, from Dan to Beersheeba—a vast no-mans land [sic], unsurveyed and unexplored" (McCullagh 1908). The way that McCullagh read, interpreted, and wrote the landscape was a result of perceptions and understandings of the land that he had formed in a European space and understood within a European context—one devoid of First Nations peoples.

Exploring some of the roots of the concept of wilderness can uncover how this construction of the land was, for newcomers, so easily transferred onto the landscapes of North America. A brief examination of the etymology of "wilderness" reveals a number of related meanings that speak to how a landscape is read as a wilderness. Wilderness is defined as "an uncultivated, uninhabited region; waste; wild ... any barren, empty, or open area, as of ocean ... a large, confused mass or tangle ... a wild condition or quality" (Webster's New World College Dictionary 1999). This definition demonstrates that "wilderness" is composed of various meanings. These layered meanings contribute to a shared cultural and social understanding of the term. A physical landscape that is perceived as being uncultivated and wild is also read as being uninhabited and thus is labeled a "wilderness."

Directly tied to this idea of the landscape as wilderness was the notion of a vast, open land waiting for colonization. This depiction is analogous to the Australian concept of a *terra nullius*, a virgin landscape (Bayet 1998; Cronon 1995). The justification behind this doctrine was that "certain societies were so primitive their land could be treated as uninhabited" (Bell and Asch 1997:52). In order for colonial powers to reshape the landscapes of British Columbia in an image that would allow for economic growth through the exploitation of natural resources, and settlement through the ownership of land, a myth of *terra nullius* was crucial. If the landscapes of British Columbia had to be conceptually emptied, then First Nations had to be conceptually removed in order to justify a social and physical removal.

The ways that First Nations were represented by Europeans at the onset of colonization "played an important part in the process of dispossessing them of their lands and pushing them to the margins of European society" (Peters 2000:46). Harris argues that

> from their earliest encounters, Europeans had begun to remake this territory in their own terms; mapping it, renaming it, claiming possession of it, bringing it within reach of the European imagination. They created a cartographic and conceptual outline of what, for them, was a new land, placing its coast and principal rivers on their maps, identifying the land as wilderness and its people as savages. These abstractions were agents of European colonialism. (Harris 1997:161)

CLEARING THE LANDSCAPE

Initial relationships between First Nations and Europeans in northern British Columbia were based on both the maritime and land-based fur trades (Ames and Maschner 2000:11–12; Miller 2000:177–178). In many ways these two types of fur trade did not directly affect the First Nations occupancy of the land; but this relatively innocuous situation changed as settlers began to move in. The newcomers no longer needed the First Nations in the area the same way that the fur trade required their presence (Cassidy 1992:12).

The political establishment of British Columbia as a province in 1871 led to a large increase in settlers, creating a new dominant society that changed the landscapes of Canada's westernmost province. Although an increase in settlers meant there were key changes to northern landscapes, the changes were not as drastic as the transformations imposed by the resource legislation, including the establishment of Indian Reserves, that followed British Columbia's entry into Canadian Confederation in 1871 (McDonald 1994:156). As European land use changed to industrial forms of resource extraction, control over the landscapes also transformed.

These shifts in power relations altered the place of First Nations in provincial society. "Respect disappeared when one side ceased to need the other, and when one side was in a position to impose its rule" (Ignatieff 2000:59–60). Through the exercise of power, the dominant society was able to take control of the land and thus inscribe itself upon the landscape. Colonial cartography drew new boundaries on the physical, social, and conceptual landscapes of British Columbia. These boundaries changed the spatiality of First Nations communities and, prior to settlers moving into new regions, served as an ideological clearing of the landscape that made it available for the "civilized" newcomers to occupy and to imagine.

The establishment of Indian Reserves was part of this process of claiming the land for the new society. The mid- to late-1800s saw the beginning of the establishment of Indian Reserves in British Columbia. The ideology behind the creation of these reserves in the preconfederation colony of British Columbia was a unique process because it was in direct contradiction to British Imperial policy. The Imperial policy of treaty making had been based on providing "homelands" for Aboriginal peoples as a result of the direct surrender of their lands. British Columbia was a remote colony and was not settled by newcomers until the final days of Imperial administration. For these reasons, the Imperial policy of treaty making was neither adhered to by the peripheral colony of British Columbia nor enforced by the Imperial core. Instead, reserves in British Columbia were created to remove First Nations from their territories, restrict their use of the land, and to create a space to "civilize" First Nations (Bartlett 1990:15–17, 60, 62). Prior to 1864, Governor Douglas did attempt to follow the Imperial policy of treaty making, but his attempts were subsequently thwarted.

James Douglas, as Governor of Vancouver Island and the mainland colony of British Columbia from 1851–1864, laid out tracts of land for southern First Nations, allowing them to have some decision making control over the extent and location of their own reserve lands (Miller 2000:186–190). By 1854, Douglas had entered into fourteen treaties with First Nations on southern Vancouver Island. He continued to attempt to follow the Imperial policy, but by 1861 Douglas was struggling with a lack of funding for the allocation of lands and a lack of support from the Imperial government (Bartlett 1990:16–17). Southern First Nations lost any control they had over land decisions when, in 1864, Douglas retired, and Joseph Trutch became the new Governor. Trutch refused to set apart any significant lands for First Nations, working within a framework of ten acres per family while arranging for the reduction in the size of the reserves that Douglas had previously established (Bartlett 1990; Miller 2000). "Under local colonial administration large areas of reserve land were alienated without the consent of the Indians, to serve settler interests" (Bartlett 1990:62).

At this time, settlers were insisting on accessing lands that they perceived as being "unused" (Miller 2000:190). Settler perceptions were encouraged by the conceptual emptying of the landscape, described above, that reinforced their preconceived European worldviews of the wilderness. Brealey (in Peters 2000:48–49) argues that "as territories became more familiar to European cartographers, First Nations were 'thematized' as archaeological objects [as] a prerequisite for mapping Aboriginal people on reserves" and that this "conceptually erased First Nations' contiguous territories and emptied spaces for settler occupancy."

The reserve system was a marginalizing and displacing strategy by the dominant colonial force of the Canadian government. The boundaries implemented with the establishment of reserves transformed Aboriginal spaces into one of a type of government administrative space classified as "reserve." As Massey (1994:254) observes, by altering spatial constructions, difference is created in the social. By altering physical and social boundaries in British Columbia, First Nations were not only physically concentrated and administratively centralized, but also conceptually bounded and relegated to the periphery of colonially defined space. Colonial perceptions of the surrounding landscape resulted in the creation of new spaces that First Nations were required to occupy on the colonizer's terms, while at the same time having to maintain or adapt their own space within the colonized one.

During the time that surveyors were mapping the landscapes of northern British Columbia for the demarcation of reserves, there was continual resistance from local First Nations. The Nisga'a and the Tsimshian of northern British Columbia, in particular, presented strong opposition to the creation of reserves in their territories in the late 1880s, including the dramatic expulsion of government land surveyors from the area of Port Essington at the mouth of Skeena River (McDonald 1985, 1990; Raunet 1996). This resistance is significant as a demonstration of the importance the territories held for the First Nations: this land was actively used and integral to their cultures. This resistance represents an early point in the ongoing struggle that continues today through the treaty process.

With First Nations cleared from the land and placed on Indian Reserves, the colonial society persisted in interrupting the remaining First Nations administration of the physical landscape through other means. In northern British Columbia, First Nations resources, including their property and use rights, were appropriated by progressive acts of legislation and regulation during the nineteenth and twentieth centuries (McDonald 1985). Regions were settled around resource-rich areas and industries, such as forestry, took over large tracts of land. These changes contributed to the physical ruin of First Nations resource sites, further marginalizing the Aboriginal presence on the land. The destruction of landscapes that had once been so familiar to First Nations forever changed the interactions these peoples had with the land and with the newcomers who were increasingly occupying that land.

The industrialization of the land in northern British Columbia was based on the perception of the landscape as being empty and unused, containing resources that would incorporate the region into the capitalist economy. The European settlement of the region involved "taming" and "civilizing" what was considered a wilderness. This was a labor-intensive undertaking that ranged from laying telegraph lines, to constructing the railway, to clearing the land for towns to house the settlers who would come to take part in the economic opportunities that the "wilderness" had to offer. Large-scale industrial endeavors, including mining and logging operations and fish canneries, were established in the region. An economic analysis describing the changing landscapes of northern British Columbia came to the conclusion that as the "Aboriginal land-scape becomes a 'wilderness'... [it will be] turned into [an] instrument of labour that will drive the new economy. And so the Aboriginal forest becomes a commercial forest under a new regime of resource management" (McDonald 2005:213). Thus, another exercise of colonial power incorporated the landscape into the dominant economy and severely affected the First Nations landscapes.

CONCLUSIONS

British Columbia is in a unique political and social position because it comprises one of the larger areas in Canada that was "not covered by historical and land surrender treaties" (Nichols and Rakai 2001:98). This province is attempting to negotiate not only its land and resources in a strictly geographical sense, but also to negotiate long-standing cultural understandings of where people belong or don't belong. Although a historical lack of signed treaties has now resulted in First Nations being strong political players in the land claims process, the fact that there was no provincial acknowledgment of Aboriginal title speaks to the existence of colonial mechanisms that allowed for this state of nonrecognition, that allowed for this landscape of clearance.

First Nations landscape perspectives are products of long-held, traditional land use values that were at one time completely unconnected from colonial-driven understandings of the North American landscape. In my ethnographic work with the Tsimshian community of Kitsumkalum, people spoke about how their families for generations had made a living from the forests of northern British Columbia and how their very identity was linked to the land (Guernsey 2004). These voices are often left out and marginalized through the reserve system and through cartography, both of which privilege a colonial voice. Prior to contact with Europeans, the landscapes of the Americas were informed and understood through Indigenous/Aboriginal perspectives and worldviews. Linda Tuhiwai Smith finds that with colonization, "Indigenous ways of knowing were excluded and marginalized" (Smith 1999:68). An "erasure," or methodical, and often unconscious, rebuilding of memory and of Indigenous history took place in many colonized areas (Bayet 1998; Cronon 1995; Sarkar 1999:405) as a result of a dominant culture's ideological inscription on the landscape.

Gary Potts's experience gives an example of one alternative understanding of the landscape, and though from northern Ontario, Canada, there are striking similarities to what I have heard from people of Kitsumkalum in northern British Columbia. In his 1998 article "Bushman and Butterfly," Potts gives the account of his struggles as Chief of the Teme-Augama Anishnabi. He recounts his experiences of struggling simultaneously with being Aboriginal in Canada and with gaining back and protecting his peoples' traditional homeland. He speaks of his connection to his land that is home. This is a place of comfort, of belonging, a place with which Potts and the Teme-Augama Anishnabi identify themselves. To Potts, changing the language used is required in changing the perceptions of the land:

> New words are the key. They can't be just technical words or scientific words ... They've got to be words that are attached to the land. And it is the case with this refiguring wilderness. You've grown from it, your descendents have grown from it, you've been part of this growth from the land as well. There is no such thing as "wilderness"... Wilderness is now losing the meaning it had for colonial purposes ... Words are the key that dismantles us, and words are the keys that can build us up as well. So it is very important that this refigured vocabulary and meaning be used. (Potts 1998:194)

From Potts's point of view, interpreting the land as wilderness is inadequate. Wilderness was a colonial tool that worked against his people. Continuing to describe the landscape in this way negates his people's relationship with the land. For his people "everything was connected to the land" (ibid.:190) and, for this reason, Potts feels that an alternative perception of the landscape is required. This example illustrates the point that "wilderness" is only one layer of meaning inscribed on the landscape.

First Nations landscapes were never read or interpreted within their own particular cultural contexts, but were read and interpreted through the colonial lens of a wilderness. Erasing First Nations landscapes and replacing them with a preconceived understanding of "wilderness" allowed the landscape to be physically, socially, and conceptually cleared for the colonial settlement of the land. Yet, First Nations landscapes were never erased; they were merely hidden by a dominant ideology. This chapter has shown how "wilderness" as a colonial metanarrative of a landscape is a cultural and social construction that was transferred onto the landscapes of northern British Columbia and demonstrates that a single landscape can in fact be multilayered and multivocal.

NOTE

1. *First Nations* is a term preferred by many Aboriginal groups in British Columbia to define themselves rather than the constitutionally defined term *Indian*.

REFERENCES

Ames, Kenneth M., and Herbert D.G. Maschner. 2000. *Peoples of the Northwest Coast: Their Archaeology and Prehistory*. Thames and Hudson, New York.

Bartlett, Richard H. 1990. *Indian Reserves and Aboriginal Lands in Canada: A Homeland*. University of Saskatchewan, Saskatoon.

Bayet, Fabienne. 1998. Overturning the Doctrine: Indigenous People and the Wilderness—Being Aboriginal in the Environmental Movement. In *The Great New Wilderness Debate*, ed. by J. Baird Calicott and Michael P. Nelson, pp. 314–324. University of Georgia Press, Athens.

Bell, Catherine, and Michael Asch. 1997. Challenging Assumptions: The Impact of Precedent in Aboriginal Rights Legislation. In *Aboriginal and Treaty Rights in Canada: Essays on Law, Equity, and Respect for Difference*, ed. by Michael Asch, pp. 38–74. University of British Columbia Press, Vancouver.

Cassidy, Frank. 1992. Aboriginal Land Claims in British Columbia. In *Aboriginal Land Claims in Canada*, ed. by Ken Coates, pp. 11–44. Copp Clark Pitman, Toronto.

Coates, Ken (editor). 1992. *Aboriginal Land Claims in Canada: A Regional Perspective*. Copp Clark Pitman, Toronto.

Cronon, William (editor). 1995. *Uncommon Ground: Toward Reinventing Nature*. W.W. Norton, New York.

Duncan, Jim. 2000. Landscape. In *The Dictionary of Human Geography*, ed. by R.J. Johnston, Derek Gregory, Geraldine Pratt, and Michael Watts, pp. 429–431. Blackwell, Oxford.

Guernsey, Brenda. 2004. Alternate Landscapes: Perceptions of a Northern British Columbia Community. In *Breaking the Ice: Proceedings of the 7th ACUNS (Inter) National Student Conference on Northern Studies,* ed. by Ryan K. Danby, Heather Castleden, Audrey R. Giles, and Jennie Rausch, pp. 74–82. University of Alberta, Edmonton.

Harris, Richard Colebrook. 1997. *The Resettlement of British Columbia: Essays on Colonialism and Geographical Change*. University of British Columbia Press, Vancouver.

Ignatieff, Michael. 2000. *The Rights Revolution: CBC Massey Lecture 2000*. House of Anansi Press, Toronto.

Lutz, Allison, Paul Simpson-Housley, and Anton F. de Man. 1999. Wilderness: Rural and Urban Attitudes and Perceptions. *Environment and Behaviour* 31(2):259–266.

Manore, Jean L. 1998. Wilderness and Territoriality: Different Ways of Viewing the Land. *Journal of Canadian Studies* 32(2):77–84.

Massey, Doreen. 1994. *Space, Place, and Gender*. University of Minnesota Press, Minneapolis.

McCullagh, James. 1908. Autumn Leaves. *Aiyansh Notes* 1(4): xii. Church Missionary Society, Wallington, Surrey.

McDonald, James A. 1985. Marginalization of a Cultural Ecology: The Seasonal Cycle of Kitsumkalum. In *Native Peoples, Native Lands*, ed. by B. Cox, pp. 109–218. MacMillan, Ottawa.

———. 1990. Bleeding Day and Night: The Construction of the Grand Trunk Pacific Railway across Tsimshian Reserve Lands. *Canadian Journal of Native Studies* 10(1):33–69.

———. 1994. Social Change and the Creation of Underdevelopment: A Northwest Coast Case. *American Ethnologist* 21(1):152–175.

———. 2005. Cultivating in the Northwest: Early Accounts of Tsimshian Horticulture. In *Keeping it Living: Traditions of Plant Use and Cultivation on the Northwest Coast of North America*, ed. by Nancy Turner and Doug Deur, pp. 240–273. University of British Columbia Press, Vancouver.

McKee, Cristopher. 1996. *Treaty Talks in British Columbia: Negotiating a Mutually Beneficial Future*. University of British Columbia Press, Vancouver.

Miller, J. R. 2000. *Skyscrapers Hide the Heavens: A History of Indian-White Relations in Canada*. 3rd ed. University of Toronto Press, Toronto.

Nichols, Sue, and Mele Rakai. 2001. Canadian Land Reform: An Overview of Aboriginal Rights and Land Claim Settlements. *Land Reform, Land Settlement and Cooperatives* 1:92–103. Food and Agricultural Organization of the United Nations, Rome.

Oelschlaeger, Max. 1991. *The Idea of Wilderness*. Yale University Press, New Haven.

Peters, Evelyn. 2000. Aboriginal People and Canadian Geography: A Review of the Literature. *Canadian Geographer* 44(1):44–55.

———. 2001. Geographies of Aboriginal People in Canada. *Canadian Geographer* 45(1):138–144.

Potts, Gary. 1998. Bushman and Dragonfly. *Journal of Canadian Studies* 33(2):186–195.

Raunet, Daniel. 1996. *Without Surrender, Without Consent: A History of the Nishga Land Claims*. Douglas and McIntyre, Vancouver.

Sarkar, Sahotra. 1999. Wilderness Preservation and Biodiversity Conservation—Keeping Divergent Goals Distinct. *Bioscience* 49(5):405–412.

Smith, Linda Tuhiwai. 1999. *Decolonizing Methodologies: Research and Indigenous Peoples*. University of Otago Press, Dunedin.

Taylor, Monique. 1998. "This is Our Dwelling": The Landscape Experience of the Jesuit Missionaries to the Huron, 1626–1650. *Journal of Canadian Studies* 33(2):85–96.

Tilley, Christopher. 1994. *A Phenomenology of Landscape*. Oxford University Press, Oxford.

Willems-Braun, Bruce. 1997. Buried Epistemologies: The Politics of Nature in (Post) colonial British Columbia. *Annals of the Association of American Geographers* (8791):3–31.

PART 3

RESISTANCE AND REVITALIZATION

CHAPTER 7

Ethnoarchaeological Study of Clearance in Palestine

Juliana Nairouz

Archaeology in Palestine has been used over the past half century as a tool to facilitate the separation of Palestinians from their land. However it is also possible, and indeed necessary, for Palestinian archaeologists to use the discipline to contribute to an increased awareness of the importance of the land to the identity and well-being of the people, as demonstrated in the following ethnoarchaeological study of stone structures in central Palestine.

This ethnoarchaeological study of a set of historic stone structures in the central West Bank of Palestine highlights the necessity of including indigenous people in archaeological research, in order to rethink the past based on the lives of the people who are still adding to the archaeological record. In addition, this study accentuates the importance of recent historic structures for understanding the history of Palestine and warns of the imminent threat to these historic archaeological resources. Archaeology, in this case, can play an important role by adding the missing links to the history that here, and elsewhere, is generally written by the powerful. Ethnoarchaeology can and should be a path for having the victim's voice heard.

While dominating some parts in Palestine in the early 1940s, the Zionist paramilitary forces initiated a campaign of changing the demographic and geographic landscape. This plan later became a methodical State transfer of the locals; when the State of Israel was established in 1948 it sponsored a program to substitute Jews for Palestinians. Thus, the first definite and noticeable form of clearing the Palestinian land was the Palestinians' expulsion from their villages and cities during the years 1947–1949. The outcome was the creation of a substantial Diaspora and a refugee camp populace.

This displacement was partially the result of people actually being forced to leave when their entire village or city was destroyed. Israeli historian Ilan Pappe describes the tactics used between April and July 1948 when armed Zionist soldiers surrounded "each village on three sides, and put the villagers to flight through the fourth side. In many cases, if the people refused to leave, they were forced onto lorries, and driven away to the West Bank. In some villages, there were Arab volunteers who resisted by force, and when these villages were conquered they were immediately blown up and destroyed" (Pappe 2004:137). Also, numerous massacres were committed by the Zionist forces, most notably the Irgun and Stern gangs, in order to wipe out Palestinians and drive them away, "the worst taking place at Sliha (seventy to eighty killed), Lod (250), and Dawayima (hundreds)" (Gelvin 2005:137), while the infamous one is the Deir Yasin massacre in which 254 civilians were killed (Gilmour 1980:62).

The larger part of the Palestinian displacement was the result of a campaign of fear. The "systematic aspect was in the methods employed of first terrorizing the population, executing a few to induce others to leave, and then inviting an official committee to assess the value of land and property in the deserted villages or neighborhoods" (Pappe 2004:139). This practice worked on the Palestinians; people fled because they were afraid to face the fate of their compatriots who were massacred. "Spurred by reports of massacres such as Deir Yasin near Jerusalem … Palestinians either fled or were driven into neighboring countries" (Oren 2003:4). Evidence for the extent of the fear tactic's success was uncovered in the ethnoarchaeological study that follows.

The result of these tactics was a dramatic transformation of the demographic and geographic landscape: a total of 450 villages and cities were depopulated and partially or entirely destroyed during the two years of 1947–1949 (Taha 2005:569). The exact number of refugees was never accurately established; the U.N. Economic Survey Mission's report in 1949 put the total at 726,000, the refugee office of the U.N. Palestine Conciliation Commission placed it at 900,000 (Gilmour 1980:74). In either case, this is a huge number of indigenous people alienated from their land. After the declaration of the State of Israel in 1948, Jews from all over the world continued to come in larger numbers to the area, replacing the locals. This demographical transformation meant that while Jews formed approximately 10% of the total population of Palestine in 1919 (Smith 2004:144), they constituted 76% of the population of Israel in 2004 (Drummond 2004:53). Thus, those who once were the majority became the minority and were labeled as non-Jews.

In the aftermath of this land clearance, some myths were introduced by Israel declaring that the land was not populated. The most famous is Prime Minister Golda Meir's statement to the *Sunday Times* on June 15, 1969, "There is no such thing as a Palestinian people… It is not as if we came and threw them out and took their country. They didn't exist."

Another example is the myth that Palestinians fled their lands voluntarily (Flapan 1987:81). Archaeological and ethnoarchaeological studies today can shed some light on such myths for the benefit of people around the world, though for Palestinians this is obvious.

Since 1949 archaeology has been used politically in an attempt to wipe out or minimize the evidence of the prior dense Palestinian population in the area that was declared Israel. Albert Glock demonstrated that, although there was plenty of cultural evidence on the ground, past Palestinian existence was not to be noticed. In his research on the archaeological surface survey conducted by the Israeli government inside the Green Line (the area declared to be Israel in 1948), a survey which filled 267 volumes, Glock wrote that

> the first volume published covered 56 square kilometers along the coast south of Haifa in the area of 'Atlit. Two villages destroyed in 1948 were included, Ayn Haud and Al-Mazar. The pottery on both sites is read as Byzantine and Arab. Of the 145 sites covered, 55 are said to have "no antiquities." These sites included many lime kilns, caves, ruins of buildings, wells, and other evidence of human activity. Amazingly 110 of the 145 sites have no names. I say "amazingly" because Arabs have a name for every plot of the land, hill, spring and any unusual feature on the landscape. (Glock 1994:81)

Thus, Palestinians are facing a challenge not only of their right of existence today, but in many cases trying to prove their existence in the past. In this case, had archaeology been used rationally, it would have helped in writing a history far from such bias.

Another tool used to further the disappearance of Palestinian patrimony has been the deliberate confiscation of Arab cultural resources by Israelis over the years. Specific examples are the large library of Dr. Tawfiq Canaan taken in 1948, the Palestinian archaeological museum and its library in Jerusalem taken over in 1967, and the library of the Palestinian research center in Beirut taken during the 1982 invasion of Lebanon (Glock 1994:71).

From 1948 on, and especially since 1967, Israel has consistently acted to further clear the land of Palestine by making it harder for Palestinians to have a normal life if they choose to stay in their native land and resist the colonial occupation. Water is one critical case in point. An Israeli military order in June 1967 stated that all water resources in the newly occupied Palestine were now owned by the State of Israel (United Nations Environment Programme 2003:21). From then to the present the limited water resources in the West Bank and Gaza have been unequally distributed. For example, in the West Bank an Israeli settler receives 92.5 gallons per person, five times as much water as a Palestinian, who receives 18.5 gallons. The minimum amount of water recommended by the US Agency for International Development and the

World Health Organization for household use alone is 26.4 gallons per person. A related issue is the wastewater from the Israeli settlements in the West Bank; in many cases it is not treated and flows freely into the nearby *wadis*, causing environmental problems (ibid.:56). Other policies of the Israeli occupation that are in part aimed at clearance are house demolitions, building new Israeli settlements or expanding existing ones on Palestinian land, uprooting trees, deportation and imprisonment, land confiscation, systematic humiliation, curfews, roadblocks, and political assassination.

One of the most recent examples of deliberate destruction of cultural heritage under the guise of military operations was in 2002, when the Israeli army raided and destroyed parts of the cores of several Palestinian cities in the occupied territories, including Bethlehem, Hebron, Gaza, Beit Jala, Tulkarm, Salfit, Jenin, and Nablus. These cities have evidence of continuous occupation that can be traced back to at least the Roman period, yet Israeli forces bulldozed parts of these historic areas into rubble. Nablus (Bshara 2005:73) experienced the most extensive damage, including the loss of domestic buildings, religious buildings, two traditional soap factories, the old marketplace, historical baths, and others. According to a study conducted by the Palestinian Department of Antiquities and Cultural Properties, the damage affected more than 70% of the historic core of the city (Taha 2005:68).

A current example of land clearance under the guise of security is Israel's imposition of a segregation wall between themselves and the majority of Palestinians. But instead of going around the West Bank on the Green Line, the wall cuts through and divides up the Palestinian area and separates Palestinians from each other and from their land and history. As presently planned, the Palestinian side of the wall will contain only 42% of the West Bank (Taha 2005:68). It also excludes from Palestinian control hundreds of archaeological and cultural heritage sites, as documented by a study carried out by the Palestinian Department of Antiquities.

Archaeological surveys indicate more than 12,000 archaeological and cultural heritage sites and features, including ca. 1,750 major archaeological sites and more than 10,000 minor sites and features in the West Bank and Gaza Strip which constitute ca. 5,600 sq km (24%) of the mandatory Palestine. The implemented and the projected wall will encircle the Palestinian population centers in a series of disconnected blocks. The total size of the area inside the wall is ca. 2,700 sq km (42%) of the West Bank which is less than 10% of mandatory Palestine. At the same time the 462 Israeli settlements inside the Palestinian areas controlled already more than 920 archaeological sites and features. After building the wall Israel will control more than 4500 major archaeological sites and features, including ca. 500 major archaeological sites, which constitute ca. 50% of the cultural resources of the Palestinian areas. (Taha 2005:68)

This apartheid wall is adding another link in the chain of landscape clearance.

Archaeology in Palestine has been a major tool with which to distance people from their homeland. Israeli archaeology has been used selectively to document specific periods of history deemed "Jewish," and sometimes to defend and justify the Zionist occupation of Palestine (Glock 1994:71). At the same time, by ignoring specific sites and specific periods within sites, it has minimized the place of the local people and their contribution to the cultural history of Palestine and thus alienated Palestinians from their cultural past. Thus archaeology, rather than being a tool to teach and link Palestinians to their past as in other societies, has been a part of the disenfranchisement of Palestinians. For decades, Palestinians have been unseen in the writing of their own history. Palestinian archaeologists have rarely had the opportunity to participate in excavations to uncover their past or to use their own perspective in interpreting it. Indeed, archaeology has often added to the Palestinians' misery because it has been used as an excuse for confiscating their land. The Israeli antiquities law allows the State to expropriate lands registered as historic sites, which make locals believe that archaeology is their enemy and that when archaeological material is found it is better to get rid of it than to report it. This has encouraged looting of sites, and made Palestinians suspicious when ethnographers or archaeologists attempt to interview them. Until the Palestinians took control of some areas, it was not easy to conduct a study in this cautious society.

In 1994 when a team of Birzeit University students, of which I was a part, started the ethnoarchaeological study in a small village in the West Bank, Israel was still in control of the entire area, and we had to find people known and trusted by the villagers to work with us before we could initiate the study. After this, however, the villagers were helpful and extremely kind. I was a member of the team that performed the archaeological field survey along with the ethnographic study of certain historic stone structures, which are abundant on the landscape in some areas. Later, in 1997–1999, I expanded on this work for my Master's thesis research at the University of Massachusetts, Amherst (Nairouz 2001). The indigenous people of Palestine provided an essential key to understanding these shadowy structures as an integral part of Palestine's agrarian heritage. This study demonstrates that ethnoarchaeological research can contribute valuable understanding to local history, especially during times of rapid transformation. I found that elder villagers knew a great deal about these now-abandoned structures.

About 10,000 historic stone structures of a type known locally as *qusur* are located in the highland areas in the West Bank; they are primarily seen in the farm areas, away from the core villages (Nairouz 2001).

These structures seem similar to much older towers built in Palestine during the Roman, Byzantine, and Crusader periods. My study focused on the village of al-Mazra'a Al-Sharqiyeh, about 20 km north of Jerusalem, and a number of the qusur within the village borders. The function of these structures was tied to the annual agricultural cycle: they were used as residences during the harvest season which starts in July/August and lasts until September/November. The structures were also used as watchtowers for the fields, and building them provided an opportunity to productively use fieldstones that had piled up during field clearing. The qusur are thus sites of primary agricultural production, marking a place where figs and grapes were cultivated, harvested, dried, and prepared for market.

AN ETHNOARCHAEOLOGICAL STUDY IN AL-MAZRA'A AL-SHARQIYEH

The ethnographic part of this study consisted of interviewing over 45 individuals from the village between the ages of 50 and 111, including 23 females and 22 males. In the archaeological surface survey of the village and its vicinity we located at least 234 structures, and conducted comprehensive studies on 56. Only 51 are included in the final interpreting process due to some missing information on five of the structures.

The stone structures at the center of this study were given different names in different areas of the West Bank. The common name in the village I studied was *saqifeh* (plural *saqayef*); saqifeh literally means "a roofed place." However, the most common name in other areas is *qasr* (plural *qusur*) meaning "palace." Some of the other widespread names used for these buildings in this village are *muntar* meaning "watch tower," *arish* or *arisheh* meaning "a thing that gives shade," *alali* meaning "a high building," and *azab* or *ma'zab* meaning "ranch." All these names were known in this village to refer to these structures. However, with more detailed study and by fitting the interviews together we found out that each of these names actually refers to specific parts of the structure.

Qusur were highly uniform in architecture (Figure 7.1). The typical building was circular, built of unworked fieldstones using no mortar, and with a corbelled roof. The circumference at the bottom typically varied from five to eight meters, diminishing upward until the last hole in the roof was capped with a single special stone. Two concentric circular walls were built using large stones, one within the other. Then the gap between the walls was filled with cobbles and pebbles. The entrances varied in architectural style: arched, rectangular, pointed, and double.

Figure 7.1 Qasr.

Windows did not exist in the traditional qasr. Built-in cupboards or niches in various sizes were found in both interior and exterior walls. These structures had a less permanent second story, a booth-like veranda which was built on a row of wooden posts positioned next to each other and wrapped with wild bushes. These bushes were mingled with plants and herbs known to possess good aromas, giving a relaxing atmosphere to the farmers who rested there.

Building a qasr was a ritualized communal process that took place in the summer following the wheat harvest and just before the time to move into the fields for tending grapes and harvesting figs. When a family decided to build a qasr, the details concerning the plans would be announced in the village center. On the scheduled day, a certain person known as a *shobash* man would stand on a high place at the suggested building site and start shobashing, which is the singing ritual of calling others to come and help. The shobash singing consisted of certain songs without using any musical instruments or any preparation in advance. Often the shobash person would compose his own words on the spot. When others heard the announcement they either came readily to help, chose not to show up, or maybe even sang back angrily to the shobash person. Those who did help were primarily family and friends; thus participation in this communal building activity might have acted as a barometer of the state of relationships between extended families (*hamulahs*) in the village.

Both men and women had active roles in all aspects of building and using the qusur. When the building process began, whole families would gather stones. Then women and children handed stones to the men, who placed them where the chief builder directed. The interviews indicate that the women's unique contribution in this early stage was to cheer on the men and encourage them to work harder by singing and ululating whenever the building process reached a significant point. This role was a successful one because if the women found someone who was not working very hard, they would embarrass him in their songs. The effect was to make all men work harder. Women's primary role came just before the building was finished, when they built a fire and prepared food for everyone who helped. Women recalled that the completion of building of the qasr marked by the laying of the final stone in the center of the corbelled roof, concluded with a celebration of singing, dancing, ululating, and the slaughter of certain animals for the feast, a custom which was also followed when finishing the building of a village house.

After the qasr was complete, women helped men in picking and selling the products while also doing all the domestic work in their qasr: gathering wood for the fire, collecting herbs for drinks and for decorating the arisheh, taking care of the children, and making handicrafts if they had time. Interviews indicate that children loved this several weeks' stay in the qusur because they had a larger space to play with other children. But they also helped their families, especially the women, with the daily work. When time came for school, children attended as usual but returned home to the qasr. Bedtime stories, usually told by grandmothers, did not change while they were out of their core village homes.

The interviews revealed that qusur were integral to grape and fig farming. People would leave their homes in the center villages and stay in these structures for 4 to 6 months harvesting grapes, figs, and sometimes olives. Grapes were the main reason for peasants to move into these structures. Grapes need attention early in the growing season. Farmers used to go to their fields before the grape harvest for a process called *tawriq*, (literally "leafing," which is to prune the vines and cover the plant with leaves and bushes in order to protect it from the sun's heat as the grapes grow). After the grapes were harvested, figs also obliged farmers to stay in the fields since they needed daily care: they ripen unevenly and thus need to be picked more often. Olives caused some peasants to stay longer in their qusur since this harvest season comes the latest. All these crops, however, could have been harvested by commuting daily from the center village if the people did not like staying in the fields. But this was not the case; interviewees insisted that those days in the qusur were the best in the year.

Although these structures were primarily for agricultural use, they also were centers of significant social activities. During the harvest, families would host parties where they would play the traditional flute (the *shababeh*) and dance the *dabkeh* (a traditional folk dance), sing traditional songs, and play games. Interviewees recalled the stay in the qusur as a fun time to which they as children greatly looked forward. Both men and women recounted songs, games, dances, jokes, and stories associated with the time they spent in the qusur. Thus it seems that village life in the qusur closely mirrored daily life during the rest of the year, except that it was regarded as a more pleasurable time.

The main structure of the qasr as described above was a part of a larger complex that was surrounded by a short wall and usually included a few of the following auxiliary installations: a chicken coop, a cattle pen, a donkey area, a well, a platform to dry figs or grapes, and a hearth. My research included archaeological mapping of these structures and interviews with older village residents who remembered using them. I investigated the function of each element of the qasr complex, the reasons for moving from permanent center village houses into the fields, the traditions and fun people had when moving into their qusur, and the reasons for abandoning the use of the structures.

Although the villagers described these days as their favorite time of the year, they abandoned their qusur completely by 1960. I found several reasons for this abandonment, both economic and political. The primary cause was a grape blight that affected the whole vine production in Palestine in the 1950s. This made it difficult for vine farmers to survive in this agricultural complex because grapes were a primary source of income for them.

Fear of the Israeli occupying forces was another important reason for farmers to stop going to their qusur. Informants said that in 1948 when the Zionists started occupying Palestine they killed and expelled many people. As mentioned earlier, Jewish forces, regular and irregular, demolished some villages completely, including Deir Yasin village, which has become infamous for the massacre committed against its people. Some of the Deir Yasin survivors fled in 1948 after the massacre to the village I studied and took refuge there. Thus these villagers were intimately informed about that massacre. Fear of falling victim to such a massacre, rather than actually being driven out, was the cause for most of the Palestinian refugees leaving their villages and cities in 1948. The case was similar in al-Mazra'a al-Sharqiyeh. Although the people did not flee their village, they did abandon use of the field structures that were in more isolated areas and therefore considered less secure.

Finally, labor emigration abroad and jobs in the newly established State of Israel were reasons that a quarter of the interviewees cited for abandonment of the qusur. The insecure business of selling grapes and figs could not compete against the Israeli labor market with its comparatively higher wages. Thus Palestinians repeated the pattern seen in other parts of the world in which modernization drives farmers off their lands to seek jobs in cities. Today these stone structures are rapidly disappearing from the landscape due to natural deterioration, purposeful removal to make room for new Palestinian construction, and purposeful clearance as part of the Israeli occupation.

CONCLUSIONS

The abandonment of the qusur in the 1950s is only another part of the long process of the separation of Palestinians from their land. As people become alienated from their land, they have also become separated from their history. Interviews with younger and middle-aged Palestinians revealed considerable ignorance about the stone structures, and the traditions and history associated with them. As the transformation of the landscape accelerates as result of both modernization and occupation, so too does the distance of Palestinian people from their own agrarian heritage. Documentation and understanding of this recent history will be essential to the people as they engage in their own nation building.

Although recent historical resources such as the qusur are not yet considered antiquities under contemporary Palestinian legislation, they are essential in contributing to the writing of Palestine's history. These resources and the history they represent are being rapidly erased as the landscape is quickly being transformed by development and occupation. The loss of these structures further alienates younger Palestinians from their recent agrarian history, and the older generation is steadily declining. These factors have significant consequences for the understanding that people bring to the prospect of independence and nation building.

Indigenous people of Palestine, in this study, proved that their connection to the land and their input in understanding such structures can play an enormous part in writing the history of their land. Also they demonstrated that relating contemporary life with older life can lead to a continuous historic connection. Indigenous peoples deserve archaeologists' recognition that their input into archaeological research can actually help in resolving some missing links from the past. Older residents, especially of the rural areas, can help in interpreting the ancestors' behaviors either because their own lives have changed less or because they still remember more traditions that have now passed away. Native peoples should always be included and recognized in archaeological research.

Despite the increasing challenges Palestinians face in their daily lives under occupation, historical preservation needs to be a primary concern as precious national historical resources face increasing threats. A Palestinian documentation center is desperately needed to save the archaeological record and the existing material evidence. Many more studies similar to this one of the qusur should be carried out in order to record the history of this rapidly changing society, especially considering the threats surrounding it. The world and the Palestinians themselves must understand that living people who are not scholars have much to contribute to understanding the history of their quickly evolving land-scape. Palestinians' sense of identity has to be protected and restored as part of their struggle for survival and in order to face contemporary political challenges. Archaeology can be a valuable tool to identify the specific form that Palestinian culture took in the past and to link the present smoothly with that past. Otherwise the radical disjuncture of the recent past with the present may contribute to the destruction of "Palestinian" as a continuing cultural entity.

ACKNOWLEDGMENTS

I would like to thank those who supported me and encouraged me to write this paper. To my teachers, Linda for her time editing and her con-structive comments, John for his helpful guidance, and my appreciation to Martin, Art, Hamed, Hamdan, and Fuad for their support. And to my husband I owe my accomplishment.

REFERENCES

Bshara, Khaldun. 2005. The Treatment of Unoccupied Spaces during the Armed Conflict in the Palestinian Territories. In *Mediterraneum tutela e valorizzazione dei beni culturali ed ambientali*, Vol. 5, ed. by F. Maniscalco, pp. 73–78. Massa editore, Naples, Italy.

Drummond, Dorothy. 2004. *Holy Land Whose Land? Modern Dilemma, Ancient Roots*. 2nd ed. Fairhurst Press, Terre Haute, Indiana.

Flapan, Simha. 1987. *The Birth of Israel: Myths and Realities*. Pantheon Books, New York.

Gelvin, James L. 2005. *The Israel-Palestine Conflict: One Hundred Years of War*. Cambridge University Press, Cambridge.

Gilmour, David. 1980. *Dispossessed: The Ordeal of the Palestinians 1917–1980*. Sidgwick and Jackson, London.

Glock, Albert. 1994. Archaeology as Cultural Survival: The Future of the Palestinian Past. *Journal of Palestine Studies* 23(3):70–84.

Nairouz, Juliana. 2001. Qusur: The Stone Structures in Historic Palestine. An Ethnoarchaeological Study of Qusur in the Village of Al-Mazra'a Al-Sharqiyeh. Master's thesis, Department of Anthropology, University of Massachusetts, Amherst.

Oren, Michael B. 2003. *Six Days of War: June 1967 and the Making of the Modern Middle East*. Presidio Press, New York.

Pappe, Ilan. 2004. *A History of Modern Palestine: One Land, Two Peoples*. Cambridge University Press, Cambridge.

Smith, Charles D. 2004. *Palestine and the Arab-Israeli Conflict: A History with Documents*. 5th ed. Bedford/St. Martin's, New York.

Taha, Hamdan. 2005. A Decade of Archaeology in Palestine. In *Mediterraneum tutela e valorizzazione dei beni culturali ed ambientali*, Vol. 5, ed. by F. Maniscalco, pp. 63–71. Massa editore, Naples, Italy.

United Nations Environment Programme. 2003. Desk Study of the Environment in the Occupied Palestinian Territories 2003. http://www.postconflict.unep.ch/publications/INF-31-WebOPT.pdf, accessed June 2005.

CHAPTER 8

The Domestication of Landscape through Naming and Symbolic Protection among the Batswapong Peoples of Eastern Botswana: Fullness and Emptiness of Landscapes in the Eyes of the Beholder

Phillip Segadika

> By building monuments prehistoric people were altering the earth. Not only were they erecting an eye-catching spectacle that attracts the visitor to this day, they made their contribution to a new sense of time and place. (Bradley 1993:2)

The quote by Richard Bradley listed above served as the inspiration for this chapter; unfortunately, not because it is particularly relevant for the Batswapong people but because it overlooks the fact that, in some societies, altering the earth is forbidden because the landscape is already full of the imperceptible. This chapter presents an analysis of the definitions of landscape and landscape history by the custodians of history in Malaka, a village of the Batswapong peoples located at the foot of the Tswapong Hills in east-central Botswana (Figure 8.1). The research was undertaken as part of the Landscape History in Botswana Project and formed part of my Masters Degree Dissertation with the University of Wales, Lampeter (Segadika 1997). Three main themes of relations with the landscape are presented and discussed: naming the landscape, symbolism and meaning tied to landscapes, and the fullness of some "empty" spaces where such landscapes are contested.

The various relations within and perceptions of an English landscape are much simpler to investigate over lengthy periods of time when compared to their counterparts in the Tswapong landscape. Needless to say, the difference is mainly rooted in the availability of literate, pictorial, and documentary sources dealing with the subject of landscape. Clark (1976), Thomas (1993), and even Cosgrove (1984) were able to refer to an array of artistic and literary data in studying the history of the English

Figure 8.1 Map of study area in east-central Botswana. (Paul Mellenhorst and Phillip Segadika).

landscape that enabled them to reach conclusions about the various changing attitudes of people to the landscape in specific time frames. For instance, Cosgrove (1984) sees Alberti's *Della Pittura* of 1435 as part of the birth of landscape art; through landscape art "the method of presenting a three-dimensional world on a two-dimensional surface was encouraged as a means towards revealing truth," thus giving rise to a perspective art (Cosgrove 1984:22). In that way the viewer is rendered outside of the history that is presented (Thomas 1993:20). This particular perception of the landscape can be placed within specific times because of the available evidence of the art. To interpret the Tswapong landscape, in contrast, we must use place-names, oral traditions, and archaeology because the inhabitants of these landscapes did not record their perceptions in writing or paintings.

It is well known that in the English language the term *landscape* is a product of the sixteenth-century painters, who derived it from the Dutch *landschap* (Hirsch and O'Hanlon 1995:2). However, at various times the landscape was perceived differently by different people; for instance, the growing interest in viewing the landscape is seen as a product of an eighteenth-century capitalist society, whereby the changing social relations allowed land to be looked on as a commodity (Bender 1993:22; Hirsch and O'Hanlon 1995:2). However, as Tilley (1994) has attempted to demonstrate, it would be fallacious to assume that some nonliterate, non-Western societies did not have particular ways of seeing the landscape just because they did not write it down or did not, as is common, make recorded literary-artistic impressions, manipulations, or representations of the landscape.

In the vernacular, the word for "land" is *lefatshe*. This *lefatshe* can refer to the physical land—that palimpsest on which all the physical features of hills, rivers, and trees are contained. The word *lefatshe* can, therefore, be used to contrast land with open waters. However, the word *lefatshe* can also be used to refer to "the earth." So, for instance, the Setswana translation of the Bible translates Genesis 1:1 as, "In the beginning God created the Heavens and the *Lefatshe* (earth/world)."

The word *lefatshe* is commonly used in defining ownership of portions of land, such as in "x's land." Since the postcolonial period, the word *lefatshe* has also been used to refer to the independent states— "countries." This is especially evident in the first line of the Botswana National anthem, emphasizing the fact that "this *land* is ours." Certainly the message of the song is partly a reaction to the preindependence struggles for land with the South African Boers and Cecil Rhodes's British South Africa Company (Tlou and Campbell 1984). In order to legitimize the ownership, the anthem declares that the "land" is a heritage that "our fathers" left for us (from our "fathers/ancestors") and a gift from God. The word *lefatshe*/land has, therefore, taken various meanings, and these meanings have expanded over time and sometimes in response to the sociopolitical and economic experiences of the peoples of Botswana.

NAMING THE LANDSCAPE

While a great deal has been written by anthropologists and theologians on personal names in African societies (e.g., Mbiti 1970; Setiloane 1986), very little has been done by Africanist landscape archaeologists on the subject of place-names (see, however, Boeyens and Cole 1995; Grant 1970; Humphreys 1993). Yet place-names very often capture people's perceptions, both concrete and abstract, of specific locations and can be highly revealing (Humphreys 1993:44). In a Northern Cape study, Van Vreeden (1961:112) was able to note that most of the Khoisan place-names had an emphasis on water, thus suggesting that water was accorded high priority by these people (Humphreys 1993:44).

The case of Batswapong culture and cosmology posits a striking similarity between naming individuals and naming the landscape. At the level of personal names, naming has a very distinct place in the traditional Batswapong culture and indeed in many African societies (Mbiti 1970). Whereas in the West emphasis may be placed especially on christening and commemoration of birthdays, traditionally Tswana societies place more emphasis on the ceremony of *mantsho a ngwana* which means literally "taking out the child." Traditionally, the ceremony takes place about three to six months after birth and the postbirth confinement period. In this ceremony, the restrictions and taboos regarding access to the new mother and baby are lifted and the child is "taken out" to the community and its name ceremoniously declared to members of the extended family, as well as being publicized in the community at large. However, in giving the name to a child the Batswapong are always reminded of the proverb "*ina lebe seromo*" (a bad name predestines bad luck). Some names may mark a historical occurrence, some may be called after a close relative or friend with hope of reliving their good "spirit" or a wish of having the newborn child take on some of their character. In a greater majority of cases the name will express optimism or the experience that one or both of the parents have had in life, had while the child was expected, or experienced at the time of birth.

When asked if there is any relationship between a person's name and his/her future character, an informant gave as her response the example of a well-known simpleton named Mokotedi from Setswana fables:

"If you call your child "Mokotedi" would you be surprised if he became a fool? How do you mean? ... A child's name should be Peace, Joy, Thanks." (Mma Tshakga, interview by author, July 22, 1996, Maghing ward, Ratholo)

It is clear, therefore, that in giving names to people, the giver (who can be a parent, relative, or friend) expresses optimism for the future of the child and the family. Among several Tswana societies, of which the Batswapong are a language group, it is common for a woman who suffers many miscarriages or infant mortalities to call her next-born child after the name of an object as a deceptive artifice against the evil spirits. This author has a cousin who is called "Bottle" because her mother suffered several miscarriages before "Bottle" was born. In some cases of naming, then, there is a desire and an attempt to control the future, to appropriate it and mould it according to the ideals or values of the giver.

These aspects to the act of giving personal names should shed light on the process of naming the landscape. In a culture that deeply believes in the landscape as being embedded with supernatural powers that are active in human relations (see the discussion on Dimomo Cave and Tshekedi's Road below), naming this active player, the landscape, is a sensitive issue that should anticipate harmony with the landscape in order to avoid any predetermination of bad luck. Selectivity in naming the landscape seems to be relevant to some aspects of the Batswapong landscape. The landscape is acquired (as with the birth of a child) and then "encultured," which in this case entails providing it with a distinct tag, a name, not just for distinguishing one place from the other, but as is the case with the Phalatswe Hills environs, also as a means of impressing some meaning on the landscape.

Phalatswe Hill: Description of the Male, Female, and Child Hills

Looking at it from a distance and from the direction of Malaka village, the Phalatswe Hill area seems to incorporate only two hills (Figure 8.2). However, the local people who traverse the area confirm the topographic maps in revealing that the area actually comprises three closely located peaks called *Phalatswe yo motonanyana* (male), *Phalatswe yo monamagadi* (female), and *Zwenene* (child or smallness). The various sizes of these hills and their relatedness are essential in the way that the local people have perceived and utilized them over the years. Male Hill itself is 3,736 m above sea level and occupies an area about 40,000 m². Female Hill is lower and smaller than Male Hill, occupying about 30,000 m² and being 3,200 m high. The highest and biggest hill is in other words the Male Hill, next in size is Female Hill, and lastly the peak known as *Zwenene*.

Figure 8.2 Female Hill and Male Hill, with the Tswapong Hills in the background to the right.

ENGENDERING THE LANDSCAPE?

In the vernacular, the gender words *tonanyana* and *namagadi* (male and female in this sense) are normally used to refer to animals. It is only on specific symbolic and personified cases that these words can be used for persons or other non-animal references. However, in the case of the Phalatswe range of hills, the use of the conjunctive *yo* instead of *ee* in the names of the hills implies that they are considered to represent both male and female human genders based on the varying sizes of the hills. This personification and the human reference are emphasized, as the smallest peak is named *Zwenene*. Though this word *zwenene* is ambiguously used to refer to "a child" in the local vernacular, the root *zwe* may be a corruption of the Kalanga *bgwe* which means hill or rock, while the repeated suffix *ne* is a common diminutive suffix.

It is established here that once named, the Phalatswe hillscape becomes a symbolic map of Malaka perceptions and ideals which include, among others, the perceived family order, status, and relationship. It is interesting that in gendering the Phalatswe Hills, there was a lack of preference for other names that would distinctly imply "male" or "female"; words such as *monona* (man) and *motszadi* (woman) are unambiguously human in reference and may have sounded inappropriate for a symbolic representation of a nonhuman, physical feature. For example, *Matlhogojane*, *Setlaboshane,* and *Mmapereko* would not be used because of their negative connotations: the characteristically male word *Matlhogojane* has connotations of failure and immaturity, while its female equivalent *Mmapereko* implies a household of confusion and anarchy. It is argued here that in choosing names with a positive association for a "male" Phalatswe and a "female" Phalatswe, there was a conscious propagation of an ideal household comprised of husband, wife, and child.

It is plausible, therefore, that the naming and sexing of the Phalatswe hillscape is a definite representation and propagation of community values and that the selection in naming is not a haphazard process but demonstrates an attempt at ensuring a harmonious relationship with the landscape. As a representation, these names can be perceived to be delivering a specific message about gender relations in the community to all who know the name of the hillscape. However, the purpose of naming is also to appropriate and monumentalize an entity, as it is something that will be recalled and remembered by future generations. This is illustrated in the riddle of the name, "*Thi ka ntobe bagologolo baswa ba e tlogela*" (the cherished thing that "those of old" die, leaving behind [virtually a literal translation]).

Therefore, naming the landscape is reminiscent of building a monument: future generations can make reference to it and the ideals for which the name stood can be perpetuated in the generations to come.

However, there is a curious naming of the smaller hill in an engendered fashion: the male hill is a higher, bigger, and more prominent feature, the female hill is relatively smaller and lower, while the child hill is considerably smaller still and sexless. This gendered naming of the hills has a striking similarity with the Tsodilo Hills World Heritage Site where the local people have attached "male, female, child, and grandchild" to the hills in relation to their sizes (Segadika 2006:33).

The Phalatswe Hill area, therefore, conjures up an image of some family order to both the male and the female, but perhaps with different implications and interpretations of such an image. Yet it carries with it the ideas of hierarchy and the power relations in society. The size and prominence of the peaks evidently determine how each should be gendered. The relationship is more explicit in the vernacular. The word for male is *tonanyana* which literally means "slightly big" and implies relatively bigger in comparison with female. The root *tona* can also be used to denote maturity, age, and the properties of being an elder and thus worthy of respect. In the word for female, *namagadi,* the suffix *gadi* connotes femininity, as in *Mohumagadi* (queen or Chief's wife), in *mogadibo* (co-wife, in polygamous relations), or in *bogadi* (dowry). This linguistic examination implies that the "male" word has immediate connotations of bigger size or higher status.

The name chosen for the smallest hill is *Zwenene.* It is interesting that this name has no connotations of biological sex. However, it would appear that in ascribing names to the landscapes it was not crucial that the small hill should be sexed, whereas it was vital that the two adult hills should be differentiated according to gender. Therefore the sexless peak of *Zwenene* implies a child whose sex remains unimportant until it is old enough to enter the world of the "contesting" male and female sexes.

It is evident, however, that the male-female relationship was not the only one that needed highlighting in the late nineteenth-century to early twentieth-century Batswapong (Malaka) landscape. An examination of the oral history seems to suggest that the set of Batswapong traditional beliefs about the ancestral spirits, the *Bapedi* cult, was facing challenges in a society that was politically subjugated, and that the cult was in need of a revival. This introduces us to two places with shared, related folklores as testimony to the supernatural powers of the ancestral spirits in the Tswapong Hills.

TSHEKEDI'S ROAD AND BATSWAPONG SUBVERSIVE RESISTANCE

Beginning in the 1860s, the Batswapong peoples were under the subjugation of Bangwato supremacy (Motzafi-Haller 1994a). The Bangwato were, by the turn of the nineteenth century, a well-organised ethnic group that always placed its capitals strategically to establish hegemony over other ethnicities in the central district of what is now Botswana, and also especially to control the contact and trade benefits of the early European travelers, wagon traders, missionaries, and colonial administration (Parsons 1973:115; Tlou 1970:102). The Bangwato insisted on receiving tribute from all their subjects, including the Batswapong peoples (Thema 1970:71). This subjugated position of the Batswapong peoples was noticed by European missionaries and early travelers, among them Shippard, who suggested that a caste system was being observed in which the Batswapong were perceived by the Bangwato to be of a "lower and inferior rank," albeit a little higher than the "Bushmen" (Botswana National Archives [BNA] 1888, Shippard Files BNA HC 24/15). The Bangwato chiefs and regents adopted Christianity, built churches and schools, and identified strategic locales for their capitals, sometimes on land that the Batswapong considered to be theirs and sacred (Figure 8.3).

One of these Bangwato-sponsored developments was a road construction project by a Bangwato regent named Tshekedi in the early 1940s. This road project was the first development that the Bangwato had undertaken on top of the Tswapong Hills, which are perceived by the Batswapong to be the abode of their ancestral spirits, the Bapedi.

Figure 8.3 Ruins of the Bangwato church built in the 1890s at the foot of the Tswapong Hills, near Malaka village, east-central Botswana.

Measured from Palapye to Moeng, this road (which is no longer in use) is about 40 km long (Thema 1970:71). Informants consistently report that the road was built by the conscript labor of age regiments drawn from different ethnic groups under Bangwato rule. A preliminary archaeological examination of the road shows that for the 40 km road to be built, considerable manpower had to be expended in breaking the stones and clearing the road of boulders, especially on the steep slopes just before Moeng, where special engineering skills were required (Segadika 1997). The tribe accepted the imposition of cattle levy, and for several months provided the regimental labor which must have been worth "several thousand Rand in man hours" (Thema 1970:71).

To fully appreciate the results of the analysis of the folklore regarding Tshekedi's Road, at least two things are necessary. First, we need to get a picture of the views and values that the Batswapong have on the Tswapong Hills. Secondly, the relationship between the Batswapong and the Bangwato at the time needs to be understood. These two factors will reveal the tripartite relationship between landscape, history, and emotion and, consequently, the development of folklore as a form of subversive resistance, where a landscape perceived by others to be empty turns out to be full of the imperceptible.

Several studies have established that the Batswapong people believe that the Tswapong Hills are the sacred dwelling place of their ancestors (Kiyaga-Mulindwa 1980; Landau 1993, 1995; Motzafi-Haller 1994a, 1994b). Their reverence of these "living dead" is still evident in the tendency by informants in the neighboring villages of Malaka, Moremi, and Ratholo in 1996 to avoid referring directly to the ancestral spirits as *Badimo*, but rather to call them the "owners of the land" (*Beng ba lefatshe*) or simply the Bapedi, after the predominant ethnic group from which most Batswapong are derived. These ancestral spirits have a form of selective omnipresence; although their domain is the hills, they can also see activities in the villages and are ready to punish those who behave in an unbecoming manner (*ba ba sa itshwareng sentle*) (compare also with Landau 1995). The role of the Bapedi ancestral spirits as a form of "guardian angel" is recounted in the personal testimony of Lelatlhego Busang, who became lost yet survived 30 days in the bush because he was fed by "invisible" hands (Lelatlhego Busang, interview by author, July 31, 1997, Moremi).

The prefix *ba* in the two words used to refer to the ancestral spirits, *Bapedi* and *Badimo*, is a personal prefix, thus emphasizing the notion of the ancestral spirits as the "living dead" (cf. Mbiti 1970). The reference to them as "owners of the land" has a number of implications. First, it is a historical reference. Motzafi-Haller (1994b) has argued that oral and written history from the various villages are consistent in relating that the first group to settle in the Tswapong Hills in the early seventeenth century was led by Mapulane, a Pedi chief. However, the reference to the ancestors as "owners of the land" can also be seen as a political statement. It implicitly stresses that the Batswapong are the rightful heirs of the land by virtue of their position as descendants of those people who first settled the hills. Archaeologists would, of course, disagree that the hills were not inhabited until the seventeenth century AD. It is within this context and that of subjugator-subject relationship that the popular folklore regarding the mysterious intervention of the Bapedi is examined.

There are several versions of the story regarding the time when the Bapedi expressed their displeasure with the building of the road, of the manner in which they are supposed to have intervened, and even multiple reasons for exactly why the Bapedi did not want the road to be built on the hills. Some of the informants (L. Busang, interview by author, July 31, 1997, Moremi; N. Busang, interview by author, July 19, 1997, Motlhabaneng) argue that in spite of the message that the road should not be built on the hills, the Bangwato regent did not take heed, "*one a re fa kere kare, kare kare*" (L. Busang, interview by author, July 31, 1997, Moremi). The implication here is that the warning was issued before the work on the road started. Yet other warnings were given while the road was being built (Mafhike, interview by author, July 27, 1997, Malaka; T. Sebetlela, interview by author, July 27, 1997, Malaka). An examination of some of the accounts suggest that another message came after the road had been built and was in use; the ancestral spirits complained about the fact that the fumes from the vehicles were irritating, "*Bapedi bane bare mosi wa dikoloi o a ba seleka*" (N. Busang, interview by author, July 19, 1996, Motlhabaneng).

All the stories, nevertheless, have Regent Tshekedi as the main character and recipient of the mysterious intervention of the Bapedi. One of the popular tales is that while Tshekedi was on his regular drive to Moeng College, his truck (*koloi*) inexplicably stopped and a sudden thick mist covered him and his companions (cf. Lesotlho 1982:7). Tshekedi restarted the vehicle, but all attempts to drive it forward to Moeng failed. It was only when he turned the vehicle back in the direction of his Bangwato capital that the truck moved. Another account mentions that while Tshekedi was driving he saw an antelope that he tried to shoot, only for it to change and reappear, first as a donkey, then as a mist, and finally as a strange-looking snake (N. Busang, interview by author, July 19, 1996, Motlhabaneng). Other accounts stress that Tshekedi became ill after this incident (Lesotlho 1982:8).

Some of the informants who worked on the construction of the road say they were compelled to this work because they had to respect the decree of their Chief, Otukile, who was under pressure of instruction from Tshekedi, the Bangwato regent, to mobilize two regiments for the building of the road.

Tshekedi's papers in the National Archives of Botswana make no reference to these alleged experiences. However, the building of the road was already unpopular, since the Batswapong of Tholo had to be relocated to a less fertile and eroded Majwaneng in order to allow passage to the envisaged school to which the road led (Thema 1970:71). The historical explanation for terminating the use of the road is that the road was becoming increasingly dangerous, especially at the Moeng slope (Thema 1970:71). However, Tshekedi does not appear to have been unpopular with other Basarwa and Kalanga subject ethnic groups (BNA n.d., Tshekedi Papers S/69/S, DFC 2/11, S266/10; cf. Gadibolae 1985:30), so that the lore could alternatively be interpreted as part of the Batswapong subversive resistance to Bangwato rule.

It is clear that the different versions of the manner of intervention by the ancestral spirits, or Bapedi, on Tshekedi's Road are not an issue to some custodians of village history. Rather, the essential aspect of the role is the intended message of the victory of the ancestral spirits in demonstrating their supernatural power in their domain, the Tswapong Hills. However, other informants insist their own version of the story is the true one. Yet others, when they hear of alternative versions of the lore, try to make sense out of the inconsistencies by integrating the various stories into a synoptic account. From the various versions propagated it seems evident, therefore, that the message of the folklore is about the power and intervention of the Bapedi in a contested Batswapong and Bangwato landscape.

The case of the Tswapong Hills suggests that landscape archaeologists should be careful when identifying the distinctiveness of "sacred" landscapes. The "sacred" Tswapong Hills are certainly considerably more than shrines where sacredness is concentrated in a limited area. Neither are the Tswapong Hills just a specific locale, as may be the case with a valley or the summit of a hill or a single cave (such as Dimomo Cave, discussed below). In the Tswapong case, a high level of respect is accorded to an entire 54 km long mountain range, occupying over 300 sq km. The whole range is perceived by the Batswapong as a sacred zone, a dwelling place of the living dead, within a greater landscape. However, it is evident that the levels of sacredness differ; for instance, other parts, such as Dimomo Cave, are so sacred that human presence is totally forbidden and considered a desecration.

Dimomo Cave and Alteration by Presence

Dimomo Cave is located on the summit of the Tswapong Hills, about 3 km south of the Malaka village (Figure 8.4). According to oral

DIMOMO CAVE

Figure 8.4 Malaka village with the Tswapong Hills, location of Dimomo Cave and Tshekedi's Road, in the background.

information, the cave was used, along with the nearby valleys, as a place of refuge during the "Matebele wars" of the mid-nineteenth century, in other words the *Difaqane* unrest of the 1820s and 1830s onwards. Informants mention that the cave is now occupied by the ancestral spirits of the caves. The Dimomo Cave was initially called *Malapile* because of the sudden tiredness and numb sensation that people felt whenever they passed by the cave. The name "Dimomo" is derived from a man of the same name who, while on his way from collecting wild fruit in the proximity of the cave, was mysteriously beaten by invisible hands and placed under a big boulder, yet not crushed. He returned to caution fellow villagers that he had been warned that the road that leads to the caves should no longer be used as it was the special abode of the ancestral spirits (M. Monyama, interview by author, July 27, 1997, Malaka).

Even though many informants from the village tell the same story, they all referred to one particular informant, Mma Masupatsela. Her late husband RaBotshelo Masupatsela, while on his regular visit from Matlhakoleng, had a mysterious accident: he was trapped under a big rock. He was lost for many days when "word" came from the indigenous priests that Masupatsela would bring "news" that they must take heed of. While underneath the rock he too was given the same warning as Dimomo, that "people are not allowed there" (*batho ga ba letlelelwe foo*). Similar stories of people experiencing mysterious events in the

Tswapong Hills, such as big boulders falling on them yet not crushing them, are also reported by Mpulubusi (1992:34).

This "out of bounds" principle regarding Dimomo Cave appears to be another form of avoiding "alteration" even by presence, implying that while the ancestral spirits did not allow the physical alteration of the range of hills through the building of the road, in the case of Dimomo, the presence of living humans is taken as a taboo (*go a ila*) and is considered an intrusion and an alteration of the "spiritual balance" of Dimomo Cave.

Further inquiries reveal that even the informants, in their total belief and reverence of the taboos, acknowledge that these restrictions have a beginning and could be placed within a time frame. Informants look at these caves as the place that protected their great grandparents during the mid-nineteenth-century wars (Mma Masupatsela, interview by author, July 20, 1996, Malaka). Therefore, the reverence given this part of the landscape may have been, in part, the result of a long-standing, but evolving, tradition of the importance of Dimomo Cave as a one-time fortress as well as a monument to those who fell during the *Mfecane* wars in the 1820s (for *Mfecane* wars see Tlou and Campbell 1984:146).

Consequently the idea of "no access" must have taken advantage of an existing phenomenon of "restricted places" among the Batswapong; for instance, the *Botsetse* (postbirth confinement period), in which only a few selected caretakers are given access to a special room that a mother and her newborn child use during the confinement period. People entering the confinement room are thought to have potentially stepped on "hot grounds" and could therefore have "hot feet." In Bantu cosmology, hot often implies impurity and danger (Comaroff 1985:81); for instance, a female in her menstrual cycle is considered "hot," as is a woman who has recently miscarried. Furthermore, the confined mother and child should not go out in public or visit since they may "step on and cross the footprints of the father," which could cause a child to be "overshadowed" (*go okangwa*) and thus fall sick. (cf. Comaroff 1985:81; Mogapi 1991:145).

To the Batswapong, landscape features have a role to play in making statements: both Tshekedi's Road and Dimomo Cave are places within the Tswapong Hills range with mysterious stories told about them regarding forms of forbidden alteration. It would appear that whereas the lore about Tshekedi's Road acted as a tool against Bangwato overlordship, the Dimomo Cave lore acted as a local testimony to the power of the Bapedi. The argument developed here is that the challenges posed by the Christianization of the Batswapong area to the Bapedi cult meant that the Bapedi cult needed a revival to contend the evangelism of the Tswapong area. This partly Bangwato-sponsored evangelization (Landau 1993:15) led in some respects to the deteriorating commitment to the cult that safeguarded the definition of the landscape history of the area from a Batswapong perspective of land ownership. Further afield, the engendered Phalatswe Hills themselves acted as reinforcements of cultural perceptions of family order.

It should be noted that when the Bangwato occupied the Batswapong landscape, they would have had grounds to legitimize their occupation. It would have been permissible for them to occupy the area by virtue of their position as the tribute-receiving overlords of the whole of the Central District of Botswana, a large area of which the Batswapong were only a part (cf. Ngcongco 1979; Parsons 1973; Segadika 1997). However, their occupation of a landscape that was already tagged with spiritual ownership claims rendered such an area a "contested landscape." The appropriation of the landscape by tying it to the Bapedi cult would have strengthened both the Batswapong popular opinion as well as claims about land ownership.

In conclusion, the case of the Tswapong Hills and environs is a classic illustration of the challenges and limitations that archaeologists would face in deciding the emptiness and fullness of landscapes. In an archaeological context, mapping the settlement patterns of the Batswapong of the Malaka area would show some places as being occupied, while others would be unoccupied or unusable, places that would be considered by the Batswapong as being fully occupied by the ancestral spirits. By the same token, the decision not to physically alter the landscape can itself be seen to be a monumental artifice based on a system and worldview that prohibits altering the earth. The notion of naming physical features in gender terminologies among the Batswapong people is not unrelated to the general cosmology of naming as found in people's names. Therefore, what are to geographers and archaeologists mere physical features could well have been used to strengthen or justify existing or expected social order and gender relations as realized in the labeling of the male, female, and child hills in relation to the sizes of the hills.

REFERENCES

Bender, Barbara (editor). 1993. *Landscape Politics and Perspectives*. Berg Publishers, Oxford.

Boeyens, Jan C.A., and Desmond T. Cole. 1995. Kaditswene: What's in a Name? *Nomina Africana* 9:1–40.

Botswana National Archives (BNA). 1888. Shippard Files BNA HC 24/15. Botswana National Archives, Gaborone Offices.

———. n.d. The Tshekedi Papers, Files S/69/S, DCF 2/11, S226/10. Botswana National Archives, Gaborone Offices.

Bradley, Richard. 1993. *Altering the Earth*. Monograph Series No. 8. Society of Antiquaries of Scotland, Edinburgh.

Clark, Kenneth. 1976. *Landscape into Art*. Harper and Row, New York.

Comaroff, Jean. 1985. *Body of Power, Spirit of Resistance: The Culture and History of a South African People*. Chicago University Press, Chicago.

Cosgrove, Denis. 1984. *Social Formation and Symbolic Landscape*. Croom Helm, London.

Gadibolae, Mabunga N. 1985. Serfdom (Bolata) in the Nata Area 1926–1960. *Botswana Notes and Records* 17:25–32.

Grant, Sandy. 1970. Place Names in Kgatleng. *Botswana Notes and Records* 2:115–119.

Hirsch, Eric, and Michael O'Hanlon (editors). 1995. *The Anthropology of Landscape*. Clarendon Press, Oxford.

Humphreys, A.J. 1993. The Significance of Place Names in Archaeological Research, with Particular Reference to the Northern Cape. *African Studies* 52:43–53.

Jackle, John, Stan Brunn, and Curtis Roseman. 1976. *Human Spatial Behavior: A Social Geography*. Duxbury Press, Massachusetts.

Kiyaga-Mulindwa, David. 1980. *Tswapong Historical Texts*. 3 vols. Botswana Collection, University of Botswana Library.

Landau, Paul. 1993. When Rain Falls: Rainmaking and Community in a Tswana Village ca. 1870 to Recent Times. *The International Journal of African Historical Studies* 26(1):1–30.

———. 1995. *The Realm of the Word: Language, Gender and Christianity in a Southern African Kingdom*. David Phillip, Cape Town.

Lesotlho, John. 1982. The Badimo in the Tswapong Hills. *Botswana Notes and Records* 15:7–8.

Mbiti, John. 1970. *African Religions and Philosophy*. Anchor Books, New York.

Mogapi, Kgomotso. 1991. *Ngwao ya Setswana*. L.Z. Sikwane Publishers, Mabopane.

Motzafi-Haller, Pnina. 1994a. The Duiker and the Hare: Tswapong Subjects and Ngwato Rulers in Pre-colonial Botswana. *Botswana Notes and Records* 25:59–71.

———. 1994b. Historical Narratives as Political Discourses of Identity. *Journal of African Studies* 20(3):417–431.

Mpulubusi, Tjako. 1992. *The Lore and Oral History of the Tswapong Hills and the Bobirwa People*. National Museum, Monuments, and Art Gallery, Gaborone, Botswana.

Ngcongco, Leonard. 1979. The Origins of the Tswana. *Pula* 2:41–46.

Parsons, Q. Neil. 1973. Khama III, the Bamangwato, and the British—with special reference to 1895–1923. Ph.D. dissertation, Department of History, University of Edinburgh.

Segadika, Phillip. 1997. Political Strategies for Domination and Resistance in the late 19th and early 20th Century Tswapong and Landscape. Paper presented to the Staff and Postgraduate Seminars, University of Wales, Lampeter.

———. 2006. Managing Intangible Heritage at Tsodilo, in a Continent of Achievements. *Museum International Journal* 58:31–40.

Setiloane, Gabriel. 1986. *African Theology: An Introduction*. Skottavile Publishers, Bramfountein.

Thema, Ben. 1970. Moeng College—A Product of Self Help. *Botswana Notes and Records* 2:71–74.

Thomas, Julian. 1993. The Politics of Vision and the Archaeologies of Landscape. In *Landscape Politics and Perspectives*, ed. by B. Bender, pp. 19–48. Berg Publishers, London.

Tilley, Christopher. 1994. *A Phenomenology of Landscape*. Routledge, London.

Tlou, Thomas. 1970. Khama III—Great Reformer and Innovator. *Botswana Notes and Records* 2:98–105.

Tlou, Thomas, and Alec Campbell. 1984. *History of Botswana*. Macmillan Press, Gaborone, Botswana.

Van Vreeden, Barrend F. 1961. Die Oorsprong en Geskiedenis Van Plekname in noord-Kaapland en die Aangrensende Gebiede. Ph.D. dissertation, University of the Witwatersrand, Johannesburg.

CHAPTER 9

Enclosing the Spirit

Peter Read

Wasta Est, the land is laid waste. The phrase is common in the Domesday Book describing the vacant fields and empty villages of England following the Norman conquest. Encroachment by the sea, by the plague. and by environmental change put an end to hundreds more English villages by 1400. But the greatest depopulator of English and Scottish villages was the phenomenon known as enclosure, by which hundreds of thousands of hectares of agricultural land were turned to pasture by their owners.

One of the earliest recorded enclosures was in 1489, when Thomas Twyford evicted the inhabitants of seven cottages. The jurors called to investigate found that Twyford had

> willfully allowed the houses to fall into ruin and turned the fields from cultivation to a feeding place for brute animals. Eighty people who worked here went sorrowfully away to idleness; to drag out a miserable life and—truthfully—so to die in misery. (cited in Read 1996:16)

Historian of British lost villages Maurice Beresford (1954) cited other reports of people evicted from their homes or villages who led "unhappy lives and truly have died in a pitiful state," or "left their houses weeping and became unemployed and finally, as we suppose, died in poverty and so ended their days." Houses became derelict, villages were abandoned, the parish church marooned in a sea of paddocks. Many English rural churches remain thus remote, and marooned, to this day.

The clearing of human living areas to put the land to another use, which we could call, analogically, enclosure, is all about us in the Western world. Very many of us are its victims. Forced evacuation and the abandonment of loved places are some of the more apocalyptic phenomena for which the twentieth century will be remembered.

And the nineteenth century, when the relentless expansion of the colonial populations of Europe seldom left the indigenous people in peace for more than a generation.

Aboriginal people have suffered more than most other Australians. To about 1920, Australia held thousands of reserves, government stations, and church missions for Aboriginal people. The earliest were Christian inspired. More commonly, by 1900, if governments wanted the Indigenous people out of the towns, they built them a station, installed a manager to keep order, and kept them there. When stations became too expensive, or uncontrollable, or the long-term aim was changed to the integration of Aboriginal people with the rest of the community, they were ejected from their homes on the reserves as forcibly as they had been forced on to them, sometimes only a generation before.

Destruction of such Aboriginal living areas has occurred in practically every generation. The first reserves were created in the period 1810–1830; almost all were abandoned by 1850 after the missionaries retired, or died, and their sponsors lost interest. The creation of formal Indigenous administrations and the shift in the 1870s to a policy of assimilation meant new reserves and greater State powers to retain inmates; but most of these reserves too had gone by the 1920s. Many were not just abandoned but physically destroyed, smashed. Warangesda on the Murrumbidgee River was closed only after the last inmates had the roofs pulled off their houses. They weren't free for long. The depression of the 1930s and government coercion drove them back onto the old reserves and some hurriedly created new ones, where they remained until after the Second World War.

By the 1950s the revised policy of stick-and-carrot assimilation demanded that Aboriginal people remaining on the broken-down reserves were again forced from their homes. At Hollywood Reserve, Yass, in southern New South Wales, the last of the reserve buildings were sold to a demolisher in 1957 while the people remained living in them. He arrived with sledge hammer and truck; the people were bundled off to another station 100 km away. But the paddock remained empty for 30 years. When I was first taken to Hollywood in 1980 by a former resident, it was still obvious, even after 30 years, that this had once been a human settlement. Concrete foundations, a road, a few bits of roofing iron, the remains of a toy pedal car. Today the site can be identified only by the one or two fruit trees which remain. Entry is forbidden, for it is private property. So is Warangesda. In 1980 that site was a sheep farm, the dormitory fallen in, the chapel stuffed with hay bales. The people and their descendants were scattered over half of New South Wales, but they never forgot their former home.

Do people care about such places? Of course they do, and older Aboriginal people like nothing better than to revisit old living areas like Warangesda and Hollywood, which are now almost always in non-Aboriginal hands. They hold memories of personal and family life; more, they are intimately linked with a collective Indigenous identity. So when, today, people revisit the old sites they are reembracing not only memories but sometimes a lost or obscured identity. An empty paddock with irises and one or two plum trees growing round the patch of grass greener than the rest becomes the focus of a pilgrimage. *So this is where grandad lived, the place he never stopped talking about.* Recently the launch of a book on the Indigenous people of the Collector region in southern New South Wales started such a rekindling. Almost all those who attended were members of the families who had once lived there.

Dennis Foley is a Gai-Mariagal (northern Sydney) Aboriginal. As a boy he used to be taken by his grandmother or uncles to visit the unofficial town camp of 20 of his countrymen and women clinging to a precarious existence near the beachside suburb of Narrabeen. They lived mainly on marine life and sold fish to the white townsfolk to buy necessities. One night in 1957 an urgent phone call told them that the local council was bulldozing the place. At dawn Dennis and his uncles rushed to Narrabeen, but too late. Almost all the people had gone. Dennis still remembers the smoke drifting from one or two places in the sandy soil where the last campfires of millennia still lay smoldering. When in 1999 he returned to this final urban settlement of his Gai-Mariagal people, he found a national sports complex in its place. He pointed out where he had camped with his uncles across the creek, where the oldest people had lived in seclusion themselves, where the smoke had come drifting from the blackened sandy soil. The people haven't returned. They were meant to be scattered, and they were. Dennis doesn't know where or even if any of the descendants of the Narrabeen town camp now reside in Sydney. He says of them, "God knows where they went to." Almost certainly they no longer identify as Aboriginal. "Left their houses weeping and became unemployed and finally, as we suppose, died in poverty and so ended their days" (Foley 2001).

That's the hard physical side of forced assimilation: smashed camps, broken toys, bulldozers at dawn. Yes, some of the camps were unofficial, or illegal, but, out of sight, they served the purposes of government well enough until policy changed or the site was wanted for development. The forced exit from the half a dozen wretched tin humpies of Narrabeen carried for the residents the same emotional weight as Chekov's *The Cherry Orchard.*

> Goodbye dear old house, old grandfather house. Winter will pass, spring will come again, and then you won't be here any more, you'll be pulled down. How much these walls have seen!

Even institutions, however much hated at the time, potentially carry an ambiguous charge to their former inmates. South Australian and Northern Territory Aboriginal girls, now known as the Stolen Generations, were taken to the Colebrook Home in Adelaide. Today there's nothing left of the buildings and grounds but an empty space. Yet the returning inmates have constructed a moving memorial garden on the site, imposing their own interpretation encapsulated in the majestic words:

> Let everyone who comes to this place know
> they are on Aboriginal land
> the site of what was once Colebrook
> Training Home where,
> between 1943 and 1972,
> some 350 Aboriginal children lived,
> isolated from their families and the beloved
> land of their ancestors.
>
> This is part of the country of the Kaurna
> people whose heritage and presence
> continues today

The destruction of Aboriginal places stemmed from the State's perception that its charges must sometimes suffer in answer to a greater cause. That's why all of us are metaphorically enclosed or may yet suffer the sting of enclosure. Or we have already been enclosed. The little town of Adaminaby in southern New South Wales was inundated in 1957 to allow the creation of an enormous irrigation and hydroelectricity dam.

Just before the advent of family motoring, Adaminaby was almost as remote from the rest of Australia as it had been half a century earlier. Seven or eight farm gates had to be opened and shut between Adaminaby and the nearest town 15 km away. But Adaminaby was peaceful and self-sufficient. One- to three-hectare farms, on which the residents maintained geese, a hayfield, or a cow, were common. A barter economy and larger farms kept many families out of debt without regular employment. On the famous, roistering Saturday nights, stores remained open till 8:30.

These are some of the residents' phrases as they recalled their town:

> We didn't have the conveniences, but we didn't look for anything better; a beautiful old town, a lot of fruit trees, pine trees, a football pitch; my grandfather had a wonderful flower garden, an orchard, a herb garden, and a wonderful lifestyle, our town was a good old country town, a quiet town, a happy town. We were not in each other's pockets. (Read 1996:76)

A second town to be destroyed was Yallourn, in the Latrobe Valley electricity-producing area of the state of Victoria. Yallourn was as planned a site as Adaminaby was unplanned. Construction began in 1921 for a town that would provide an attractive living area for the Victorian State Electricity Commission (SEC) workforce needed to produce brown coal briquettes and power. In the opinion of the town planner Helen Weston, Yallourn was one of the brightest flowerings of the garden city movement interpreted in Australia. An English urban expert designed a town for 1,000 people amidst the stringybark and messmate trees that would enable workers to live close to, but not be dominated by, the enormous open-cut mine. Long, straight roads were avoided in favor of shorter streets leading to a civic square. The famous cinema was the most magnificent in rural Victoria. The sports oval one of the finest in the country. The Melbourne Symphony Orchestra played in the town hall. The SEC provided for Yallourn residents the English-style, steeped-roof houses and, for their gardens, soil, deciduous trees, plants, timber edgings, and manure to relieve the stiff, infertile clay.

But the increased demand for post–World War II electricity put an end to Adaminaby and Yallourn equally.

Yallourn lived by electricity as well as died from it. Day and night, its residents heard the grind of the coal dredgers digging out the coal, the whistle and rumble of the train taking the coal to the briquette factory and the power plant. Every year the sound was a little louder. Every year the mine approached the town a little closer. For in the 1930s, just ten years after its construction, SEC engineers found that the brown coal seam which gave Yallourn its purpose continued underneath the planned town itself.

It was 1949 when Leo Crowe, who owned land near Adaminaby, pulled up his horse to ask a stranger what he was staring at through his binoculars. "That's where they're going to put the dam." Others were as incredulous as Leo when they heard the news that the Snowy Mountains Authority intended to flood the Eucumbene Valley to produce hydroelectric power. The townsfolk were shown a marked post to indicate the proposed high-water mark, and assured that everyone would have to leave and their town destroyed.

Yallourn residents heard the news of the destruction of their own town just as suddenly. The announcement was contained in the SEC's newspaper *Live Wire* in October 1961 under the headline "Playing Field to Go First. Yallourn's 1995 demolition." As at Adaminaby, some refused to believe or to comprehend. Surely a town of 6,000 people could not be moved just to get at four years' coal reserves? The public buildings were so massive and so expensive. How could they possibly be demolished? But Yallourn's destruction came much sooner than 1995.

The Snowy Mountains Authority made much of the new town that would replace Adaminaby. For the first time residents would enjoy mains electricity, running water, and sewerage. Wooden houses capable of being moved would be trucked to the new town site, while public buildings like churches and banks would either be moved or rebuilt. The massive public relations exercise implied that those who stood in the way of national progress were selfish or patriotic.

The capacity of authority for crushing local attachments to the doomed towns was reinforced by its language. In films, speeches, and leaflets the Snowy Mountains Authority used phrases like "it was necessary" for the dam construction to commence, as if bulldozers obeyed some natural phenomenon like gravity. It referred to the "loss," not the destruction, of the old town, the changeover to the new as the old town "submerged," not died. The "transfer" was usually presented in the passive voice: "the site was chosen," "procedures were explained," "difficulties were overcome." The project was "necessary," it was "more than justified." An orderly and irreversible program was implied in "the decision taken, planning began." In the euphoria of postwar reconstruction, the Authority maintained that "modern machinery and skilled people could provide water to quench Australia's fiery heart" (Read 1996:80–83).

There was not much of the national agenda that could be offered to justify the destruction of Yallourn. The SEC's arguments were economic. The town was "ageing," the coal was under it, and "failure to exploit it would cause unemployment and blackouts." The most economically rationalist position was that "in principle nothing should be allowed to interfere with the production of coal mining, with its allied operations of electricity and briquette production, to the utmost economic limit." Community anxiety, lulled by the faraway date of 1995, returned when the SEC announced that, instead, it would "begin to remove" the town almost immediately. A "Save Yallourn" committee was formed in November 1968, whose members sang to the tune of "Yankee Doodle":

> Let's gather round the old town square
> Our voices raised in protest
> We'll sing its praises loud and clear
> To save it from the dozers. (Read 1996:84)

Memories converge on the last few months of Adaminaby. In the wet spring of 1956, roads turn to mud as residents stare at their neighbor's house grinding past the front door, then at the empty site. Soon a second space appears on the other side. The diminishing village begins to resemble the open valley slope it had been a century earlier. One by one the shops close, some to reappear in the new town six kilometers away, some to vanish altogether. The post office closes in September. "New Adaminaby" becomes "Adaminaby," and "Old Adaminaby" ceases to exist. The last house is jacked up in November. An Authority publicity photograph records the triumph of the cottage perched atop the semitrailer, but the background inadvertently reveals the agony of a dying town: empty footpaths, collapsing verandahs, naked interiors, piles of debris, exposed ceilings.

By December 1957 the water is rising at the dam wall by 30 cm a day. The farms and orchards along the river are gone and the water is creeping towards the town site itself. All that remains are outhouses, foundations, chimneys, immovable stone cottages, roads, and trees. Lanes, dusty for a century, are tinged with green. Fruit trees have their best, but briefest, season. The last balls, churches services, dances, and picnics are over. People dig roses out of the gardens for their new dwellings. They calculate the height of the water by watching it rise up the pine trees at the back of the recreation ground. All at once the pines die. The fruit trees, too, die before they vanish. Among the sharpest memories are those of frequently returning to the water's edge to stare at what will soon be nothing. The evicted residents stand in fascination, dismay, anguish, or horror before the scummy water inching towards what remains of their homes. Look, it's lapping at the back fence, creeping up the garden, swirling round the outhouse, eddying round the lintel, muddying the fireplace, splashing about the chimneys. Oblivion.

Yallourn residents too watched in alarm and distress as one by one the wooden houses were jacked up, sometimes split in half, and towed away. At first the removals were violently opposed, but in January 1974 the Victorian premier declared that "the town must go." The Gippsland Trades and Labour Council called it "a terrible act of vandalism," but the SEC, seemingly as inexorable as the waters of Lake Eucumbene, advertised for the demolition of the first eight brick buildings. University students squatted in empty houses. People already shifted returned on weekends to watch the destruction. Bernadette O'Loughlin recalled, "It was very sad. With it went all my memories. I'd like to take my children back and say 'this is where I had my childhood,' but I can't, it's really sad." Her family bought timber from the demolished high school and a load of the distinctive Yallourn bricks from the town center to use in their new home. After the last visit together to the old home, Bernadette's father, still working at the factory, reported fresh developments to the others. "Now the roof's gone." When the house went he returned to dig up the camellias and roses. "The buildings were part of your life."

Another youngster was Alan Lucas. He too "watched the heart of it go. The shops, they were the first." One day he passed the half-wrecked cinema, once the pride of the valley. It was where he had had his first date. He clambered over the wreckage and souvenired a copper number from the back of one of the seats. "It was a solid memory, a connection." Watching the town die like this, he said, was like "watching a friend die of cancer." A third evicted resident, David Andrew, returned to the site in 1979 to find electricity trainees taking lessons in the library and sheep grazing in the school playground. The family home was vandalized, and a barbed wire fence ran through the middle of what had been his mother's treasured garden. The front gate and fence remained. He had himself photographed standing in front of them.

The historian Connerton noted that sometimes community memory is a struggle against state power and forced forgetting (Connerton 1989:15). So at Adaminaby. The Snowy authorities did their best to eliminate memories of the old town. It tried to change the name of the new town to Chifley, and the old town to Coolawye. It discouraged reunions, "Back To Adaminaby"'s, and memorials where the now deserted road points to the glittering lake. The much-coveted new housing blocks overlooking the lake above the old town were available only to those already living 30 km away, which disqualified former old town residents. The mood of the residents became steadily one of disappointed resignation: "Mixed feelings now, a bit of sadness" or "I don't know how to explain, it's just that we were happy there and satisfied to stay put." Outsiders who watched the death of Adaminaby pinpoint the malaise: "to a certain extent they're grieving; they're in deep mourning; a very severe shock and they never recovered from it." The residents of Old Adaminaby remain distressed, reflected in a kind of emotional paralysis, because they were never allowed to mourn their town. Forty years after its destruction, there were few picnics beside the old town, or pilgrimages, or heritage walks; no wreaths floating, no museum, no map, not a solitary sign beside the scattered half-dozen houses and the silent lake. "I don't like going back to a ghost town and see the road suddenly disappear and go nowhere." This is not the slow peaceful decline of other country towns.

When, in 1983, during the worst drought since the dam was filled, the water level dropped so far that those who used to live in the higher part of the town saw the foundations of their houses reappear, "like a corpse from a grave," as one resident put it. Flowers appeared in the same beds where they had bloomed a generation earlier. People knelt in prayer in the ruins of the church, picnicked in their gardens, or were photographed standing on the muddy steps of what were once their front doors. At the conclusion of the twenty interviews I conducted with former residents I often read a verse from a poem written by a resident of a nearby pastoral property:

The stations, farms, the sheds, the barns
Are all awash in the deep waters.
While ghosts of men swim through the glen
Drowned faces haunt their sons and daughters. (Read 1996:96)

Yallourn was different. Community feeling was better coordinated and more articulated. A plainly expressed economic interest was easier to

denounce than the claims of a national interest, and the residents reinforced each other in their denunciations of the SEC. The "Save Yallourn"
committee produced a book of stories. A community theater production
The Yallourn Story was performed by the former residents to packed
houses in 1988. In the play's final moments the long-time resident Jean
sweeps the floor for the last time as she resists her children's attempts
to get her to leave. A chorus of ghosts, accompanied by drum beats,
chants:

> A dying house in a dying town
> A dying house in a dying town
> And memories are ghosts that won't lie down.

The last words of the play

> Jean: Just go and let me be, will you? I'll be ready by the time you get back.
> John (son): Come on. But she can't even sit down. The house is empty.
> [exit]
> Jean: Empty ... Empty he says. Ha. Fifty years of memories. Empty! (Read
> 1996:98)

The curtain falls on Jean still sweeping the floor.

Yallourn people bought their houses and reerected them sometimes
hundreds of kilometers away. Others who could not afford to buy tried
to find out where in the nearby towns the new owners had erected their
houses and photographed them. They dug out plants from the garden,
they souvenired bits of their houses and the public buildings, they bought
bits of demolished buildings and laid new paths with old Yallourn bricks.
Sociologists who interviewed many former residents concluded that they
had not suffered much pain or grief. Perhaps, in the light of what we
now know about the long-term effects of the loss of place, the judgment
was rather premature. Yet it is true that Yallourn residents probably
were less traumatized because they were allowed the emotional space to
speak and write about their feelings, and continued to do so. Yallourn
people were more numerous and better educated than Adaminaby's residents, and the mass rallies, protests, committees, interviews, and the play
gave them confidence in their own sense of belonging and the value of
the place they had lost.

Yet to visit today any of these towns which once existed is to take
a journey to nothing. Warangesda is a farm. Hollywood is a paddock.
Narrabeen is a fitness and sporting center. At Adaminaby on a still,
cloudless day in midsummer, the deserted road still slips into the sleeping
lake. Roads at the site of Yallourn terminate just as abruptly at the edge
of the open cut, the big, black hole. Viewers at the lookout stare into the

vast coal face, and reflect that somewhere in that suspended dust, there in that empty space, was once their town of Yallourn.

Human habitations always are important, not only for the emotions invested in them by their residents, but because precise locality represents universal as well as human values. The Australian poet Douglas Stewart urged us to mourn the drowned Snowy Mountains town of Jindabyne.

Finally for the mystery and the pathos
That seep from earth and bubble out from water
In any place where men have lived and bred
And feuded with each other. (Stewart 1967:28)

Yet conductors of Australian Environmental Impact Statements into, say, the feasibility of destroying a dozen suburban streets for a freeway extension, are still not required to enquire into the emotions of those whose homes and neighborhoods will be destroyed.

Are local places important? Yes, because an ordinary home or suburb, once loved, transcends particularity for as long as the person who formed the attachment values that bond. Each construction of event, experience, memory, and place is unrepeatable.

Australia is not, of course, alone. Environmental psychologist Gerda Speller found in her studies of destroyed English villages that few people were offered counseling for the grief they felt over loss of place, nor were their psychological needs ever considered to be an issue by the authorities. Speller concluded, "Rather than deny a problem exists, we need to articulate it and find ways of building a supportive structure" (cited in Beresford 1954).

Loss of loved place is not the sole province of prehistory, nor of the modern age, but of historic time past and future. Grief for lost place seems much more analogous to grief for dead people than professional carers have allowed. We need to advance place-bereavement as a continuing theme of contemporary distress. We are all subject to enclosure.

REFERENCES

Beresford, Maurice. 1954. *The Lost Villages of England*. Lutterworth Press, London.

Connerton, Paul. 1989. *How Societies Remember*. Cambridge University Press, Cambridge.

Foley, Dennis. 2001. *Repossession of Our Spirit. Traditional Owners of Northern Sydney*. Aboriginal History, Canberra.

Read, Peter. 1996. *Returning to Nothing: The Meaning of Lost Places*. Cambridge University Press, Melbourne.

Stewart, Douglas. 1967. *Collected Poems 1936–1967*. Angus and Robertson, Sydney.

CHAPTER 10

New Places for Old: The Reinhabitation of Cleared Landscapes in Northern Scotland

Olivia Lelong

In 1997, I spent six weeks walking along the northern coast of Sutherland, the county that forms the northwestern part of mainland Scotland (see Figure 10.1). Our brief was to survey the 100 km stretch of coast from the Kyle of Durness on the west to Torrisdale Bay on the east, recording all the archaeological remains along the coastal fringe on behalf of Historic Scotland. One day, while working along the edge of Lamigo Bay in the area known as Skerray, my colleague and I observed several puzzling structures on one of the crofts. Nestled in a narrow gully, above cliffs that plunged to the sea, were several stone settings and little drystone structures shaped like boats, their prows pointing out to sea. Boat-shaped settings are known in Scotland (for example, on the island of Hirta in the St. Kilda Archipelago) and are usually thought to be prehistoric, although these did appear rather fresh. We duly recorded them anyway. Later, we discovered that a few years earlier a sculptor, visiting a neighboring croft, had gone up to the gully and begun to rearrange several lambing shelters he found there into ship shapes. But the crofter had objected because the shelters had been built by her father and she wanted them preserved as they were—the archaeology of the previous generation.

This story captures a few of the different currents that run through the inhabitation of this part of Scotland today. In this case, they involve personal histories, agricultural regimes, aesthetic responses, and archaeological interests. These and other concerns sometimes conflict, sometimes converge, in the reinhabitation of landscapes that have seen radical changes over the last two hundred years in terms of settlement pattern, economic character, and social fabric.

I want first to define the term "inhabitation" for the purposes of this paper. By inhabitation I mean not simply or necessarily the physical act of living in a place, although inhabitation can arise through or coincide with that. Rather, I mean a person's *engagement* with a place. This can happen on various levels (intellectual, economic, or aesthetic, for

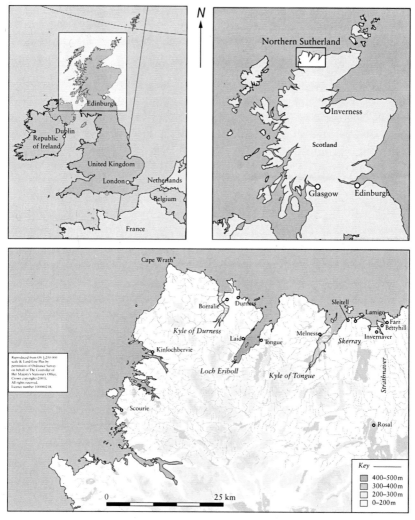

Figure 10.1 Location of project area, northern Sutherland, Scotland.

example) and it can be mediated through different kinds of knowledge and experience (personal, historical, scientific, and so on). Through this engagement, those who are reinhabiting cleared landscapes such as the ones in northern Sutherland create new senses of place, and in doing so make them their own. In this paper, I begin by reviewing the nineteenth-century changes in northern Sutherland's landscapes that took place as a result of the Highland Clearances. I then examine the ways in which people in the present are reinhabiting those cleared landscapes and endowing them with new meanings.

CLEARING THE LAND

The eighteenth and early nineteenth centuries brought profound social and economic changes to the Highlands, culminating in the Clearances of many Highland straths (valleys). The history of that period has been well covered elsewhere (e.g., Bangor-Jones 1987; Richards 1982), and I will only briefly review it here.

In the second half of the eighteenth century, landowners throughout Scotland came under increasing economic pressure to turn their estates into profitable ventures. In areas such as Sutherland, where feudalism had long been established, wealth had previously been measured less by monetary surplus and more in terms of agricultural produce and men who could be mustered to fight for the laird. However, Highland landlords had begun to have stronger links with lowland urban centers and wished to maintain lifestyles like the ones practiced there. In addition, the military emasculation of the Highlands after the failed Jacobite uprising of 1745 made the military strength of Highland lairds increasingly irrelevant. At the same time, the growing populations of many townships were causing serious famines, which some of the landowners helped to alleviate, and agricultural improvers were arguing for more efficient land use to increase productivity (Richards 1982:60). As a result of all these factors, by the late eighteenth century Highland landlords needed transferable capital more than they needed tenants.

During the first few decades of the nineteenth century, many landowners throughout Highland Scotland evicted the tenants farming their land in joint tenant farms, or townships, in order to create sheep farms for profit. In some cases, tenants were relocated a short distance away in newly created villages, while in others the evictions were more drastic. In Sutherland, many tenants occupying the more fertile straths were relocated to newly established crofts, or individual smallholdings, along the rugged coast. The clearances in Strathnaver in northern Sutherland, carried out by Patrick Sellar on behalf of the Duke and Duchess of Sutherland (the Staffords), have come to have almost iconic historical status, partly because of the brutality with which they were sometimes carried out (see Basu 2001).

The Staffords also subjected their tenants to an extraordinary experiment in social and economic engineering. Between 1807 and 1821 they moved up to 15,000 people from the straths to new lots on the north coast. These lots were much smaller than the township lands they had jointly farmed, and the Staffords planned that in order to feed themselves, the people would have to take up fishing. This, they believed, would give tenants a more secure living than subsistence farming and would also develop the fishing industry as a source of income for the estate (Fairhurst 1964:1).

James Loch, factor (agent) for the estate after 1816, foresaw the tenants' future prospects with confident clarity. He wrote:

> I am particularly anxious that their [new] lots should be so small as to prevent their massing any considerable part of their rent by selling a beast, their rent must not depend on that. In short I wish them to become fishers only, but if you give them any extent of land or of Commonality they will never embark heartily on that pursuit. (quoted in Richards 1982:318–19)

Contemporary accounts by the parish minister, Donald Sage, and other observers describe the disbelief, the anger, and the kind of stupor in which people left their homes in Strathnaver and went (often on foot, carrying their possessions) to unfamiliar coastal settlements like Bettyhill, Farr, Kirtomy, and Strathy. Sage described the prospect these tenants now faced:

> Some miserable patches of ground along the shores were doled out as lots, without aught in the shape of the poorest hut to shelter them. Upon these lots it was intended that they should build houses at their own expense, and cultivate the ground, at the same time occupying themselves as fishermen, although the great majority of them had never set foot on a boat in their lives. (quoted in Mackenzie 1883:36)

Estate records show that townships were deliberately split up, with families from each township sent to several different places on the coast, thus tearing apart the social fabric (National Library of Scotland, Sutherland Estate Papers, Deposit 313, acc. 1015). The former system of shared arable land (known as "run rig") and common grazings was replaced by small, individual crofts, many on exposed headlands. The poor quality of the limited arable land and the restrictions on grazing meant that, as Loch had planned, tenants could no longer make a living purely from farming (Hunter 1976:27).

The intended alternative confronted them inescapably here. One can imagine the effect on people who had lived all their lives inland, some of whom had perhaps never seen the sea before, of seeing the land abruptly ending and giving way to a constantly shifting liquid plain that stretched ahead to the horizon, so different from the restricted views and undulating topography along the valleys. The sea along this coast can be unpredictable, as people learned to their cost: contemporary accounts describe newly relocated tenants being swept away by waves while fishing from the rocks, collecting birds' eggs, or inspecting their new lots (Macleod 1841:26).

In order to have any sustainable contact with the sea, these people had to learn its strength and rhythms. Where before they had synchronized the cycles of their working lives with those of the sun, now they had to match them to the rhythms of the moon as well. They had to learn the habits of tides and to predict how they changed over the days and seasons. Equipped with this knowledge, they would know when the surf retreated, making it safe to forage and exposing shellfish for food or bait and seaweed for fertilizer. They needed to learn which kinds of shellfish were suitable for bait and which for food, where to find them and how to use them; for instance, how to chew limpets and spread the pulp on the water to attract fish to shoreline rocks (Fenton 1992:139). Some would have practiced line fishing, going out daily in small, single-masted boats equipped with oars to catch whitefish (Gray 1978:16–17). The daily and annual routines of life would have changed, especially for those who took up fishing full time (a more common occurrence on the sheltered east coast than on the exposed north). The seasonal herring fishing, with work for men at sea and for women at the gutting, replaced the summer practice of taking stock to graze for several weeks at the shieling grounds.

In order to venture out on the sea on either a daily or seasonal basis, people had to acquire the skills and confidence to handle boats, as well as detailed knowledge of the local currents, reefs, and safe landing places. In conceiving their plan for a new fishing industry, the Staffords had failed to take into account the extremely hazardous nature of the north coast where, during one early nineteenth-century winter, storms destroyed about 100 boats along a 30-mile stretch (Macleod 1841:27). Some people never got accustomed to such an unfamiliar element. An elderly lady in Bettyhill lived most of her life on Eilean nan Roan, a small island off Skerray, the descendant of people who had been relocated there. She recently said that even in her lifetime, people on the island hated the sea and boats so much that they avoided going to mainland whenever possible. When it was unavoidable, they would get into the boat, lie down in the bottom, cover their faces with their coats and howl for the duration of the journey (P. Rudie, personal communication 1998).

Uncertainty about the success of fishing and concern for those at sea must have bound together the families in the newly created communities in novel configurations. The communal effort required in fishing, perhaps mirroring to some extent the efforts of communal farming, might have had a similar effect. Some, especially younger people, did take to fishing and the general industry of fish curing, although for those on Sutherland's north coast the distance from markets meant it was only profitable at a very small scale (Macleod 1841:27; Smout 1998). Those who were settled on the east coast, where the harbors were naturally better and enhanced by estate improvements, seem to have taken more readily to fishing. Everywhere, however, the herring fishing declined later in the nineteenth century when the shoals went elsewhere (Gray 1978:13). Along the north coast, many people emigrated after a few years, having tried to make a living on their new crofts and failed (Macleod 1841). Others persisted, and during the nineteenth century a crofting landscape replaced the earlier settlement pattern.

MONUMENTS TO CLEARANCE

Having briefly reviewed the history of the Clearances in northern Sutherland, I want now to examine the ways in which people have reinhabited those landscapes. One of the most profound ways centers on the history of the Clearances, and their effects both on descendants remaining in the area and on the landscape today.

In 1810, Benjamin Meredith produced a map called "The Heights of Strathnaver" to complement an agricultural survey on behalf of the estate. His map shows the 50 or so townships that peppered the sides and floor of the valley at the time of the first Clearances (see Fairhurst 1968:137, 142). By 1821, these were ghost towns, inhabited only by sheep and scattered shepherds. Few traces survive of the townships today. In the early twentieth century, the Sutherland estate created crofts in Strathnaver, hoping to encourage people to move back in and increase the land's profitability after the sheep farms failed to produce the immense profits that nineteenth-century improvers had envisaged. The new crofters cannibalized the township remains for stone to build new farm buildings, dykes, and enclosures, and other aspects of this new, more intensive phase of land use also helped destroy older remains (Temperley 1977). Today, Strathnaver is still occupied by sheep farms and sporting estates.

However, in the upper valley the remains of several townships do survive well, thanks largely to the interest and archaeological work of Horace Fairhurst in the 1960s. In particular, his excavations at Rosal ensured its protection from Forestry Commission planting in the vicinity. The township occupies an area of undulating ground, enclosed by a drystone ring dyke. Today commercial forestry laps its edges, exaggerating the encircling effect of the dyke and blocking views across the strath; as Fairhurst pointed out, when it was occupied Rosal would have looked like a green island in the surrounding moorland (Fairhurst 1968:138).

Rosal township now forms part of the Strathnaver Trail, an archaeological and historical route established for tourists by the Highland Council Archaeology Service, and it is one of the most famous monuments to the Highland Clearances. Plaques guide the visitor through the township, describe its agricultural regimes and the excavation results, and recount the violent manner of its clearance under Patrick Sellar. At the other, seaward end of Strathnaver is the Bettyhill Museum, in a former church beside the beach at Farr. Another monument to the Clearances, it tells the story of the evictions that still figure so strongly in folk memory and family histories in the area. The museum contains a tapestry made by local schoolchildren depicting scenes from the Clearances and their aftermath.

The most prominent monument is the all-but-deserted landscape of the valley. It is difficult to overstate the consciousness of people living in the area today, particularly those descended from evicted families, of that tumultuous period in its history. Not all of them want to remember it. In 1989, the then-chairman of the Highlands and Islands Development Board suggested that the archaeological remains of cleared townships should be "cleared away" because they were "psychologically debilitating" (quoted in Gibson 1996:55). Basu (2000:226) has described the remains of cleared townships as "unintentional monuments," open to individual interpretation, experience, and creation of a sense of place. When explanatory plaques are erected at sites like Rosal, they become "closed" sites of memory, intentional monuments that are narrated and interpreted for the visitor.

Some of the most striking unintentional monuments to the Clearances are the settlements created to receive those who were evicted. The broad, rocky headland known as Skerray, to the west of Strathnaver, contains archaeological remains from the period following the Clearances, in which that landscape was intensively reworked. For example, the entire loch of Blár Dubh was drained in the early nineteenth century and the basin and sloping ground to its north were divided into the strips typical of single crofts; that area of Skerray is even today locally called "Lots" rather than its official name of Achtoty. At Modsarie, Achnabat, Clasheddy, Torrisdale, and Eilean nan Roan, the re-allocation of land transformed the map into ladder-like patterns of long, thin fields.

In 1750, Skerray included eight settlement clusters supporting 20 small tenants, who all had proportions of the arable land according to their rents; the Mackays of Skerray, tacksmen (chief tenants) to the Reay estate, held the wadsett or mortgage (Caird 1987:49). When the leases expired in 1820, some removals took place. Then, in 1826, after the Reay estate was sold to the Duke of Sutherland, the crofting system was introduced (although it had already been planned for some time), and the lots at Achtoty and Modsarie were created in the drained basin of Blár Dubh and on reclaimed moorland respectively (Caird 1987:42–46).

Here, as elsewhere along the coast, estate factors (agents) had ambitious plans for a greatly expanded fishing industry. As elsewhere, those plans were not realized: the newly created crofts were too small to support families on agriculture alone, but the fishing was neither reliable nor safe enough to encourage a large-scale industry. An 1828 census lists only seven boats in Skerray, and in 1851 there were some resident fishermen listed in the census but recorded as having gone to fish in Wick, while 11 fishermen from Aberdeen were temporarily based at Port Skerray (Caird 1987:50).

The settlement at Sleitell, which was created to house cleared families, is the best-preserved piece of the immediate post-clearance landscape in Skerray, by virtue of its having been abandoned in the 1950s. It is bounded on three sides by high moorland. On the seaward side is a narrow, rock-bound beach with a natural slipway leading through the bedrock; the rest of Sleitell's coastal strip consists of cliffs. The tiny inlet, which faces northwest into prevailing winds, could never have provided much shelter for boats, and the Sleitell Rocks at its mouth create a dangerous wave (G. Lockhart, personal communication 1998).

Sleitell opens suddenly like a broad green bowl after kilometers of empty, bleak moorland. The settlement is striking for what is absent: the strip fields ubiquitous elsewhere in the crofting landscape. A few buildings are scattered on the upper slopes of the valley to the east and west. A lochan fills its lowest part, and there are lazybeds (spade-dug cultivation plots) along the cliff tops and peat cuttings in the moorland around. Some of the buildings were clearly houses; there are gable chimneys, the remains of iron stoves, a rusted bedstead. They are built of dry stone, and most still stand to the original height of the wall. These walls would certainly have been strong enough to take the weight of a roof. However, all of them have couple slots built into their fabric, and in several cases the timber couples themselves survive, weathered and decaying in the walls. Couples (crucks) were crucial elements in the architecture of pre-Clearance Highland houses: they supported the roofs, as the walls (then built of stone, turf, or a combination) were not load bearing (Noble 1984:69).

The presence of couple slots built into walls where none were needed might reflect a transition between pre- and post-Clearance architecture, between tenants' conceptions of what the fabric of a house should be and landlords' or factors' ideas about improved building techniques. Many landlords encouraged tenants to alter the manner in which they built, abandoning the old stone footings and turf or stone superstructure for more strongly-built, mortared houses. The Sleitell buildings may reflect the tenants' own compromise, or perhaps a refusal to give up the security that couples had always meant: they held up the roof. The presence of couples here is also striking because of the entirely treeless character of the surrounding landscape. The closest woods today are ca. 3.5 km to the southwest, around Strathtongue. Tenants evicted to Sleitell would have had to fetch timbers from there by a more circuitous route, perhaps by sea.

Today, Skerray's population has declined from over 500 in 1926 to about a fifth of that (Caird 1987:50). But, as in Strathnaver and other communities in Sutherland, its inhabitants are trying to reclaim economic power and a sense of ownership of the land in the face of monolithic landlords. The economic unit known as a croft, an individual small-holding occupied by a tenant, was introduced here after the Clearances (although crofts had existed previously in some other parts of Scotland). In itself it was a radical departure from the joint tenant farms that were typical of the northern Highlands. Now it is a concept with its own momentum, as crofters attempt to marry it to their own aspirations and their now-established relationships to the land.

LIVING FROM THE LAND

At the time of writing, Len Mackay still lived on a croft at Invernaver, in the mouth of Strathnaver, the valley of the River Naver. His ances-tors were evicted from Rosal to this croft, where he was born. He is known locally as Len Naver, to distinguish him from the myriad other Mackays in the area. At well over 70, he could often be found riding a quad bike across his fields in search of an errant cow, followed by a yapping sheepdog. Like other crofters with whom he shares common grazings, he was enraged at the Sutherland estate's sale in 1998 of a house at Crossburn, which forms part of the common grazings, as a holiday cottage. He speaks out for the need for land reform and the integrity of crofting as it is practiced today. "Crofting has to be kept in the hands of practical crofters—not the theorists," he says. "If it doesn't involve sheep and cattle then it won't be crofting as we know it" (North Sutherland Duthchas Project n.d.). This is a person not longing for some imagined pre-Clearance paradise, but attempting to drive his own way of life forward into the future.

To the west of Strathnaver, on the Kyle of Tongue, is the small croft-ing community of Melness, composed of about 100 families. Many are descended from people who were removed here during the Clearances. In 1995, the Melness crofters took the opportunity, offered by the owner of Hope and Melness Estate, to buy a portion of it, the Crofting Estate of Melness. In doing so, they followed the lead of crofters in Assynt and on the island of Eigg, both in western Scotland, in community buyouts. As a result, they now have control over their joint grazings, income from rents, land rights and the shooting lease, and the potential to develop wind farms, native woodlands, and other commercial initia-tives (Brennan n.d.). The Land Reform (Scotland) Act, passed in 2003, established the rights of communities to buy agricultural land. Although the Act still requires a willing seller, it represents an important shift away from historical perceptions of crofting communities' rights and owner-ship potential (Scottish Government: Rural Development n.d.).

Elsewhere, however, crofting communities in northern Sutherland meet opposition to moves toward local economic self-determination. People attempting to make a living as individual farmers or communities sometimes find themselves in conflict with larger institutions concerned mainly with profit.

The village of Laid is a steady trickle of crofts along the road that follows the western side of Loch Eriboll; like Sleitell and Bettyhill, it was created during the Clearances. Those evicted here found themselves on acid, sloping ground bordering a long, deep body of green-blue sea water, hemmed in by high, heather-clad mountains. Important archaeological remains, including a souterrain and a wheelhouse, attest to thriving Iron Age communities here some two thousand years ago. Loch Eriboll is a natural harbor, so deep that during World War II, Allied warships routinely sheltered in it and the German U-boat fleet surrendered here in May 1945. Allied seamen would come ashore from their ships and, climbing a mountainside on the western side of the loch, would spell out the names of their ships in white quartzite boulders. Local schoolchildren still ascend the hill every year and paint the stones white to keep them brightly visible. Among the names spelled out in stones is that of the HMS *Hood*. After leaving Loch Eriboll for the last time in May 1941, the *Hood* headed out into the North Atlantic. She engaged the German battleship *Bismarck* in the Denmark Strait and was sunk, with all but three of her crew of 1,418 lost. Her name, along with those of the others, has become part of the archaeology of Laid.

The community at Laid is actively attempting to have all of its 18 crofts permanently reinhabited after a period of population decline. In the early 1990s it had only three resident families, but by 1999 this had increased to seven, with prospects of others joining the community and a number of houses being refurbished (*West Highland Free Press*, October 22, 1999), and the community is still slowly growing. Local attempts to invigorate tourism, a potential economic lifeline, have included a rare-breeds farm and several bed-and-breakfast establishments, as well as aquacultural projects. During the 1997 survey, as my colleague and I made our way along the coast at Laid, we recorded some linear sweeps of seaweed-covered stone in the shallows that, to our eyes, had all the appearance of nineteenth-century fish traps. Less than an hour later, we met the man who had built them. He invited us into his office, in the cabin of a beached fishing boat, for a cup of tea. Hugh McLenan had that year established an oyster farm along the shore of the loch. He showed us water-filled containers of thousands of tiny, button-like spat that he would deposit in the shallows within the protective stone arms as soon as they were old enough: his seed corn for a future crop of oysters, destined for expensive restaurants in Glasgow, Edinburgh, and London when they came to maturity in a few years' time.

The Laid community have expressed interest in buying the Laid Common Grazings, which are part of the Durness Estate. They have met opposition from the landowner, a foreign-registered company that plans to establish a superquarry to exploit the mineral wealth of the rocky massif on which the ships' names are written in stone, and a marine terminal in Loch Eriboll to transport quarried pegmatite. The Laid Grazings Committee vigorously opposes the plans (which have not so far met success in the planning process) on the grounds that a super-quarry would have overwhelming and adverse effects on local tourism and on shellfish farming. The effects of dust produced by the quarry on plankton in the loch and of the toxins from sea-going vessels would, they argue, seriously damage the economic prospects of these local industries and destroy the beauty and tranquility that draws so many visitors to the lochside (Laid Crofting Township 2002). The estate has since attempted to meet the community halfway, offering it the opportunity for a buyout while retaining control of the mineral wealth: negotiations continue.

CREATING MEANING FROM THE LAND

These examples of large and small economic concerns across northern Sutherland—of large landowners and industrial concerns sometimes working with and sometimes battling crofters who are trying to prosper on a more modest scale—are one aspect of the reinhabitation of the cleared landscapes. Another, quite different but equally vibrant aspect is expressed through the coast's artistic community.

The most arresting sight in Laid, one that causes most drivers' heads to turn, is that of a small, natural, heather-covered mound in a paddock beside the road. The mound itself is unremarkable, but sprouting from it are numerous flexible metal poles, each taller than a tall man and topped by a large ceramic ball glazed in deep blue, green, or purple. The poles bend in the wind and under the weight of their heads (Glob n.d.). These are the creation of a potter whose relationship with her surroundings best encapsulates that of many contemporary artists with the landscapes of northern Sutherland. Lotte Glob, daughter of the late Danish archae-ologist P. V. Glob, has been working in the area around Durness for many years. Along with other artists and craftspeople, she helped establish the Balnakeil Craft Village in a complex originally built to house military staff manning the radar station on Faraid Head, to the west of the village of Durness.

In her pottery, she consciously draws on the materials, colors, and moods of the surrounding landscape. Walking into the mountains, she gathers local rocks and incorporates them into ceramic sculptures, letting the rocks partly vitrify and meld with the clay. Some of her sculptures she leaves high in the hills, letting them become part of the landscape or be altered by the elements. She creates hollow ceramic balls ("Floating Stones") that float in water; she drops them into peaty lochans in the hills, or arranges them on a beach, photographs them, and lets the tide take them away.

Lotte is part of a vibrant community of artists living and working along Sutherland's northern coast. Balnakeil is home to one cluster, and Skerray to another. At Skerray, a traditional early nineteenth-century building has been carefully restored and rethatched as a community hall, and local residents often invite obscure musical groups from Third World countries to perform there. The Lockharts, artists and residents of a croft at Lamigo, banished sheep from their land and planted native trees with assistance from Scottish Natural Heritage in an attempt to return the land to its former, pre-Clearance character. They also diverted the Modsaridh Burn, which flows through their croft, into a large, hand-dug Celtic knot which can, they believe, be seen from passing airplanes. In another act of landscape reworking that involved people from all along the coast, crofters built a crannog (an artificial island typical of Scottish Iron Age settlement) in Loch Crochach, in the Skerray hinterland, by digging a deep ditch to turn a small promontory into an island. They ceremoniously planted native species of trees on the crannog and dropped Lotte Glob's ceramic balls into the water around it.

These and other artists are drawn by the area's great beauty, a stunning study in contrast between dark, looming mountains, creamy-pink beaches, and turquoise sea. Those drawn by these extraordinary physical characteristics also include members of the scientific community. Northwestern Scotland, including this area, has recently been named a "geopark" for its rich geological heritage (European Geoparks Network 2008). Certain parts of northern Sutherland are highly valued by Scottish Natural Heritage for their diversity of habitats for flora and fauna.

For example, on the headland centered around Loch Borralie, on the west side of the Kyle of Durness, the solid limestone geology has created a fertile, green, and freely draining area of ground, an unusual pocket of lushness in the generally acid northern Highlands. The ground is not only agriculturally productive, it also sustains a remarkable diversity of habitats, including fixed dune grasslands, shifting dunes with marram, limestone pavements, alpine calcareous grasslands, and heathlands. Because of this, the headland has been classified as a Site of Special Scientific Interest, and parts of it are candidates for Special Conservation Areas due to their rarity in Europe. Scottish Natural Heritage (SNH) therefore plays an important role in the management of the headland. Its interests sometimes conflict with those of the Keoldale Sheep Stock Club, tenants of the headland with grazing rights, as sheep can damage the fragile habitats. The club in turn leases the land from the Ministry of Defense, which runs a bombing range on the opposite side of the Kyle.

Similarly, at Invernaver there is a glacial outwash plain of sand-covered boulder clay, the unlikely setting for an abundance of fragile plant life, in particular mountain plants found at sea level. Here are rare examples of plants like mountain aven, creeping willow, and crowberry. The machair around Bettyhill supports purple oxytropis, Scottish primrose abound on the sea-facing slopes at Torrisdale and Lamigo, and marram grass covers the fragile dune systems at Invernaver and Farr (Kenworthy 1982:88–98).

These landscapes bring me to why I originally came to northern Sutherland: its archaeology. The glacial outwash plain at Invernaver was home in the past to prehistoric and late Medieval communities, who have left stone-built Bronze Age roundhouses, burial cairns and cists, an Iron Age broch and Medieval metal-working sites littering its surface, exposed in the sand, half excavated by the wind (Lelong 2002). The valley of Strathnaver may be relatively bare of pre-Clearance townships, but it contains a wealth of Neolithic chambered tombs, Bronze Age agricultural settlements, Iron Age brochs, and early Christian chapel sites, as well as possible Norse settlement sites that may have been occupied well into the Medieval period (Lelong 2003). Another remarkable concentration of archaeology occurs on the western side of the Kyle of Durness, on the headland centered around Loch Borralie, where the fixed dune grasslands are eroding to reveal abundant prehistoric buildings and land surfaces, along with late Norse to Medieval longhouses and shieling structures (the latter used for shelter during summer transhumance) (Lelong and MacGregor 2004). This rich archaeological heritage is currently the subject of a long-term research project exploring the early to late Medieval occupation of northern Sutherland, the Strathnaver Province Archaeology Project (Gazin-Schwartz and Lelong 2004; Lelong and Gazin-Schwartz 2005; http://www.northsutherlandarchaeology. org.uk).

Community groups across northern Sutherland have recently renamed their region "Mackay Country," emphasizing its unique historical status as the Medieval province of Strathnaver (Mackay Country Community Trust n.d.). This "brand" was invented in the hope that it would create a stronger sense of shared identity among the region's communities, promote the area's great natural beauty and heritage to visitors, and provide resources and inspiration for those working in business and tourism. The Mackay Country concept may have originated as a marketing ploy, but it has since found its own momentum. Its many strands include a project to draw together all existing historical research on the area and build upon that with fresh ethnographic, historical, and archaeological research.

A month-long event in 2005 drew together exhibits of photographs, artifacts, and personal accounts by local people, along with performances by musicians and bards and talks on traditional medicine and plants, archaeology, and emigration.

CONCLUSIONS

To many visitors these seem all but empty lands—the primeval, romantic wilderness perceived by Victorian poets and artists. But these lands are anything but empty. They are constantly being reinhabited by those who live and work in them today, who invest them with their own concerns, ideas, and perceptions. These acts of engagement take many forms. Some focus around economic concerns: the desire to survive on a small scale, through fishing or farming or tourism, or the desire to exploit the area's natural resources on a larger, industrial scale. Other forms of engagement express scientific interest, focusing on research into and protection of those natural resources. Still others are aesthetic responses to the area's unusual beauty. Some are intellectual or personal responses—or a combination of the two—to the region's history, in particular the dramatic upheavals from the widespread Clearance of its hinterland in the early nineteenth century. And others focus on its archaeological remains, the traces of the area's long and varied past, of millennia of inhabitation.

The Clearances of the early nineteenth century have had a permanent effect on the physical character of settlement pattern and land use and on the psyche of families descended from those evicted. However, through these acts of engagement, people are creating their own, new, and evolving senses of the place—living landscapes in the present.

ACKNOWLEDGMENTS

I would like to thank Gavin MacGregor, Janet Hooper, and Tony Pollard for various discussions on the subject of this paper, and Ingrid Shearer for preparing the illustration.

REFERENCES

Bangor-Jones, Malcolm. 1987. The Strathnaver Clearances. *North Sutherland Studies*. Scottish Vernacular Buildings Working Group. Edinburgh.

Basu, Paul. 2000. Sites of Memory–Sources of Identity: Landscape-Narratives of the Sutherland Clearances. In *Townships to Farmsteads: Rural Settlement Studies in Scotland, England and Wales*, ed. by J.A. Atkinson, I. Banks, and G. MacGregor, pp. 225–236. BAR British Series 293. Archaeopress, Oxford.

Basu, Paul. 2001. Hunting Down Home: Reflections on Homeland and the Search for Identity in the Scottish Diaspora. In *Contested Landscapes: Movement, Exile and Place*, ed. by Barbara Bender & Margot Winer, pp. 333–348. Berg, Oxford.

Brennan, Mark. n.d. Melness Crofters Estate, Sutherland—A New "Crofting Community Landowner." Caledonia Centre for Social Development, http://www.caledonia.org.uk/socialland/melness.htm, accessed April 30, 2008.

Caird, J.B. 1987. The Making of the North Sutherland Crofting Landscape in the Skerray District. *North Sutherland Studies*. Scottish Vernacular Buildings Working Group, Edinburgh.

European Geoparks Network. 2008. European Geoparks. http://www.europeangeoparks.org, accessed April 30, 2008.

Fairhurst, Horace. 1964. The Surveys for the Sutherland Clearances 1813–1820. *Scottish Studies* 8:1–18.

———. 1968. Rosal: A Deserted Township in Strath Naver, Sutherland. *Proceedings of the Society of Antiquaries, Scotland* 100:135–69. Edinburgh.

Fenton, Alexander. 1992. Shellfish as Bait: The Interface Between Domestic and Commercial Fishing. In *Scotland and the Sea,* ed. by T.C. Smout, pp. 137–153. John Donald, Edinburgh.

Gazin-Schwartz, Amy, and Olivia Lelong. 2004. Borralie, Durness: Data Structure Report 2004. GUARD 1634. Glasgow University Archaeological Research Division, Glasgow.

Gibson, Rob. 1996. *Toppling the Duke: Outrage on Ben Bhraggie?* Highland Heritage Books, Evanton, Ross-shire.

Glob, Lotte. n.d. Sculpture Garden. http://www.lotteglob.co.uk/gsculpt.htm, accessed April 30, 2008.

Gray, M. 1978. *The Fishing Industries of Scotland, 1790–1914*. Oxford University Press, Oxford.

Hunter, James. 1976. *The Making of the Crofting Community*. John Donald, Edinburgh.

Kenworthy, B. 1982. Plant Life. In *The Sutherland Book*, ed. by D. Omand, pp. 88–103. Northern Times, Golspie.

Laid Crofting Township. 2002. Laid Crofting Township, Sutherland. Blackpark, http://www.drive.to/laid, accessed April 30, 2008.

Lelong, Olivia. 2002. Writing People into the Landscape: Approaches to the Archaeology of Badenoch and Strathnaver. Ph.D. dissertation, Department of Archaeology, University of Glasgow.

———. 2003. Medieval (or Later) Rural Settlement in the Highlands and Islands: The Case for Optimism. In *Medieval or Later Rural Settlement in Scotland: 10 Years On,* ed. by S. Govan, pp. 7–16. Historic Scotland/MSRG, Edinburgh.

Lelong, Olivia, and Amy Gazin-Schwartz. 2005. Borralie, Durness: Data Structure Report 2005. GUARD 1925. Glasgow University Archaeological Research Division, Glasgow.

Lelong, Olivia, and Gavin MacGregor. 2004. Gallant Country of Corn: Making Sense of a Multi-period Landscape on the Kyle of Durness, Sutherland. In *Modern Views— Ancient Lands: New Work and Thought on Cultural Landscapes*, ed. by E. Carver and O. Lelong, pp. 11–22. BAR British Series 377. Archaeopress, Oxford.

Mackay Country Community Trust. n.d. At Home in Mackay Country. http://www.mackaycountry.com, accessed April 30, 2008.

Mackenzie, A. 1883. *The History of the Highland Clearances*. 2nd ed. A. Maclaren, Glasgow.

Macleod, Donald. 1841. *Gloomy Memories in the Highlands of Scotland*. Sinclair, Glasgow.

National Library of Scotland. n.d. Sutherland Estate Papers. Deposit 313. Edinburgh.

Noble, Ross. 1984. Turf-Walled Houses of the Central Highlands. *Folk Life* 22:63–83.

North Sutherland Duthchas Project. n.d. North Sutherland: Our Place in the Future. http://www.duthchas.org.uk/pdfs/area_value/NorthSutherlandValueState.pdf, accessed April 30, 2008.

Richards, Eric. 1982. *A History of the Highland Clearances: Agrarian Transformations and the Evictions 1748–1886*, Vol. 1. Croon Helm, London.

Scottish Government: Rural Development. n.d. Land Reform. http://www.scotland.gov.uk/topics/rural/land, accessed April 30, 2008.

Smout, T.C. 1998. *A History of the Scottish People 1560–1830*. Fontania Press, London.

Temperley, A. 1977. *Tales of the North Coast*. Luath Press, Inverness.

CHAPTER 11

The Devonshires Held This Trench, They Hold It Still: Cultural Landscapes of Sacrifice and the Problem of the Sacred Ground of the Great War 1914–1918

Jon Price

This paper considers the issue of the landscape of the Great War from a British perspective. This is not a purely academic question. In North America battlefield memorials are largely protected landscapes that are managed as cultural resources. In Europe the memorials are mainly cemeteries, and preserved battlefield landscape is rare (Franza and Johnson 1996). Despite, or because of, this, in Europe cultural resource management issues concerning the Great War battlefields are live and attracting attention. Self-defining descendants, descendant organizations, national governments, and professional and amateur archaeologists are all involving themselves to a greater or lesser extent, depending on their status and power, in the process. Although the landscape of the western front is now heavily populated, it is a landscape of clearance. The static warfare of 1914–1918 created a devastated landscape drastically different from any previously experienced. The millions of soldiers who lived there owned the new battlefield landscape, unlike the previous inhabitants or those who subsequently cleared and resettled it. The battlefield landscape has now almost disappeared, but it remains a heavily charged symbolic and sacred landscape for the descendants of the soldiers.

At the end of the Great War, the land along the line of the western front in France and Belgium was devastated by bombardment, littered with unexploded ordnance, and contained the unlocated bodies of millions of soldiers from around the world. Almost a quarter of a million British Imperial troops still have no known grave, and the number is greater for the French and Germans. Civilian populations were exposed to the unprecedented carnage of the war through volunteering, conscription, and media exposure. This led, during the war, to the development of a view of the war effort as a form of sacrifice, and invested the battlefields, as locus of activity, with a sacred quality. This view revealed itself in publications such as *High Altars* (Oxenham 1918) and in guides for tourists/pilgrims (Michelin 1917). Initially a proposal was seriously considered to maintain the "Red Zone" of the battlefields as a monument, and this chimed with the immediate postwar feeling for the landscape as a place of pilgrimage.

The apparently shattered landscape was dotted with cemeteries. At first these cemeteries contained some individual family input, with relatives buying and inscribing memorials (Depoorter et al. 1999). It rapidly became clear, however, that the bodies of the soldiers no longer belonged to their families; they were official property, to be commemorated in official monuments (Gough 2004). This led to an increasing number of memorials being placed on the battlefields, commemorating the activity of individual regiments or of groups of individuals from a particular town. These memorials were not part of the States' response to the war, being instead raised by subscription. The monuments had similarities to the war memorials being erected in towns and villages in the home countries, and to the rolls of honor held by commercial and industrial companies (Gough 2004), with the difference that one of their functions was to validate the sanctity of particular locations. This validation is made explicit at Mansell Wood, where the memorial reads, "The Devonshires held this trench. The Devonshires hold it still." The sacrifice of the soldiers of the Devonshire Regiment sanctifies the landscape, and as sacrificial victims they are charged with maintaining that sanctity.

At first it was believed that the battlefields had been devastated beyond renovation and recovery, but by the late 1920s veterans began to worry that reclamation and reconstruction, driven by economic factors, would leave very little trace of the site of their endeavors (Dyer 1994). The British erected monuments to their missing soldiers, of which the largest, at Thiepval, has inscribed on it the names of more than 76,000 missing soldiers. Sites such as the Canadian memorial at Vimy, the Newfoundland memorial at Beaumont Hamel, and the South African memorial at Delville Wood were designed to maintain the position of the landscape as consecrated and protected from profane activity. Economic pressure meant, however, that across most of its extent, the Red Zone was gradually returned to farming, industry, and housing use.

As the war falls beyond living memory the approach to the landscape, the monuments, and the human remains has begun to alter. Symbolism alters its meaning through time, and the symbolic landscapes of the post-Great War period are now part of a different set of economic and political realities (Saunders 2000).

For British visitors the western front continues to be a sacred landscape of remembrance, but the social and political landscape has changed in the intervening 90 years. This is now a place where, instead of responding to the impact of current events on personal experience, visitors create and explore their personal and cultural identities in response to a symbolic landscape of historical events (Saunders 2000). This process can now be seen online in the numerous websites recording these visits. Some of these sites are clearly individual statements, or the work of military enthusiasts, but many more, such as the Marple Remembers site (Rice 2003), form part of a town's or village's larger web presence and can be considered as a further attempt to reify cultural memory.

Within the sacred landscapes, the monuments and memorials are subject to a constant evolution of meaning (Gough 2004). Despite Belgian proposals to declare parts of the battlefield a World Heritage Site (Fabiansson 2005), this is not a likely development. To minimize conflict between interested parties, a management solution taking into account current use and current values, as well as original intent, is necessary. Veterans Affairs Canada, the body charged with the management of Canadian sites in Europe, has attempted to adopt this approach in its recent programs of restoration and reorganization of Great War memorials.

At Vimy the memorial park commemorates the actions of the Canadian forces. The site is composed of a large wooded area, several cemeteries and memorials, and the massive Vimy monument. Construction of the monument began in 1925 on land given to Canada by the French government, and the monument was unveiled in 1936. The monument lists the 11,285 Canadian soldiers who have no known graves.

A restoration program was started at Vimy in 2005. The leaflet issued to explain the closure during restoration work explains that

> as the memorial at Vimy Ridge has been designated a Canadian national historic site, it is important to preserve its historical and cultural integrity. This restoration project will ensure that the original conception for the site of artist and architect Walter S. Allward is upheld. (Veterans Affairs Canada 2004)

Despite the emphasis within the renewal project on taking into account the original commemorative intent which encompasses the creation of national identity, the preplanning for the project included significant attempts to deal with broader issues of usage. As a result, the question of how the continuing use of the site as a sacred place of pilgrimage and commemoration by non-French users can be integrated and reconciled with a recreational use by local French people, who view it as a rare open and accessible space in an urban and agribusiness-dominated landscape, and with how far landscape conservation responses should be driven by the conflicting requirements of user groups and owners (A. King, Director Beaumont Hamel, and A. E. Puxley, Director European Operations, Veterans Affairs Canada, personal communication 2003).

As this management development process takes place across the battlefields, interested groups are becoming more vociferous and active in their attempts to control the management interventions which take place. An increase in interest in the sites, evidenced by the range of guidebooks available, such as *Walking the Somme* in the Battlefield Europe series (Reed 1997), and by the development of archaeological approaches to the battlefields (Brown 2005; Desfossés et al. 2000; Price 2004, 2006; Saunders 2002) has begun to accelerate this debate.

In France and Belgium work has been carried out in advance of high speed rail link, motorway, and industrial developments. In general this work has been undertaken by official government-sponsored archaeological bodies. In Belgium this has partly been a response to amateur exploration that had been received critically in the United Kingdom (Harvey 2000).

So far the debate has taken place in the context of managing threats to physical remains and the management of official monuments and cemeteries; however, the particular nature of the sites and their usage requires an approach which takes into account their perception in nonofficial and nonorganized ways. One archaeological approach is driven by political perceptions, and brings global perspectives on archaeology into the European theater:

> It is significant that the rise of contestatory archaeological narratives of the past has found its most virulent form in places where the discordance between colonial master narrative and local indigenous identities has been greatest … the call for contestatory histories in the west—working class histories, gender, race, etc.—has emphasized struggle in the narrative at home as well. (Rowlands 1999)

As an example of these contestatory narratives impacting on the management of Great War heritage, a monument to those soldiers executed during the war for desertion has already been paid for by public subscription and erected in Britain (Black 2004), but it is clear that visitors to the battlefields may well press for something similar there as well (Shot at Dawn Campaign 1999). Archaeologists working in this field need to position themselves in relation to this broader political debate. An international, British-based team, No Man's Land, has begun to work in ways which may perhaps do this (Brown 2005; No Man's Land 2007; Price 2004, 2006). In 2007 the beginning of a multivocal approach to the archaeology was made (Brown and Plugstreet Team 2007), but as yet there has been no statement from archaeologists along the lines of that made by the Ludlow Collective:

> In the Colorado Coal Field War Project we have built an archaeology that working people can relate to both emotionally and intellectually. It is one of the few archaeological projects devised in the United States that speaks to working-class people. (Ludlow Collective 2001)

This position is likely to change. The reason for this change is related to an area where archaeology claims expertise: death, mortuary ritual, and the sacred. So far the management issues have involved emotive and strongly held views, which are often described in terms of sacredness and sacrifice but which are actually discussed in the context of historical "fact" (disputed or not) and mainstream logic. The actual sacred nature of sacred landscapes, and the responses to them, must also be addressed. Discussions of the management of sacred sites by heritage professionals have so far tended to focus on the relationship between Western/ modern society (seen as value neutral) and tribal/traditional groups (seen as descendant and value-driven) in postcolonial situations (Carmichael et al. 1994). It is, however, becoming clear that perceptions of sacredness drive responses to heritage amongst various groups within Western/ modern society as well (Blain and Wallis 2004).

How should the question of sacredness be addressed in respect to the landscapes of the Great War? Although it is clear that the whole landscape of the battlefields may be considered sacred, as in the original plan for retaining the Red Zone, this approach has already officially been abandoned. Alternatively, the sacredness of specific sites that have particular significance might be accepted. "It is after all not possible to treat every bit of earth with the same degree of respect" (Hubert 1994). In a sense this is what has happened at Vimy, Beaumont Hamel, and Delville Wood. A perimeter has been drawn around a section of the battlefield. Within is sacred ground, outside is agricultural land. This approach does not take into account personal responses to the sacred, but is driven by pragmatic and bureaucratic concerns.

To understand the issue of sacredness we need to consider the drivers in people's response to, and presumption of, sacredness. People can consciously inscribe sacredness into, or attach sacredness onto, landscapes, or they can have a perception that landscapes are inherently sacred (Blain and Wallis 2004). In the case of the Great War, they might attach sacredness as a result of historical narrative, or they may perceive it because of landscape or cultural signals which sensitize them to sacredness.

In the case of perception, the omnipresence of specifically designed cemeteries is guaranteed to have this effect. Although these sites are formal and the dominating rituals are formal, the behavior of visitors indicates a much deeper response. Touching war memorials, and in particular touching the names of those who died (Dyer 1994; photograph in Rice 2003), and inserting paper poppies in crevices between the stone panels on the memorials to the missing are clear evidence of personal ritual responses to sacredness.

Sacredness attached to landscape can also generate ritual response. At Sunken Lane, near Beaumont Hamel, two companies of Lancashire Fusiliers advanced into machine gun fire at the start of the July 1916 Somme offensive and were wiped out in seconds. Unlike at the nearby memorial park, no landscape preservation has taken place, and there are no official memorials apart from the cemetery around 80 yards away, where most of the bodies lay in the open for a year after the battle. At the lane, an unofficial shrine is renewed on a regular basis (Figure 11.1). To all intents and purposes this appears similar to a pagan tree shrine: an

Figure 11.1 Unofficial shrine at Sunken Lane, Beaumont Hamel, Departement du Somme. Here, on July 1, 1916, the Lancashire Fusiliers suffered 486 casualties in a few seconds as they emerged from their forward positions to advance on the German lines. The small cemetery, which marks the furthest point they reached, around 30 yards from the start line, is a standard Commonwealth War Graves Cemetery and so has no information on the action. There are no other official monuments at the site. The shrine, which has similarities to a pagan tree shrine, appears to be renewed on a regular basis.

unofficial personal response to sacredness of place. In management terms it is also a deposit of "ritual litter" (Blain and Wallis 2004).

The response to the recovery of dead soldiers missing since the war is one of the drivers in the developing debate surrounding the management of the battlefields. This is not a debate between Western scientific and tribal sacred views. The archaeologists are themselves part of various communities for whom the landscape and remains are sacred. They participate in official ceremonials of reburial when bodies are uncovered during excavation. They also engage in private rituals during excavation (Martin Brown, personal communication 2005; Anonymous, personal communication; and personal experience).

Archaeologists in this field are working within a grey area of ethics and sacredness. "To disturb the dead is a taboo deeply ingrained in any culture where burial is the norm" (Boyle 1999), and the more recently they died, the greater the transgression. This leads to a situation where archaeological investigation on the battlefields in advance of development is carried out in the almost certain knowledge that bodies will be found, yet that statement cannot be included in the project design as a purpose since this would transgress taboos, and laws. Prospecting for missing soldiers is not an allowable objective in France and Belgium, despite the fact that the knowledge that they are there is often a driver in requiring archaeological work in the first place.

This has produced situations such as the fraught and complex activity surrounding a likely mass grave, identified as Australian but actually likely to contain more British troops, at Fromelles in France. Parties involved include the Australian government, British archaeologists, the French government, and enormous amounts of strongly expressed opinion by internet discussion groups (Billson 2007; Stephens 2007). In the United States, official and private concern about the location and recovery of the 102,000 American soldiers missing in the twentieth-century wars has meant that since 2003 a significantly resourced military archaeological unit, the Joint POW/MIA Accounting Command (JPAC), work previously carried out by the Central Identification Laboratory in Hawaii (CILHI), operates to locate and recover missing personnel (JPAC 2005; Swift 2003). In Europe the scale of the task and the culture of the governments concerned make such a development unlikely.

We cannot treat the sacred landscapes and the missing soldiers only with dispassion, logic, or legal precedent. Places of death are inevitably sacred. Places of mass death are more so. The sacred nature of these places is also overlain with politics. There was no universal male, let alone female, suffrage in Britain or Germany. In Britain at the start of the Great War only 59% of men could vote, and in Germany elections to state governments were based on class (Müller 2003). Millions of men went to their deaths as a result of decisions in which they had no part. In a discussion of personal narrative, Hynes says that

> each narrative among the thousands that exist of modern wars, commemorates one life lived in the mass action of a modern war, that each is a monument of a kind to that one soldier, or sailor, or pilot, and to no one else, and that by existing they refute and subvert the collective story of war that is military history. Not one of these men was necessary to the war he fought, not one affected the winning or losing; individually they were irrelevant. But they were there; they bear witness to their human particularity. (Hynes 1999)

The archaeological recovery of the bodies of individual soldiers, and their identification through forensic work, is a physical manifestation of this reclamation of individuality. In the case of the "unheroic dead who fed the guns" (Sassoon 1983), their individuality is reclaimed, in contrast to the collective dominance of the monuments to the dead. Siegfried Sassoon, war poet and decorated war hero, wrote a poem in 1927 after attending the opening ceremony of one of those, the Menin Gate, a memorial listing almost 55,000 soldiers with no known grave (Sassoon 1983:153). Sassoon makes clear his distaste for the memorial, and suggests that the dead soldiers who "struggled in the slime" should "rise and deride this sepulcher of crime." Perhaps one of the tasks archaeologists should carry out in the sacred landscapes of the Great War battlefields is to help those dead rise up.

REFERENCES

Billson, Bruce. 2007. Minister to Support Further Examination of Suspected Fromelles Mass Burial Site (Media release by the Hon. Bruce Billson, MP, Minister assisting the Minister of Defense). http://www.defence.gov.au/minister/Billsontpl.cfm?CurrentId = 6886, accessed August 11, 2007.

Black, Jonathan. 2004. Thanks for the Memory: War Memorials, Spectatorship and the Trajectories of Commemoration 1919–2001. In *Matters of Conflict: Material Culture, Memory and the First World War*, ed. by Nicholas Saunders, pp. 134–148. Routledge, London.

Blain, Jenny, and Robert J. Wallis. 2004. Sacred Sites, Contested Rites/Rights: Contemporary Pagan Engagement with the Past. *Journal of Material Culture* 9(3):237–261.

Boyle, Angela. 1999. A Grave Disturbance: Archaeological Perceptions of the Recently Dead. In *The Loved Body's Corruption*, ed. by Jane Downes and Tony Pollard, pp. 187–199. Cruithne Press, Glasgow.

Brown, Martin. 2005. Journey Back to Hell: Excavation at Serre on the Somme. *Current World Archaeology* 10:25–33.

Brown, Martin, and Plugstreet Team. 2007. Plugstreet. http://plugstreet.blogspot.com, accessed August 10, 2007.

Carmichael, David L., Jane Hubert, Brian Reeves, and Audhild Schanche (editors). 1994. *Sacred Sites, Sacred Places*. Routledge, London.

Depoorter, Ch., Stefaan Cossey, and Willie C. Tillie. 1999. 1914–1918 De Oorlog Achter Het Front. Kring voor Heemkunde "Aan de Schreve," Poperinghe.

Desfossés, Yves, Alain Jacques, and Gilles Prileaux. 2000. Premières recherches sur le grand guerre dans le Nord-Pas-de-Calais. *Archaéologie* 367(Mai):32–38.

Dyer, Geoff. 1994. *The Missing of the Somme*. Hamish Hamilton, London.

Fabiansson, Nils. 2005. The Archaeology of the Western Front 1914–1918. http://web.telia.com/~u86517080/BattlefieldArchaeology/ArkeologENG_3B.html, accessed February 27, 2005.

Franza, Mary E., and Ronald W. Johnson. 1996. Commemorating 20th Century Wars. *CRM, The Journal of Heritage Stewardship* 19(9):5–8.

Gough, Peter. 2004. Corporation and Commemoration: First World War Remembrance, Lloyds TSB and the National Memorial Arboretum. *International Journal of Heritage Studies*. 10(5):435–456.

Harvey, Oliver. 2000. Ghouls Dig Up Bodies of Our Hero Tommies: Trading on the Sick Black Market. *The Sun*, November 11.

Hubert, Jane. 1994. Sacred Beliefs, and Beliefs of Sacredness. In *Sacred Sites, Sacred Places*, ed. by David L. Carmichael, Jane Hubert, Brian Reeves, and Audhild Schanche, pp. 9–19. Routledge, London.

Hynes, Samuel. 1999. Personal Narratives and Commemoration. In *War and Remembrance in the Twentieth Century*, ed. by Jay Winter and Emmanuel Sivan, pp. 205–220. Cambridge University Press, Cambridge.

Joint POW/MIA Accounting Command (JPAC). 2005. Until They Are Home. Joint POW/MIA Accounting Command, JPAC. http://www.jpac.pacom.mil/index.htm, accessed February 27, 2005.

Ludlow Collective. 2001. Archaeology of the Colorado Coal Field War 1913–1914. In *Archaeologies of the Contemporary Past*, ed. by V. Buchli and G. Lucas, pp. 94–107. Routledge, London.

Michelin at Cie. 1917. *Battlefields of the Marne 1914*. Michelin et Cie., Clermont-Ferrand.

Müller, Sven Oliver. 2003. *Die Nation als Waffe und als Vorstellung: Nationalismus in Deutschland und Grossbritaninnien im Ersten Weltkrieg*. Vandenhoeck and Ruprecht, Göttingen.

No Man's Land. 2007. No Man's Land: The European Group for Great War Archaeology. http://www.redtwo.plus.com/nml, accessed August 10, 2007.

Oxenham, John. 1918. *High Altars, the Battlefields of France and Flanders as I Saw Them*. Methuen, London.

Price, Jon. 2004. The Ocean Villas Project: Archaeology in the Service of Remembrance. In *Matters of Conflict: Material Culture, Memory and the First World War*, ed. by Nicholas Saunders, pp. 179–191. Routledge, London.

———. 2006. Orphan Heritage: Issues in Managing the Heritage of the Great War in Northern France and Belgium. In *Past Tense: Studies in the Archaeology of Conflict*, ed. by Tony Pollard and Ian Banks, pp. 181–196. Brill, Leiden.

Reed, Paul. 1997. *Walking the Somme*. Battlefield Europe Series. Leo Cooper, Barnsley.

Rice, Ian. 2003. Marple Remembers, The Somme 2002, Ypres 2003. http://www.marple-uk.com/ianrice/index.htm, accessed February 27, 2005.

Rowlands, Michael. 1999. The Politics of Identity in Archaeology. In *Social Construction of the Past: Representation as Power*, ed. by George C. Bond and Angela Gilliam, pp. 129–143. Routledge, London.

Sassoon, Siegfried. 1983. *The War Poems*. Arranged and introduced by Rupert Hart-Davis. Faber and Faber, London.

Saunders, Nicholas J. 2000. Bodies of Metal, Shells of Memory: Trench Art and the Great War Re-cycled. *Journal of Material Culture* 5(1):43–47.

———. 2002. Excavating Memories: Archaeology and the Great War, 1914–2001. *Antiquity* 76(1):101-108.

Shot at Dawn Campaign. 1999. Shot at Dawn. http://www.shotatdawn.org.uk/, accessed February 27, 2005.

Stephens, Tony. 2007. Under the Fields of Fire. http://www.smh.com.au/text/articles/2007/07/23/1185043033540.html, accessed August 11, 2007.

Swift, Earl. 2003. *Where They Lay: The Search for Those Who Fell in Battle and Were Left Behind*. Bantam Press, London.

Veterans Affairs Canada. 2004. Restoration Project Leaflet. http://www.interlog.com/~fatjack/vimy/vimybrochure.htm, accessed February 27, 2005.

Winter, Jay. 1995. *Sites of Memory, Sites of Mourning: The Great War in European Cultural History*. Cambridge University Press, Cambridge.

———. 1999. Forms of Kinship and Remembrance in the Aftermath of the Great War. In *War and Remembrance in the Twentieth Century*, ed. by Jay Winter and Emmanuel Sivan, pp. 40–60. Cambridge University Press, Cambridge.

CHAPTER 12

Archaeological Taxonomy, Native Americans, and Scientific Landscapes of Clearance: A Case Study from Northeastern Iowa

Larry J. Zimmerman and Dawn Makes Strong Move

This is a story of removal and return, one version of the complex pasts of a landscape in the northeastern part of what now is known as the state of Iowa in central North America. The Missouri River delimits the land on the west, as does the Mississippi River on the east. Although they are no longer present in the state, the state derives its name from the Ioway (also spelled Iowa) nation,[1] the primary tribe living in the area before the arrival of European and American invaders. What happened in Iowa to American Indians[2] living there is a story typical of many states, especially in the eastern United States. Native Americans had been part of these lands for at least 12,000 years and longer by the reckoning of their oral traditions. The waves of immigrant European colonizers from the sixteenth century onward, however, brought massive, mostly negative, changes to the cultures living on the prairies and in the eastern woodlands of North America.

By both accident and by plan, the colonizers removed Indian people from their ancestral lands. From the "Trail of Death" for the Potawatomi in 1837, to the "Trail of Tears" for the Cherokee in 1838–1839, to the "Longest Walk" of the Navajo people in 1863–1864, stories of removal and horrible suffering abound in American Indian history. From the perspective of the colonizers, the act of removal physically, emotionally, and legally severed the ties of people to their lands, allowing non-Indians to own the "empty" lands.[3] Similar, though less dramatic, removals occurred in the northeastern Iowa region. These actions now seem reprehensible by any standard, and realistically, they are not reversible. In fact, in some ways attempts to sever the ties of Indian people to their lands really has not ceased. Unintentionally, but unfortunately, archaeology's practice of "scientific colonialism"[4] has played a continuing role in the process.

That archaeology does much to alienate Indigenous peoples is by now a truism. Concerns of Indigenous peoples about proper treatment of remains of their ancestors and sacred objects are well known (e.g., Thomas 2000), as are worries that their stories will be told by others (e.g., Zimmerman 2001a). A few problems are more subtle, but when exacerbated by political concerns about questions of cultural affiliation in land claims or repatriation, they come into greater clarity. One such problem—and one focus of this paper—is that because some archaeologists cannot produce unequivocal evidence of cultural affiliation, they are reluctant or unwilling to make definitive statements that link groups that were formerly living in a region to the archaeological remains found there. Thus, as well as having been forcibly removed from their traditional lands by Euroamerican colonists, some American Indian nations now must deal with archaeologists who have created an "intellectual" landscape of clearance by taxonomically severing the ties of a tribe to the lands and works of their ancestors.

By way of example, this paper summarizes a complex tale about two kinds of removal, one physical and the other intellectual, from one particular landscape of clearance, Iowa's Neutral Ground, and an archaeological manifestation on its periphery, Effigy Mounds National Monument (Figure 12.1). The story is about four American Indian nations—the Ioway, the Ho-Chunk (Winnebago), the Meskwaki, and the Eastern

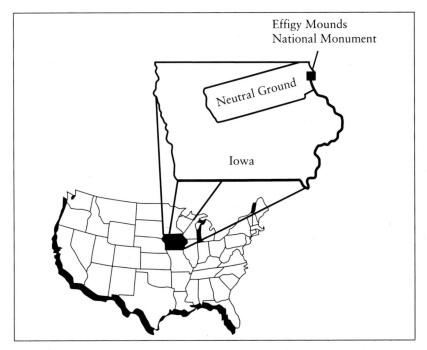

Figure 12.1 Effigy Mounds National Monument and Iowa's Neutral Ground.

Dakota—and their residence in, and removal from, northeastern Iowa, as well as their desire to reconnect with that land. A common theme for many American Indian groups—almost bordering on stereotype—is that they always have been people of the land. They declare that although they may now live in urban centers or on lands forced upon them by Euroamericans, they cannot and will not forget the lands of their ancestors. There can be no emotional or intellectual separation from these places. That land is their history, their identity, and their lives. What this story hopefully will show is that such declarations are not hyperbole. By the time the story is through, there should be clear understanding that landscapes of clearance mean only that Indian people themselves have been removed from their lands, but their emotional links remain. In northeastern Iowa, those links have been especially powerful.

This version of the story begins with a discussion of the role of taxonomy in colonizing Native American pasts, using an archaeological culture history of northeastern Iowa to demonstrate the problem. The tale, however, has an ending that is happy (or at least satisfying) and relates an odd kind of return and restoration of these people to their land, an ending in which archaeology also has played a key role.

TAXONOMY

Many archaeological taxonomic systems have at their heart a notion of time that is linear.[5] Taxonomy linguistically partitions the past into temporal segments that imply cultural beginnings and endings rather than presenting cultures as continuous and cumulative. In the United States, these segments are marked as distinctly named cultural complexes, phases, or traditions. Most archaeologists probably intuit otherwise, but because of gaps or a lack of clarity in data, these taxa tend to imply that one group has vanished or has been displaced by another. Archaeologists go so far as to use terms such as "collapsed," "disappeared," or "vanished" when describing culture histories of some landscapes and speak of sites as being "ruins" or "abandoned."[6] Even where archaeologists can use the direct historical approach (see Fagan 2005:40–42 for a description), they sometimes have trouble making connections between historically known tribes and those more distant in time. Oddly echoing the Whorf hypothesis (Whorf 1956), the point here is to suggest that taxonomy predisposes archaeologists to see culture histories as discontinuous rather than as a continuous evolution of groups that frequently reposition themselves on the land as they adapt to changing natural and cultural environments. In other words, as archaeologists come to the linguistic partition of a taxon in a culture history, they must "clear the landscape" before they can move to the next taxon.

To complicate the matter, archaeologists have inherited a system of tribal names from colonial times that does not reflect the realities of Native American social organization either before or after European Contact. One problem, which seems relatively innocuous for archaeologists (though not for Indians!), is that the names Euroamericans used for each Indian nation usually were not the names a people used for themselves.[7] A greater problem is that the seemingly simple act of naming a tribe created something of a fantasy: tribal names promoted an idea that tribes were discrete entities when often they were not. In reality, ethnic boundaries were vastly more fluid than most archaeologists seem to realize. For example, tribes might take in enemies as captives or slaves and fully absorb them, but continue to recognize their group of origin well beyond the time of the event and the lives of the individuals involved.[8] Names applied at Contact also tended to link tribes to particular spatial units, when the reality is that many groups also were vastly more mobile than most archaeologists admit.

To summarize, all of this has a great deal to do with how archaeologists view American Indian ethnogenesis. Whether the result of scientific taxonomy or based on common tribal names, nomenclature has contributed to the creation of landscapes of clearance. If groups are seen as discrete temporal and spatial entities, they may be thought of as having disappeared from a landscape when in fact there may have been cultural continuity in a particular place. Reality demonstrates that groups move in and out of a landscape or coalesce and diffuse; ethnic boundaries and tribal memberships change through time in response to natural and social pressures. The result is a vastly more complex cultural landscape than most imagine, and archaeologists dealing with northeastern Iowa demonstrate many of these points nicely.

The section that follows will seem "old fashioned," a recitation of traditional culture history and taxonomy for the northeastern Iowa region. The purpose is to show the complexity of archaeological views of ethnogenesis. Knowing the taxonomy is important for understanding how we think about a region. For northeastern Iowa, taxonomy seems to have emphasized the discontinuities as much or more than it has the continuities, helping to create the intellectual landscape of clearance.

ARCHAEOLOGY, PREHISTORY, AND ETHNOGENESIS IN NORTHEASTERN IOWA

By the time the effigy mounds were built, people had lived in the northeastern Iowa area for nearly 10,000 years. The landscape provided vast resources from the Mississippi River and its many tributary streams, as well as from the deep-cut valleys, a land known as the Driftless Zone because it was bypassed by the continental glaciers of the Pleistocene. About 80 miles west of the river, the land smooths into gently rolling flatlands. During this span of time, people lived in the region as successful foragers exploiting the wide variety of animals and plants in the area.

Starting about 500 BCE, cultures in the area started to change, and over the next 1,500 years developed pottery, hunting with the bow and arrow, construction of burial mounds, and the domestication and cultivation of plants. Archaeologically the cultural tradition in this area is known as the Woodland, usually subdivided into Early (500 BCE–100 BCE), Middle (100 BCE–300 CE), and Late (300 CE–1000 CE). Burial mound building began in the Early Woodland, but sites are poorly known in northeast Iowa. By Middle Woodland there was a vast trade network in exotic raw materials, part of the so-called Hopewell Interaction Sphere, and a well-developed mortuary complex with intensive mound building. Although the peoples of northeastern Iowa were a part of that widespread cultural complex, relatively little of it is directly evidenced in the area. However, the Late Woodland was a time of change, with the introduction of the bow and arrow and cultigens, especially maize, around 800 CE. Mound construction continued, with large clusters of mounds reflecting social aggregation and intensive ritual usage. (See Perry [1996] for summary of Woodland tradition in Iowa. For a detailed coverage of Woodland in the Effigy Mounds area specifically, see Green 2001:39–41).

An intriguing variant of the Late Woodland that developed in the Driftless Zone (incorporating parts of the neighboring states of Wisconsin, Illinois, and Minnesota) was the Effigy Mound complex. Although people lived a primarily foraging life with limited horticulture, their culture was similar to other eastern woodland areas. They practiced a microband-macroband subsistence pattern, living in dispersed groups much of the year, but coming together for fish and shellfish collection by the streams and nut harvesting in the uplands. During these times they were heavily involved in the construction of large mounds in the shape of birds, panthers, bears, and other animals (Figure 12.2). These rarely were burial mounds; the people continued to bury their dead in conical or linear mounds. More likely, people participated in a large ritual complex having to do with renewal, and they perhaps used the clusters of effigies to mark clan territories.

After 1000 CE, during the last few hundred years before European Contact, there were significant cultural changes brought by the development of two other cultural complexes near the region, the Middle Mississippian and the Oneota. The Middle Mississippian derives from the people living farther south along the Mississippi River in and around

Figure 12.2 Aerial photograph of the Marching Bear group at Effigy Mounds National Monument, with bird and bear effigies and two linear mounds outlined in lime. (National Park Service).

Cahokia, a chiefdom with large populations, social stratification, and a vast material culture complex based mostly on maize horticulture. Their influence was widespread and profound on most Woodland peoples. They had multiple centers that certainly had an impact on local Woodland populations (see Pauketat 2004 and papers in Pauketat and Emerson 1997 for an excellent summary).

Appearing around 800 CE and lasting until around 1650, just before European Contact, Oneota cultural origins are less clear. Oneota is a very diverse and diffuse culture extending all the way to the Great Plains hundreds of miles to the west, but concentrated around the southern portion of western Great Lakes region. There are three general views on Oneota origins (see Overstreet 1997 for an excellent summary). One is that people bringing new ways migrated from the south, with their point of origin unclear but likely directly from Middle Mississippian centers. Another sees Oneota as degenerating from Middle Mississippian centers such as that at Aztalan in contemporary Wisconsin. The third is that local Woodland peoples of the Effigy Mound culture transformed their ways due to Mississippian influence. There certainly appears to be a continuation of Late Woodland peoples alongside Oneota, and these Late Woodland peoples were themselves at least somewhat involved with the powerful Middle Mississippian interaction sphere, exchanging goods with Cahokia and its outliers at centers near contemporary La Crosse, Wisconsin. Oneota culture also was agriculturally based, with large villages often located on or near open river terraces and floodplains. There is evidence of increasing hostilities that may have resulted in group fission. As time passed, Oneota appears to replace Woodland, at least in some areas. Effigy mound construction ceased with Late Woodland peoples, but conical burial mounds, mostly scattered, continued to be built into the 1600s. Comments in David Overstreet's (1997:252) recent summary on Oneota are revealing:

> Perhaps there is a shred of truth in all three models, or perhaps the Oneota tradition has its roots and branches in processes and contexts not yet fully discerned in the archaeological record ... Unfortunately, conclusive evidence is lacking to prove beyond a reasonable doubt one model over another.

As Overstreet (ibid.) also notes: "The conclusion of the Oneota tradition ... is as problematical as are its beginnings."

Oneota cultures evidently developed into the widely-dispersed Siouan-speaking peoples of the region, those met by the first Europeans who came into the area, but as Overstreet (1997:252) notes, "these assumptions are based more on historical records than on hard archaeological data." Few archaeologists are definitive, but most probably would agree that Oneota is closely related to the historically known Siouan speakers and perhaps some other non-Siouan groups. These include the Chiwere-Winnebago (with common tribal names such as Ioway, Otoe, Missouria, Winnebago) and Dhegiha (common tribal names: Omaha, Ponca, Osage, Kansa, and Quapaw), but some Oneota peoples may have been Algonkian speakers (common tribal names: Miami and Illinois).[9]

The problem is that the archaeological evidence seems to belie the historical evidence. When Overstreet (1997:254) discusses the problem, he use phrases such as "Of equal significance to understanding Oneota prehistory in Wisconsin is their rapid decline and abandonment of the region sometime prior to A.D. 1650." Yet the Winnebago were in place, with relatively large numbers, when encountered by Nicolet in 1634 and still there, though with smaller numbers, when visited by Perrot in the 1650s. Overstreet attributes at least part of the demise to diseases that came immediately in advance of white contact.

In other words, by some ways of seeing the data there appear to be two gaps—that is, taxonomic landscapes of clearance—between Late Woodland Effigy Mound culture and Oneota culture and then later between Oneota and the historically known Siouan-speakers of the region. The latter gap is at the juncture of what American archaeologists have usually called the "prehistoric" and the "historic," which is in itself a kind of taxonomic clearance whereby the prehistoric, based on interpretation of a material culture record, is swept away intellectually by the historic, based on material culture plus a documentary record usually created by non-Indians. As for the record created by Native oral traditions, archaeologists rarely believe that it contains useful historical information.[10] The archaeological versions of pasts emphasize discontinuity rather than continuity (which is emphasized in oral tradition) for little reason other than the taxonomic structure archaeologists use in the region. Real discontinuity came with physical removal of tribes from their homelands.

FROM PREHISTORY TO HISTORY: PHYSICAL REMOVAL FROM THE LAND

Even before the establishment of the United States as a country, tribes along the east coast of North America were being pushed from the lands of their origins. Those with direct contact with whites were pushed off their homelands into lands to the west that were already occupied by other groups in a kind of "domino effect" that led to intertribal conflict as well as conflict with Europeans. The intent in this section is to summarize the complexity of the actual process of clearance as the Euroamericans moved into the area and is in no way meant to be a complete history. At the same time, this section will discuss some of the archaeology that has helped to document clearance.

Initially, European contact in northeastern Iowa was primarily through trade. By 1673, the Jesuit seminarian and fur trader Louis Joliet and his companion, Jesuit priest Father Jacques Marquette, had floated down the Wisconsin River to the Mississippi, seeing the high bluffs but not the effigy mounds the Indians had built there (Hancock 1913:12). By 1685, the French trader Nicholas Perrot traveled to the upper Mississippi River area to promote peace and trade with the Ioway nation, the primary residents of Iowa, successfully negotiating treaties and alliances with the tribes of the region whereby the tribes eventually acknowledged as the possession of France all of the lands drained by the upper Mississippi River. By 1700, the fur trade was in decline. The influence of the French, who never truly dominated the region due to aggressive activity from the Indians, began to diminish (HRA Gray and Pape 2003). Although northeastern Iowa was used for hunting and occasional settlement by a number of other tribes, the major nations, those with substantial connections to the land, that play a role in this story are four: the Ioway, the Fox or Meskwaki, the Eastern Sioux or Dakota, and the Hochungra, more often known as Ho-Chunk or Winnebago.[11]

The Ioway

The tribal traditions of the Ioway, who call themselves *Páxoche,* say that their clans agreed to form a People, the *Honga* (the Great Nation), and that their roots are at *Moka-Shutze* (the Red Earth), probably a location along the Wisconsin shore of Lake Michigan. They also say that some of their ancestors built mounds in the shapes of animals along the Great River (the

Mississippi), or *Nyitanga* as they called it (Foster 1996:1, 1999). They are related to the Chiwere-Siouan (Oto, Missouria, and Ho-Chunk) speakers of the region and traditionally call the Oto "brothers" and the Ho-Chunk "fathers." Although some archaeologists are hesitant to link Oneota sites to historically known tribes as discussed above, Wedel's (1976) use of the Direct Historical Approach clearly drew the connection between the Ioway and Oneota sites of the taxon "Orr phase" along the Upper Iowa–Root River drainage region of northeastern Iowa and southeastern Minnesota.

Michel Accault, a French fur trader, likely visited these Ioway villages on the Upper Iowa River between 1677 and 1680, when the Ioway were drawn into trade for bison hides, possibly shifting their settlements westward to take better advantage of bison herds (Alex 2000:218). By the late 1600s they appear to have abandoned their villages along the Upper Iowa, relocating to northwestern Iowa and southern Minnesota. Hostilities with Algonquian-speaking peoples pushed them even further west near their Oto and Omaha allies, where they began to infringe on the territory of the Dakota with whom relationships had been good (Alex 2000:219). They settled along the Missouri River until the late 1760s but hunted throughout Iowa, with their presence recorded in villages along the Mississippi, Iowa, Grand, Des Moines, and other rivers into the 1820s. The peripheries of their territories had been claimed, shared, or contested by many other groups, and there were hostilities. Ioway numbers were diminished from epidemic diseases, and they ceded land to the US government between 1824 and 1836, eventually giving up claim to all land east of the Missouri River and moving into what is now Nebraska and Kansas. By the late 1800s they had been moved to the Indian Territories in present-day Oklahoma.

The Meskwaki

In early relationships with the tribes of the region, the French particularly were plagued by the Sauk and their allies and kin, the Fox (who call themselves Meskwaki), who first met the French in 1666 to the east in their homelands along the St. Lawrence River Valley and in the states of Michigan and Wisconsin. According to their oral tradition, *Wisaka* created the Algonquian-speaking Meskwaki along the east coast of the continent after the Manitou spirit beings destroyed the land and everything on it. *Wisaka* remade the land and all living things, so they call themselves Meskwaki, or the "Red Earth People." By the late 1670s they had villages along the Fox River in Wisconsin. Their territory was substantial, and their traditions claim that the Ioway granted them territory in Iowa, which brought them into conflict with the Illinois and Miami. The latter allied themselves with the French to exterminate the Meskwaki.

The Sauk and Meskwaki went to war with the French in the so-called Fox Wars (1701–1742), creating long-term animosity toward the French (Johnathan Buffalo, personal communication 1999). By 1776, continual pressure on the Meskwaki and Sauk eventually pushed them west into northeastern Iowa (Mason 1988:89). They claimed hunting lands along both sides of the Mississippi River all the way downstream to the mouth of the Des Moines River, putting them in direct conflict for lands with the Dakota (sometimes called the Santee).

They and their Sauk allies signed six treaties with the US government from 1800 to the 1830s. The Sauks, under their chief Black Hawk, tried to resist American incursion into Sauk lands in Illinois, which led to the so-called Black Hawk's War of 1832. The Meskwaki and other Sauks remained neutral, but after Black Hawk's defeat ceded their lands along the eastern border of Iowa, moving to a small reserve. From the time of the war until they were relocated outside Iowa, they shifted settlements and ceded more lands until they were removed from the state between 1836 and 1842.[12] However, though officially removed, some stayed and others returned (Green 1976). In 1856 the Meskwaki purchased land in the state under the authorization of the Iowa state legislature, where they remain today.

The Dakota

The Dakota are part of the larger groups of Dakota-Lakota-Nakota Siouan speakers, of the Seven Council Fires. Although many of the Sioux, especially the Lakota, share a story of origins in the Black Hills of South Dakota, many speak of a great circular migration that may have brought them from the east. Gibbon (2003:38–46) proposes a model for the origin of the Dakota out of a wild rice–gathering complex called Psinomani near the Mille Lacs Lake, Minnesota, area which he says "suddenly replaced this Terminal Woodland lifeway about AD 1300" (Gibbon 2003:38). By the late 1600s they had regular interactions with the French. Although most of their villages were in Minnesota, they claimed hunting lands along the Mississippi all the way south to the mouth of the Des Moines River, which put them into competition with the Sauk, Fox, and other tribes. Some claim that their western migration took them to the area of contemporary La Crosse, Wisconsin, where they established villages. They gave land to the Ho-Chunk, who at the time had no land. When the Ho-Chunk wanted to marry into the tribe, the Dakota refused and moved west again, leaving the land to the Ho-Chunk.

They lived with years of difficult interaction with Euroamericans and other tribes, and in the Mendota (1837) and Traverse des Sioux (1851) treaties they ceded all lands in Minnesota and Iowa except for small reservations along the Minnesota River and farther northwest. After years of being cheated of land and food, the groups took part in a last, desperate act of resistance: the Dakota Uprising of 1862. Their rebellion collapsed and the government confiscated all their lands. Many were incarcerated for a time, then moved to South Dakota to the Crow Creek Reservation and from there to the Santee Reservation in Nebraska. Four small reservations remain in Minnesota and South Dakota.

The Ho-Chunk

The Ho-Chunk or Hochungra, according to tribal historian David Smith, are descended from the mound-building cultures of eastern North America. Some accounts place their origins at Red Banks on the Door Peninsula on the western shore of Lake Michigan, and others have them migrating from the southeast seeking new territory to settle and hunt. All accounts put them in place in Wisconsin before the seventeenth century (Smith 1986). The Ho-Chunk certainly were one of the more powerful groups in the region, strong enough to keep out the Ojibwe who pushed toward the south. Even so, the stress on territory and population pressure may have caused them to seek relief by pushing south themselves into regions occupied by the Illinois Confederacy. The group began to fragment, and this may have caused the split with the Ioway, Oto, and Missouria sometime around 1570.

The effects of the French fur trade started to have an impact on the Ho-Chunk by the early 1600s, when the Ottawa and Huron, linked with the Ojibwe, tried to open trade with them. Jean Nicolet was the first European to contact the Ho-Chunk, arranging a treaty to allow trade between them and the Ottawa, Huron, and Ojibwe. In 1635, a small-pox epidemic killed all but 16,000 Ho-Chunks. In 1638, the Ottawa, Potawatomi, Kickapoo, Sauk, and Meskwaki united against them. The Ho-Chunk chose to focus on the Meskwaki, with the three largest Ho-Chunk villages concentrated for defense. In 1638, with 12,000 people confined in a relatively small space, another smallpox epidemic devastated them; only 6,000 survived. Continued warfare reduced their numbers to fewer than 500 survivors, who were involved in complex relations with other groups well into the 1700s.

Warfare caused the Sauk and Meskwaki to flee west into Iowa, leaving territory for Ho-Chunk expansion and a rebound in population. Over the years, shifting alliances saw them allied to former enemies, siding with the British in the War of 1812. Though the war essentially ended in a stalemate between the British and Americans, the tribes suffered total defeat. The Ho-Chunk signed a peace treaty with the Americans in 1816, but remained suspicious and hostile, charging tolls for Americans to travel through their lands. A huge intertribal council in 1825 attempted to end fighting between the tribes and in 1830 created a 40-mile-wide buffer zone between the Dakota and the Meskwaki and Sauk in northeast Iowa, the Neutral Ground, into which the Americans proposed to move the Ho-Chunk.

Over the next 15 years the Ho-Chunks were forced to surrender most of their lands, which they resisted. After the 1827 Winnebago War resistance collapsed, and in 1832, the Winnebago ceded all their lands east of the Mississippi River and agreed to move to the Neutral Ground in Iowa, although some remained in Wisconsin. One fourth of the Ho-Chunk died in an 1836 epidemic, and after a second treaty in 1837, the Winnebago agreed to move to the Neutral Ground, which had already been reduced in size. By 1842, approximately 2,200 Ho-Chunk moved to the Turkey River Subagency in northeastern Iowa, where they had to be protected from the Meskwaki and Sauk near a military post, Fort Atkinson. More than a thousand Ho-Chunk had remained in Wisconsin, however, and the military had to keep those in the Neutral Ground from moving back to Wisconsin. With Iowa statehood in 1846, the Ho-Chunk were first moved to Minnesota in 1848–1849, which ended the threat from the Meskwaki and Sauk, but they were placed as a buffer for a second time, in this case between the Dakota and Ojibwe. Some Ho-Chunk managed to remain in northeast Iowa for more than a century.

With the Dakota Uprising in 1862, the Ho-Chunk were forcibly rounded up and moved to the Crow Creek Reservation with the Dakota. Under terrible conditions, some moved back to Minnesota and Wisconsin, but the 1,200 who remained at Crow Creek finally left as a group for their own reservation in eastern Nebraska. Life there was not easy, and the government planned once again to use them as a "buffer tribe," this time in North Dakota. They refused, and many tried to return to Wisconsin, where in 1875 the government stopped forcing them to return to Nebraska and purchased homesteads for them in Wisconsin. During the 1880s more than half returned to Wisconsin, with the rest staying on the reservation in Nebraska.

ARCHAEOLOGY, THE NEUTRAL GROUND, AND DOCUMENTING TRIBAL CONNECTIONS TO A LANDSCAPE OF CLEARANCE

The government established the Neutral Ground as a place the Sauk, Meskwaki, and Dakota could enter only if permitted by negotiation. This 40-mile-wide strip of land stretched from the northeast corner of Iowa in a southwesterly direction to the upper fork of the Des Moines River. In the treaties the Ho-Chunk signed in 1832 and 1837, they were to move from Wisconsin lands and occupy the easternmost 35 miles of the Neutral Ground. They were forced to move to it in 1842. Fort Atkinson had been built in 1840 to keep tribal members in place around the Turkey River Subagency (one of two Ho-Chunk agencies in the Neutral Ground). A Winnebago School and model farm were set up, but most Ho-Chunk didn't participate. They didn't have enough food, weren't protected from the Sauk and Meskwaki, and were exposed to sales of alcohol by whites. Events overtook the facilities, and in 1848–1849 Fort Atkinson was abandoned, the Winnebago School was moved to Minnesota, and by terms of a treaty in 1847 the Winnebagos gave up their rights to land in the Neutral Ground.

Although their occupancy of the Neutral Ground was brief, material culture remnants of their occupancy were substantial and have been investigated archaeologically, presenting interesting views of a landscape of clearance. Fort Atkinson itself has been the subject of extensive archaeological investigation; archaeological field schools have been conducted on the site many times, one as recently as 2005, and also a National Park Service remote sensing workshop.[13] Away from the Fort, two field schools investigated the lands of the Turkey River Subagency and Ho-Chunk linkages to the Neutral Ground. In a limited way, the field schools worked to restore the Ho-Chunk, Meskwaki, and Dakota to the archaeology of this complex cultural landscape.

The University of Iowa and the Office of the State Archaeologist of Iowa offered the field schools in 2000–2001 to address American Indian concerns about archaeology directly. Students had regular interaction with Native Americans concerned about archaeology and Native American scholars who were trained as archaeologists, as well as with other individuals representing particular viewpoints about the project or about archaeology. Native American youth from the Iowa First Nations summer program at the University of Iowa also spent time working with field school students. Many of the Indian people involved in the project were descended from the tribes represented in the Neutral Ground.[14] Both years the students worked with descendant communities of Native Americans and of non-Indians whose ancestors had worked at Fort Atkinson. Materials recovered from excavations demonstrated the interactions of both groups. Doershuk, Peterson, and Fishel (2003) have presented a paper on the excavations, the source of the summary below.

Some historical sources indicate that during the eight years the Ho-Chunk lived in the Neutral Ground they had at least 14 villages, and perhaps as many as 22, near Fort Atkinson, each associated with a leader's name. One such camp was that of Whirling Thunder, whose village totaled 177 people. Also in the area was the Hewitt-Olmsted trading post, a government-licensed, permanent place for trade with the Indians.

Sites were rich, with excavations at the Hewitt-Olmsted trading post uncovering building foundations confirming the location of the post, as well as copious items used in trade with the Indians. Other excavations have confirmed the locations of several of the Winnebago camps, including what appears to be Whirling Thunder's village about two miles away. In this area there is also a non-Indian settler's residence dating to the time just after the Winnebago were removed. That site had an almost complete absence of trade goods and according to current local residents was an almost ideal location for a postremoval land claim. At site 13WH158 excavators found a wide range of materials from the time of the Neutral Ground, including fragments of ball clay pipes, a variety of glass and metal, gun parts, glass and shell beads, porcupine quills, and a range of construction materials including brick, flat glass, and nails. The excavators have debated whether this is a Winnebago settlement or another trading post (Doershuk, Peterson, and Fishel 2003:6).

What should a landscape of clearance such as the Neutral Ground look like archaeologically? Investigators should expect a wide range of site types and locations that reflect millennia of occupation by Native American residents, followed by a small number of sites reflecting trade-associated contact with Euroamericans. As the landscape became contested by different groups moving into the area (such as occurred with the Meskwaki), archaeologists should expect to see a number of sites that would appear to be "out of place," that is, different enough from those cultures that developed *in situ* to be recognizable as incongruous.

Once the Neutral Ground was established, we might expect substantial differentiation of settlement types, which these preliminary results seem to suggest, in terms of military, native, and commercial non-Native types. Certainly during the occupancy of the Neutral Ground around 1840 only the Winnebago, government employees (military, subagency workers, and families), licensed traders, or approved missionaries were allowed in the area, and the material culture reflects that fact. The Winnebago camps and traders' facilities seem to have few or no military or religious items, and though archaeologists have found no missionary sites, the other types are certainly present, though the Native and trader sites are not easy to differentiate. Following the abrupt abandonment by the military and Native peoples, which is clear in the archaeological record, we would expect the incursion of non-Native settlers, for which we also have evidence.

EFFIGY MOUNDS, CULTURAL AFFILIATION, AND INTELLECTUAL RESTORATION

The removal of the Ho-Chunk from Iowa's Neutral Ground marked the end of a substantial Indian presence in the region for nearly 150 years. A few Ho-Chunks stayed in the area for a few decades, and the Meskwaki purchased land for a settlement just outside the Neutral Ground in 1856.[15] In one sense, the Indian heritage of the state is considered to be an important part of Iowa's story, with most contemporary Iowa citizens knowing that the state is named after a formerly resident tribe. Many Iowans also know of and speak with some pride about the state's only National Monument at Effigy Mounds.

Effigy Mounds National Monument, a park of nearly 1,500 acres, preserves 206 known mounds, 31 of them effigies of animals such as birds, bears, and panthers. The rest are conical and linear mounds used primarily for burials. Their construction, as noted above, is well-documented archaeologically to be part of the Woodland tradition. The first suggestion to establish a national park in northeastern Iowa came in 1901, only about 60 years after the removal of the Ho-Chunks from the Neutral Ground. Discussion and legislative wrangling about the nature of the park and what should be included continued for nearly 50 years, and much of the discussion focused on preservation of the mounds. In 1949, President Truman signed a proclamation establishing Effigy Mounds National Monument, and since that time land donations and purchases have added to the monument's size.[16] Archaeological research on the monument has documented the mounds and excavation their contents.

In 1990, with the Native American Graves Protection and Repatriation Act, federal agencies were to inventory their collections, work to repatriate biologically or culturally affiliated human remains, grave goods, and sacred objects to American Indian people, and consult with concerned Native American tribes. As part of this process, the National Park Service conducted two investigations at Effigy Mounds National Monument regarding cultural affiliation. Henning (1998) completed the inventory of remains and Green et al. (2001) examined the cultural affiliation of the effigy mounds themselves. Although no archaeologists saw the mounds as being anything other than created by ancestors of contemporary Native Americans, examination of archaeological reports demonstrated the taxonomic issues discussed above, and the reports were not definitive about which tribes specifically could be associated with the construction of the mounds. Reports did, however, suggest the possibility of linkages to the Siouan-speaking tribes. Ethnographic information was more provocative and ultimately clearer in providing answers about affiliation.

Interviews with personnel at the monument showed how complete the removal of Native Americans from the creation of the mounds has been in the minds of some members of the general public. In one instance, park rangers reported that members of the Church of Jesus Christ of Latter Day Saints claimed that the mounds had been built by their ancestors, following a pre-twentieth-century idea that Indians were descendants of the Lost Tribes of Israel. This notion was part of speculation from the 1800s and earlier about the origin of the numerous and often spectacular mounds and other earthworks found over most of eastern North America. The so-called Moundbuilder Myth (Silverberg 1968) claims that the Indians were not capable of such constructions so Europeans, who were then later displaced by the Indians, must have been responsible. In another instance, rangers reported that practitioners of so-called New Age spirituality believe the effigy mounds to be some sort of power point or vortex with a spiritual energy connecting all of humanity, thus seeing the mounds as the creation of the entire human species or of mystical powers and so a public heritage.

However, these unusual ideas aside, there was information that demonstrated direct cultural affiliation with the Siouan-speakers of the region. Ethnographer Paul Radin (1923) had reported early in the twentieth century that the Winnebago claimed their ancestors had built the effigy mounds and other mounds in the region. As part of the affiliation report (Green et al. 2001), researchers also interviewed members from the tribes discussed in this essay. Ho-Chunk people describe the effigy mounds area as a sacred place where holy people went to gather certain plants and understood the mounds to be made by their people. An Ioway elder woman from Oklahoma reported that her clan had stories and a song about one particular bear effigy, and during an event at the monument described below, she made a special point of visiting that mound. Another Ioway elder also reported links between his clan and the mounds and how the mounds still hold a special place in traditions. At the same time, an interview with a Meskwaki tribal member showed that they recognized the sacred nature of the mounds, but realized that the mounds were built well before the Meskwaki entered the area and made no claim of affiliation. Similarly, the Dakota also make no claim to the mounds, but see them as sacred. While none of this proves affiliation of the Ho-Chunk and Ioway with the effigy mounds, the link seems fairly clear: archaeology suggests long-term occupation of the region by ancestors of the Siouan-speaking Winnebago and Ioway people, and both nations claim affiliation to the effigy mounds, having extant oral traditions that relate directly to them. If nothing else, this provides limited intellectual restoration of the Ho-Chunk and Ioway to the land of their ancestors and their creations upon it.

CONCLUSIONS

Landscapes of clearance can be created by removing people from their homes and lands, but clearance also can be accomplished intellectually by denying the ancestral ties of a people to their lands. Such has been the case in Iowa's Neutral Ground where, at least for a time, four tribes claimed lands and from where all were eventually removed to make way for Euroamerican settlement. For the Ioway and Ho-Chunk, clearance also has been intellectual, as the linguistic and temporal partitions of archaeological taxonomy mostly have failed to acknowledge that ancestors of the two groups built the effigy mounds. Physical removal from a landscape, as with the Ioway, Ho-Chunk, Dakota, and Meskwaki in northeastern Iowa, is often dramatic and certainly traumatic for those removed. Unfortunately, the archaeological record usually fails to document the difficulties encountered. At the same time, however, historical records discuss the removal of tribes from the Neutral Ground, and archaeological investigations show both the abrupt beginnings of the Neutral Ground's use and the abrupt abandonment and departure of the military and Ho-Chunk people from the area.

Having ancestors intellectually removed from the landscape, as the Ioway and Ho-Chunk do in the case of their cultural affiliation to the effigy mounds, is certainly less traumatic than physical separation but works no less efficiently to sever ties of a people to their lands. A combination of 150 years of physical separation from the land and archaeological methodology have worked to allow dominant-society archaeologists to disconnect the mounds from the tribes, even though tribal oral tradition has consistently said that the ancestors of the tribes made the mounds. However, at least a symbolic restoration recently occurred and has been maintained since then.

In 1999, Effigy Mounds National Monument hosted two linked events meant to bring back a presence of the Indian groups. One was a public seminar commemorating the fiftieth anniversary of the monument. Pete Fee, an Ioway who has moved back to the state, and David Smith, a Winnebago tribal historian, both spoke at the session, recounting their people's connection to the mounds and the role the mounds played for their cultures. The second was an Indian Heritage Festival attended by many Indian people, but also by non-Indians from the region. There were cultural presentations, including demonstrations of crafts by Ioway, Meskwaki, Ho-Chunk, and Dakota people. There was also a demonstration powwow, showing dance styles of tribes in the region, traditional and contemporary dance regalia, singing and drumming, and traditional stories. This was followed by a similar cultural event in 2001, and in 2004 Effigy Mounds hosted another Indian Heritage Festival along with an academic symposium about sacred sites. Several of the participants in that session were Dakota people who talked about the difficulties of sharing sacred sites like the effigy mounds with non-Indian people. The Ioway, Ho-Chunk, Dakota, and Meskwaki were back.

EPILOGUE

The hills are steep there, really more like bluffs, and the valleys deep and long, opening onto the Mississippi River. A few feet north of a brown, brick National Park Service Interpretive Center on the valley floor are millennium-old, conical burial mounds. Three hundred feet or so above, on top of long, narrow ridges on both sides of the valley, are more mounds. Many are conical, but there are large earthen birds, bears, and panthers. All kept silent watch on the activities starting below.

Anticipation was palpable as Kate Miller, then Superintendent at Effigy Mounds National Monument, stepped to the microphone to start the festivities. The sun just setting and the river flowing gently by the monument as 500 or more Native American and non-Native audience members seated themselves on the grassy slopes of the natural amphitheater. Kate first welcomed all, then introduced Pete Fee to ask a blessing.

Pete was dazzling in his people's traditional dress, his head shaved but for a small lock in the back, emphasized by his porcupine- and deer-hair roach and eagle feathers. His head and face were dramatically painted half red with yellow dots and half black. Pete is a tradition-oriented Ioway, who a few years before had moved back to Iowa, returning to the original lands of his ancestors. Pete is descended from the very people who had a role in building the mounds, his ancestors likely buried in some of the conical mounds. His presence on the stage was extraordinary as he asked blessings for the people and event. As he ended, he stated simply, but with extraordinary eloquence and power, "When I am here, the spirits of our ancestors are all around me."

For the next few hours songs echoed through the hills, the drums a powerful heartbeat and the songs alive and joyous. One ranger noted that as he did his evening rounds of the monument, he could hear the music everywhere, sometimes miles distant. The past was clearly present as the mounds—no longer silent—sang their joy for the return of their relatives for the first time in more than 150 years!

ACKNOWLEDGMENTS

William Green has been an excellent sounding board for ideas for many of the concepts in this paper and has proven to be a superb scholar of the region. John Doershuk, Cindy Peterson, and Rich Fishel provided generous permission to cite their unpublished work and were great teachers and organizers for the field schools mentioned in the article. Johnathan Buffalo generously shared time with our students and willingly related the history of his people. The authors feel fortunate to have been a part of those field schools. Phoebe O'Dell, Pete Fee, and Lance Foster have proven very generous and insightful in their discussions of the Ioway. Joe Williams, Tom Sanders, and Tom Ross have provided guidance for information about the Dakota. Kate Miller and Phyllis Ewing, Superintendents at Effigy Mounds National Monument, showed great wisdom in developing and continuing the Indian Heritage Festival. Lori Stanley of Luther College and Ken Block from Effigy Mounds were instrumental in making the festival work. Dennis Lenzendorf at Effigy Mounds knows everything about the place and willingly shares it.

NOTES

1. Readers should be aware that although many American Indian groups are often called "tribes" in both conversation and legal convention, many "tribes" feel the term to be derogatory because it connotes them as "primitive." Many use the term "nation" to combat that connotation and to force recognition of their sovereignty. That recognized, the terms will be used interchangeably in this paper.
2. American Indian, Native American, and Indian are used interchangeably in this paper to refer to the Indigenous people of North America, present before the arrival of people of European heritage.
3. In several cases, the immorality of such removals was recognized by many Euroamerican people of the time, and in a few cases, as with the Navajo, people were restored to their lands. For a good summary, see Trafzer (2000), especially chapters 3–10.
4. Following Galtung (1967), Hymes (1974:49) defines scientific colonialism as the process whereby the center of gravity for acquisition of information about a people is located elsewhere than with the people themselves.
5. Kehoe (1998:100–105) provides an intriguing history of taxonomy, which includes a discussion of the origins of one of the first American taxonomic systems, the MTS or Midwestern Taxonomic System. The MTS has its origins in the region discussed in this paper.
6. These word choices in themselves can be alienating to Indigenous people (see Colwell-Chanthaphonh and Ferguson 2006).
7. Names first used by Euroamericans were often those given to a tribe by people of other nations, sometimes by their enemies. Tribes usually called themselves names that would translate roughly as "the people" or "human beings." Though the stories vary, one common example is "Sioux," which is based on an Algonquin word (probably Ojibwe or Blackfoot), tribes who were often enemies of the Sioux. The word meant "lesser adder," or roughly "snake," a word considered to be derogatory and dehumanizing. The people now called the Sioux tend to use the name of their particular dialect—Nakota, Dakota, or Lakota—or the name of their "council fire" such as Inhanktonwan (Yankton) or Hunkpapa, or even their band names. See Sutton (2000:9–10) for a more complete explanation.
8. The Meskwaki, for example, have stories about capturing a group of Ioway women and absorbing them into their group. Even today people are recognized as being descended from that group of women (Johnathan Buffalo, personal communication 1996).
9. Please note that, for reasons discussed in note 7, the matter of the common names listed here for these groups is complex. For an excellent discussion of the archaeological complexity of these groups and their Oneota links see the papers in Henning and Thiessen (2004).

10. See discussions by Echo-Hawk (2000), Mason (2000, 2006), and Whiteley (2002) for detailed treatments of the utility of oral tradition in archaeology and Vansina (1985) for a more general discussion of the historical attributes of oral tradition.

11. Each group's story is vastly more complicated than can be related here. The intent is to show how each group had and has connections to the northeastern Iowa landscape. See Zimmerman (2001b) for longer versions and his References for more thorough histories based on primary sources.

12. Gourley (2003) documents the arduous movements of the Meskwaki in the 1840s, especially in 1845.

13. Relatively few publications have come out of the recent research. See Merry 1988 and Merry and Green 1989 for a list of pre-1990 sources.

14. Dawn Makes Strong Move, for example, is a member of the Ho-Chunk nation and a trained archaeologist who served as a consultant, working directly with students. Johnathan Buffalo, the Meskwaki tribal historian, worked with students on the Meskwaki settlement near Tama, Iowa. Dr. Leonard Bruguier, a Yankton Sioux historian, visited the students in the field and gave lectures, emphasizing oral tradition. Larry Zimmerman, John Doershuk, Richard Fishel, and Cynthia Peterson served as codirectors of the field schools.

15. As of 2004, the population on the Meskwaki settlement outside Tama, Iowa, was approximately 700, with the remainder of the tribe's enrolled members about double that, most living off-settlement in the state.

16. For a more detailed history of the monument see HRA Gray and Pape 2003, especially Chapter 8, Movement for a Park, at http://www.nps.gov/efmo/web/hrs/hrs8.htm (accessed March 14, 2006).

REFERENCES

Alex, Lynn M. 2000. *Iowa's Archaeological Past*. University of Iowa Press, Iowa City.

Colwell-Chanthaphonh, Chip, and T. J. Ferguson. 2006. Rethinking Abandonment in Archaeological Contexts. *The SAA Archaeological Record* 6(1):37–41.

Doershuk, John F., Cynthia L. Peterson, and Richard L. Fishel. 2003. The Northeast Iowa Neutral Ground: Identifying 1840s Native and Euro American Archaeological Components. Paper presented at the 49th Annual Midwest Archaeological Conference, Milwaukee. http://www.uiowa.edu/~osa/gcp/reports/JFD CLP RLF MAC 2003.pdf, accessed February 20, 2006, and cited with permission.

Echo-Hawk, Roger. 2000. Ancient History in the New World: Integrating Oral Traditions and the Archaeological Record. *American Antiquity* 65(2):267–290.

Fagan, Brian M. 2005. *Ancient North America*. Thames and Hudson, London.

Foster, Lance. 1996. The Iowa and the Landscape of Southeast Iowa. *Journal of the Iowa Archeological Society* 43:1–5.

———. 1999. *Tanji na Che*: Recovering the Landscape of the Ioway. In *Recovering The Prairie*, ed. by Robert F. Sayre. University of Wisconsin Press, Madison and online at http://ioway.nativeweb.org/iowaylibrary/tanji.htm, accessed March 7, 2006.

Galtung, Johann. 1967. After Camelot. In *The Rise and Fall of Project Camelot: Studies in the Relationship between the Social Sciences and Practical Politics*, ed. by I. Horowitz, pp. 281–312. Cambridge, MIT Press.

Gibbon, Guy. 2003. *The Sioux: The Dakota and Lakota Nations*. Blackwell Publishing, Malden, MA.

Gourley, Kathy. 2003. Migrations of the Sauk and Meskwaki in the mid-1840s: The Emigration of 1845. *Journal of the Iowa Archeological Society* 50:223–228.

Green, Michael. 1976. "We dance in opposite directions": Meskwaki (Fox) Separatism from the Sac and Fox Tribe. *Ethnohistory* 30:129–140.

Green, William. 2001. Native Peoples in the Study Region: Culture History. In *Effigy Mounds National Monument Cultural Affiliation Report* by William Green, Larry Zimmerman, Robin Lillie, Dawn Makes Strong Move, and Dawn Sly-Terpstra. Research Papers Vol. 26, No. 3 (Vols. 1 and 2), pp. 35–43. Office of the State Archaeologist of Iowa, Iowa City.

Green, William, Larry Zimmerman, Robin Lillie, Dawn Makes Strong Move, and Dawn Sly-Terpstra. 2001. *Effigy Mounds National Monument Cultural Affiliation Report.* Research Papers Vol. 26, No. 3 (Vols. 1 and 2). Office of the State Archaeologist of Iowa, Iowa City.

Hancock, Ellery M. 1913. *Past and Present of Allamakee County, Iowa*, Vol. 1. S.J. Clarke, Chicago.

Henning, Dale R. 1998. Recommendations to NAGPRA Summary and NAGPRA Inventory, Effigy Mounds National Monument. Report prepared by the Quaternary Studies Program, Illinois State Museum, Springfield.

Henning, Dale R., and Thomas D. Thiessen (editors). 2004. *Dheigihan and Chiwere Siouans in the Plains: Historical and Archaeological Perspectives*, Memoir No. 36. *Plains Anthropologist* 49(192), part 2.

HRA Gray and Pape. 2003. *Figures on the Landscape: Effigy Mounds National Monument Historic Resource Study.* National Park Service Midwest Regional Office, Omaha. http://www.nps.gov/efmo/web/hrs/hrs5.htm, accessed October 5, 2005.

Hymes, Dell. 1974. The Uses of Anthropology. In *Reinventing Anthropology*, ed. by D. Hymes, pp. 3–82. Vintage Books, New York.

Kehoe, Alice. 1998. *The Land of Prehistory: A Critical History of American Archaeology.* Routledge, New York.

Mason, Carol I. 1988. *Introduction to Wisconsin Indians.* Sheffield Publishing, Salem, WI.

Mason, Ronald J. 2000. Archaeology and Native American Oral Tradition. *American Antiquity* 65(2):239–266.

———. 2006. *Inconstant Companions: Archaeology and North American Indian Oral Traditions.* University of Alabama Press, Tuscaloosa.

Merry, Carl A. 1988. The Archaeology of Fort Atkinson (13WH57): A Guide to Sources. In *Archaeological and Paleoenvironmental Studies in the Turkey River Valley, Northeastern Iowa*, ed. by W. Green. Research Papers Vol. 13, No. 1, pp. 66–81. Office of the State Archaeologist of Iowa, Iowa City.

Merry, Carl A., and William Green. 1989. Sources for Winnebago Prehistory in Northeastern Iowa, 1837–1848. *Journal of the Iowa Archeological Society* 36:1–8.

Overstreet, David F. 1997. Oneota Prehistory and History. *Wisconsin Archeologist* 78(1–2):250–297.

Pauketat, Timothy R. 2004. *Ancient Cahokia and the Mississippians.* Cambridge University Press, Cambridge.

Pauketat, Timothy R., and Thomas E. Emerson (editors). 1997. *Cahokia: Domination and Ideology in the Mississippian World.* University of Nebraska Press, Lincoln.

Perry, Michael. 1996. The Woodland Period. Office of the State Archaeologist, Iowa City. http://www.uiowa.edu/~osa/learn/prehistoric/wood.htm, accessed August 20, 2005.

Peterson, Cynthia L. 1995. The Turkey River Winnebago Subagency (13WH111), 1840–1848: Phase II Archaeological Testing at Locus A and Surrounding Subagency-Era Sites. *Contract Completion Report 441.* Office of the State Archaeologist, Iowa City.

Radin, Paul. 1923. The Winnebago Tribe. *37th Annual Report of the Bureau of American Ethnography for the Years 1915–1916*, pp. 33–550. Smithsonian Institution, Washington, DC.

Silverberg, Robert. 1968. *Mound Builders of Ancient America: The Archaeology of a Myth.* New York Graphics Society, Greenwich, CT.

Smith, David L. 1986. The Events Leading up to the Permanent Split within the Winnebago Tribe, 1800–1816. Master's thesis, Department of History, University of California, Los Angeles.

Sutton, Mark Q. 2000. *An Introduction to Native North America.* Allyn and Bacon, Boston.

Thomas, David H. 2000. *Skull Wars: Kennewick Man, Archaeology, and the Battle for Native American Identity.* Basic Books, New York.

Trafzer, Clifford E. 2000. *As Long as the Grass Shall Grow and the Rivers Flow: A History of Native Americans.* Harcourt, Fort Worth.

Vansina, Jan. 1985. *Oral Tradition as History.* University of Wisconsin Press, Madison.

Van der Zee, Jacob. 1915. "The Neutral Ground." *The Iowa Journal of History and Politics*, 13(3):311–348.

Wedel, Mildred Mott. 1976. Ethnohistory: Its Payoffs and Pitfalls for Iowa Archaeologists. *Journal of the Iowa Archeological Society* 23:1–44.

Whiteley, Peter. 2002. Archaeology and Oral Tradition: The Scientific Importance of Dialogue. *American Antiquity* 67(3):405–415

Whorf, Benjamin L. 1956. *Language, Thought, and Reality.* John Wiley and Sons, New York.

Zimmerman, Larry J. 2001a. Usurping Native American Voice. In *The Future of the Past: Archaeologists, Native Americans, and Repatriation,* ed. by T. Bray, pp. 196–184. Garland Publishing, New York.

———. 2001b. Tribal Culture Histories. In *Effigy Mounds National Monument Cultural Affiliation Report,* by William Green, Larry Zimmerman, Robin Lillie, Dawn Makes Strong Move, and Dawn Sly-Terpstra. Research Papers Vol. 26, No. 3 (Vols. 1 and 2), pp. 45–64. Office of the State Archaeologist of Iowa, Iowa City.

Zimmerman, Larry J., John Doershuk, Cindy Peterson, and Richard Fishel. 2002. Unraveling Tensions Between Communities: Archaeological Field Schools and American Indian Concerns. Paper presented at the Towards a More Ethical Mayanist Archaeology conference, University of British Columbia, Vancouver.

Index

abandonment, 13–14, 17, 19, 25–26, 29–30, 33–35, 39–41, 49
Aboriginal people, 89
  in Australia, 155–157
  colonialism and, in Canada, 114
  reserves, in Canada, 118
  Stolen Generations of, in Australia, 156
  as term, 122 n. 1
  titles to land, in Canada, 113, 115, 120
  understanding of landscapes, 121
  See also Indigenous, First Nations
absentee landowners, 30
Accault, Michel, 198
Adaminaby, NSW, Australia, 157–162
Adrian IV (Pope), 52, 66
Afrikaans, 93, 94, 103
agriculture, 27, 29–30, 33, 35, 37–38, 53, 56, 78
  colonial, in South Africa, 92
  effect of restructuring, in South Africa, 94
  movement away from, 166–168
  Palestinian, 131, 133–136
ancestors, 31, 42, 76, 81, 157, 204–207
  dwelling places of, 41
  sprits of, in Botswana, 145–152
apartheid, 92
  Group Areas under, 90
  Homelands under, 90, 92
Arab cultural resources, 129
assimilation, 155–156
avoided landscapes, 30–31, 35–36, 40, 41

Bangwato, 145–152
Bapedi cult, 145–152
Batswapong people, 139–152

Belgium, 183
belonging, sense of, 14, 16–17, 18, 23, 81, 121
Bender, Barbara, 17
Bettyhill, Scotland, 168
Black Hawk (Sauk chieftain), 199
Black Hawk's War, 199
Black Hills, 199
Boers, 87, 92, 141
Botswana, 139–153
British Columbia, Canada, 112–123
British settlers, in South Africa, 90, 92, 141
Bushmen, 77, 146
  diffusionist and evolutionary interpretation of engravings of, 98–99, 106
  in historical records of Driekopseiland, 91, 94
  identity of, 105
  place-names and, 90
  rock art, 87
  See also Khoisan

Cambrensis, Giraldus, 49, 50, 55, 56–60, 63, 68
cartography/cartographers
  in Canada, 117–119, 121
  in Ireland, 50, 60
  in South Africa, 76, 82
  See also maps
Certeau, Michel de, 16
Christian Europe, 50–51, 59–60, 66, 68
Christianity/Christianization
  in Botswana, 146, 151
  in Ireland, 17, 64, 66
Church of Jesus Christ of Latter Day Saints, 204
closing deposits, 41
Colebrook Home, Adelaide, Australia, 157

colonial(ism), 14, 18–21, 23
    Anglo-Norman, in Ireland, 49–51,
      55, 67–68
    archaeology and, in South Africa,
      71, 73–74
    and clearance, 31–32
    conceptions of land use, in
      Canada, 114, 120–121
    as ideological clearance, 56, 62,
      65
    ideology of wilderness, in Canada,
      113, 116–117, 121
    landownership and: in South
      Africa, 78, 94; in Canada, 113,
      119
    material culture and, in South
      Africa, 93
    in Palestine, 129
    racial taxonomy and, in South
      Africa, 104, 105 n. 1, 106 n. 4
    in South Africa, 87, 91–92, 106
      n. 6
    use of literature and maps for: in
      Ireland, 58–62, 65; in South
      Africa, 90; in Canada, 118
colonization, 20–21, 31, 50, 52–53,
    55–56, 58, 61, 67–68
    "scientific," 190
"Coloured," 93–94, 103
conflict, 27, 29–31, 40–42, 54
conquest, 31–32, 42
conservation, 20, 72, 78–79, 112
"contested" landscape, 14, 16, 18,
    21, 113
    in Botswana, 139, 149, 152
continuity, 16, 30, 40–41, 196
    narrative of, 183
    of occupation, in Palestinian
      cities, 130
Cork, Ireland, 53, 57, 64
Crannog, 53, 175
crofting, 169–174
    community buy-outs of crofts,
      172–174
Crow Creek Reservation,
    200–201
Crusades, 51, 55, 59, 62

Dakota people, 1862 uprising of,
    200–201
decision making, locus of, 28, 30–32,
    35–36
descendants
    archaeology and identity among,
      104–105, 202
    and heritage, in Scotland, 26, 39,
      168–169
    separation from heritage, 92, 97,
      155–156
    in South Africa, 78, 90, 102, 103
Des Moines River, 199
diamond mining, 87, 92–93, 97
diaspora, 18, 23, 104, 127
Difaqane, 91, 150
Dimomo Cave, *140 (map)*, 149–151
dispossession of landscape, 18, 19
    in Canada, 117
    among Khoisan, 92–93, 106 n. 6,
      160 n. 7
Douglas, James, 118
Driekopseiland rock engravings,
    87–110
Driftless Zone (North-Central North
    America), 194
Dublin, Ireland, 52–54, 57, 63
dwelling, 16, 82, 83

Effigy Mounds National Monument,
    191, *195*, 204, 206–207
emigration
    Palestinian, 135
    in Scotland, 34, 39, 56
enclosure, 154
engendering of landscape, 144–145
ethnic corporatization, 79
ethnoarchaeology, 127–129, 131–137
ethnogenesis, 193–196
eviction, 14, 17, 31, 37–38, 42, 50,
    154, 160, 166
exclusion from landscape, 14, 22
    in South Africa, 90
expulsion
    defined, 31–32
    Palestinian, 127, 135
    in Scotland, 36–39, 40, 42

farming. *See* agriculture
Fee, Pete, 206–207
First Nations, 19, 21
   colonial removal of, 118, 120
   colonial representations of, 117
   perceptions of the landscape, 114,
     116, 120–122
   reserves and, 119
   resistance to colonialism, 119
   territorial rights of, 113, 120
   treaties with, 118
   See also Aboriginal *and entries for*
     individual groups
fishing, 166–168
FitzGilbert de Clare, Richard, 54
folklore, 21
   Batswapong, 145, 147–149
   Khoisan, 101
   Scottish, 35–36, 40
Fort Atkinson, 201–202
Fox Wars (1701–1742), 199
France, 51–52, 54. *See also Chapter 11*
French in North America, 197–200
fur trade, 117, 197–198

Gaza, 129–130
gaze, 82, 83
ghost towns, 161–162, 169
GIS, 72, 75
Glob, Lotte, 174–175
   "Floating Stones," 175
Glock, Albert, 129
Great Zimbabwe ruins, 79
Griqua, 91–92
Griqualand West, 88 *(map)*, 89
   Fig. 5.2 caption, 92

Ha-Tshirundu Mountains, 76, 77, 79
Henry II (King of England), 52, 54,
   55, 58, 64
heritage
   destruction of, 130
   management, 103–104
   tourism, 72, 74–75, 183–184
Hewitt-Olmsted trading post, 202
Ho-Chunk (Winnebago) people,
   198–206

Hollywood Reserve, NSW, Australia,
   155
home, 14, 16, 18, 21, 23, 121
homelessness, 18
Hopewell Interaction Sphere, 194
human remains, 180–181, 191
   recovery of, 185–186

Iceland, 66
ideological clearance, 50, 56, 118
image
   of Africa, 77, 79
   of Ireland, 50, 56, 58–59, 62,
     65–68
   of the past, 72–75, 77, 82
   of wilderness, 116
Indigenous
   alienation of by archaeology, 190
   historical complexity of identity,
     in South Africa, 100, 104
   knowledge, in South Africa, 90,
     93, 101–102, 104
   people, in South Africa, 75, 77,
     87, 98
   relationships with colonists, in
     South Africa, 91
   See also Aboriginal people, First
     Nations, *and entries for*
     individual groups
intellectual clearance, 191–193, 206
Iowa, Neutral Ground, 201–206
Ioway people, 197–198, 205–207
Ireland, 49–70
   Anglo-Norman invasion of, 50,
     52, 54, 55, 64
   Gaelic, 52–54, 57
   medieval, 49–70
Israel
   Antiquities Laws of, 131
   archaeology in, 129
   creation of, 127
   demography, 128
   land clearance, 130–131
   settlements in West Bank, 129–130

Joint POW/MIA Accounting
   Campaign (JPAC), 186

Karretjiemense, 92–94
Khoisan (Khoe-San), 87
  archaeological record and, 92, 103
  as creators of rock art, 97, 99,
    103
  historical records of contact,
    90–91
  idiom and lore of, 93
  place-names, 90, 141
  racial taxonomy and, 92, 94
  ritual and beliefs of, 100–101
  terms for 105 n. 1
  See also Bushmen
Kousop, 89
Kwinda Tshirundu, 76–81

La Crosse, Wisconsin, 195, 199
Laid, Scotland, 173–174
land claims/land restitution
  in South Africa, 71, 72, 78, 79,
    104, 106 n. 7
land ownership
  attitudes towards, in Canada, 113
  Batswapong conceptions of, 152
  changes in: in Scotland, 31, 37;
    in South Africa, 92, 94
  rock art as "title deeds" for, 87,
    89–90, 105
language, loss of, 93
language of clearance, 121
lefatshe, 141, 147
Limerick, Ireland, 53, 63, 64
Limpopo
  Province, 71–86
  River, 76
loss of place, 162–163
Joliet, Louis, 197
Ludlow Collective, 184

MacMurchada (Dairmait), 54
mantsho a ngwana ceremony, 141
maps, mapping, 17, 19–21, 169–170
  colonial: in South Africa, 72–77,
    81–83, 90, 92; in Canada,
    117, 119; in Ireland, 49–51,
    56, 58–68

massacre, Deir Yasin, 128
mass gravesites, 186
McGregor Museum, Kimberley,
  South Africa, 96–97
Meir, Golda, 128
Melness, Scotland, 172
memorialization, 40
memory, 16–18, 22–23, 33, 39, 170
Meskwaki (Fox) people, 198–203
Mfecane wars, 151
Middle Mississippian society,
  194–195
migration, 13, 23
  in South Africa, 98–99
Mille Lacs Lake, Minnesota, 199
missionaries, 64, 91–92, 106 n. 6,
  116, 146
missions, 91–92, 106 n. 6
modernity, 78
monuments, 22, 39, 95–96, 97, 170,
  181–183
  natural places as, 144, 151
motte and bailey, 50, 55, 63
Moundbuilder Myth, 205
Murphy, Andrew, 60, 61, 65

naming
  of the landscape, 139–142,
    144–145, 152
  of Native American groups, 193
Napier commission, 33–34, 38–39,
  42
Narrabeen, NSW, 156
narrative, personal, 187
national parks, 26
  in South Africa, 79, 103
nationalism, 18
nation building, 71, 136
Native American Graves Protection
  and Repatriation Act, 204
Natives Land Act (South Africa), 94
Neutral Ground. *See* Iowa, Neutral
  Ground
Nisga'a, 116, 119
Norse settlement sites, 176
Nzhelele River, 76, 79, 84

Occupied Territories. *See* Palestine
Ojibwe people, 200
oral history, 32, 40, 72, 76, 81
  in Botswana, 145, 147, 149
Orser, Charles, 13, 42
other/otherness, 50, 56, 58, 60–61,
  65–67, 68, 71, 75

Palestine, 129–130
  abandonment of *qusur* in, 135
  Antiquities Laws of, 136
  archaeology in, 127–138
  Department of Antiquities, 135
  depopulation of, 128–129
  Israeli settlements in, 129–130
Patrick, Saint, 64
Perrot, Nicholas, 196–197
Phalatswe Hills, *140 (map)*,
  143–145, 152
phenomenology, 16
Philip, John, 91
pilgrimage, 62, 65, 156, 181
"place-bereavement," 163
population, 29–30, 51, 53
  of Israel and Palestine, 128
postcolonial, 14, 23
  archaeology, 72, 83–84
Potts, Gary, 121
propaganda, 57–60
Psinomani (ancestral Dakota cultural
  complex), 199
Ptolemy, 61, 67

qusur, 127, 131–132, 134–137

Raasay, Isle of, Scotland, 32–39, 41
  ACFA surveys of, 32–33, 35
  Hallaig, 36–39
Rainbow Nation (South Africa), 104
refugees, 23, 103
Renaissance, 58, 60
repatriation, 204
representations, 50, 56, 58, 60,
  62–63, 67
  of community values, 144
  of culture, in South Africa, 105

reserve
  Aboriginal, 155
  Indian, 117–119, 121
  Khoe-San, 106 n. 6
  land, 77–79, 81
ritual, 18, 30, 31, 40–41, 81
  in building *qusur*, 133
  Khoe-San, 100–102

sacred landscapes
  in Botswana, 146, 147, 149
  of remembrance, 181
  as a result of historical narrative,
    184
safaris, 77
saqifeh, 132
Sassoon, Siegfried, 187
Sauk people, 199–202
Schiffer, Michael, 27, 41
Scotland, 52, 62
  Highlands, 164–177
  Highlands and Islands
    Development Board, 170
  Highland Clearances, 37–39,
    165–173
  Highland Council Archaeology
    Service, 169
  Mackay Country, 176
  medieval, 33, 35, 176
Setswana, 141–142
settlers, 20, 21, 77, 78
Siouan-speaking tribes, 196,
  204–205. *See also* Dakota
Skerray, Scotland, 170–171, 175
Sleitell, Scotland, 171
Smith, David (Winnebago tribal
  historian), 200–206
Smuts, General Jan, 96
Snowy Mountains Authority,
  158–159
spatial/social relations, 15, 193
Stafford family, 166
Stonehenge, 17–18
stone structures, 56, 76, 79
  boat-shaped, in Scotland, 164
  See also qusur

storytelling, 83
Stow, George, 87–91, 101–102, 105, 105 n. 2, 106 n. 5
Strathnaver Trail tourist route, 166–167, 169–172, 176
Strongbow. *See* FitzGilbert de Clare, Richard
supernatural, 28, 30–31, 36, 102
  powers in landscape, 142, 145, 149
Sutherland, Scotland, 164–176

taboo, 30, 40, 41, 142, 151, 186
terra nullius ("virgin landscape"), 117
Theal, George, 98, 104
Topographia Hibernica, 50, 55–67
tourism, 71–72, 75, 104, 115, 169
  heritage, 74–75
treaty, in Canada, 113, 118–119
Trekboers, 87, 91–92
Trutch, Joseph, 118
Tshekedi's Road, 145–149, *150*, 151–152
Tsimshian, 113, 119–120
Tswana, 91–92, 141–142
Tswapong (geographical area), 139–140, *140 (map)*, 145–149, *150*, 151–152
Tuan, Yi-Fu, 16
Turkey River Subagency, 201–202

"uninhabited" landscapes, 50, 67, 113, 116–117

Venda-language speakers, 76–77, 81, 84
Victorian State Electricity Commission (SEC), 157–158
Viking towns, 53, 64

Warangdesa, 155
Waterford, Ireland, 52–54, 57, 63, 64
West Bank, 127–132
Wexford, Ireland, 52–54, 63, 64
Whorf hypothesis, 192
Wildebeest Kuil Rock Art Center, *88 (map)*, 97, 99, 103, 105, 106 n. 9
wilderness, 26, 77, 79
  changes in attitudes towards, 114, 117, 119
  etymology of, 116
  ideology of, 112–116
  Indigenous attitudes towards, 121
  taming of, 120
  uses of, 115, 120
  values attributed to, 114–115, 120
Wilman, Maria, 96, 99
Woodland society, 194–195
World Archaeological Congress (2003), 13
World Heritage Site
  uKhahlamba, *88 (map)*, 103
World War I (The Great War), 180–187
  battlefield at Sunken Lane, 185
  Canadian memorial at Vimy, 181–182
  Devonshire memorial at Mansell Wood, 181
  management of battlefields, 182–184, 186
  Menin Gate Memorial, 187
  "Red Zone," 181, 184
World War II, 173

Xhosa, 91

Yallourn, Victoria, Australia, 157–163

Zimbabwe, 77

About the Authors

AMY GAZIN-SCHWARTZ is Associate Professor of Anthropology at Assumption College in Massachusetts and, with Olivia Lelong, codirector of the Strathnaver Province Archaeology Project. She has interests in the archaeology of rural settlement and life and in the intersections between folklore and archaeology. In addition to research in Strathnaver on medieval rural Scotland, she has done archaeological fieldwork on the island of Raasay, Scotland, with the Association of Certificated Field Archaeologists and in other parts of Great Britain and the northeastern US. She is coeditor (with Cornelius Holtorff) of *Archaeology and Folklore* (Routledge 1999).

BRENDA GUERNSEY is an MA candidate at the University of Northern British Columbia, Canada. Working with the Tsimshian First Nation community of northern British Columbia, her main areas of research deal with issues of identity, place, and decolonization. She has also worked as the Director/Curator of Heritage Park Museum in Terrace, British Columbia, and is currently working in the same region as a consultant conducting cultural heritage research for local communities and community organizations.

NEELS KRUGER is affiliated with the Department of Anthropology and Archaeology, University of Pretoria, South Africa, where he is a junior lecturer. He is an MA candidate in archaeology specializing in the late Iron Age and Colonial periods of Southern Africa. He is specifically interested in the frontier societies of South Africa's northern interior and the Limpopo River Valley, where he has been doing research for the past five years.

OLIVIA LELONG began working in archaeology in 1993 and has conducted research mainly in Scotland and England, with brief periods of work in France and the US. She was awarded an M.Phil. in 1993 and a Ph.D. in 2001, both from the University of Glasgow, Scotland. She has worked for Glasgow University Archaeological Research Division since 1997. Her doctoral research addressed the long-term occupation and reoccupation of particular landscapes in the central and northern Highlands of Scotland. Olivia codirects (with Amy Gazin-Schwartz) the Strathnaver Province Archaeology Project, which is investigating evidence for medieval settlement in the northern Highlands of Scotland. She also has ongoing research interests in the late first millennium BC and the first millennium AD, with major excavations at Iron Age sites in the Shetland Islands and southeast Scotland. She has strong interests in public archaeology, in forging links with local communities, and in finding the relevance of archaeological research to contemporary life.

DAWN MAKES STRONG MOVE is a member of the Ho-Chunk Nation and a trained archaeologist who has worked for her tribe in a variety of capacities related to cultural resources.

KATHRYN MATHERS teaches in the Introduction to the Humanities program at Stanford University, California. She has examined the representation of the past in South African museums and is currently interested in the contradictions between the goals of cultural and heritage tourism and the actual impacts of this industry on tourists and on the communities that they visit. The paper "Natives, Tourists, and Makwerekwere: Ethical Concerns with 'Proudly South African' Tourism," coauthored with Loren Landau, was published in *Development Southern Africa* in 2007. She is still affiliated with the Department of Anthropology and Archaeology, University of Pretoria, South Africa.

DAVID MORRIS is Head of Archaeology at the McGregor Museum in Kimberley, South Africa, and a Ph.D. candidate at the University of the Western Cape in Cape Town. His research focus is rock engraving sites of the Northern Cape, South Africa; he studied the site of Driekopseiland for a Master's thesis. His interests include public archaeology, and he was closely involved in developing the Wildebeest Kuil Rock Art Center outside Kimberley. He is coauthoring a book on rock art of the Karoo, and a monograph on Wildebeest Kuil as part of a Franco-South African *Groupe de Recherche International* partnership and research program.

JULIANA NAIROUZ is a mother of two boys and resides in San Jose, California. Juliana graduated with a bachelor's degree in Anthropology and Archaeology from Birzeit University, and then obtained her MA in historic archaeology from the University of Massachusetts, Amherst. Juliana worked as the Archaeology Outreach Supervisor for the Palestinian Ministry of Tourism and Antiquities. In the US she worked as a teaching assistant at the University of Massachusetts, then as an intern in the US Fish and Wildlife Service in Hadley, Massachusetts. She has conducted several fieldwork projects in archaeology and ethnography, including at Ain Ghazal (a Neolithic site) in Jordan and salvage excavation sites in Jericho (different eras) and other cities in the West Bank. Ms. Nairouz has presented her ethnoarchaeological work at several meetings on archaeology, including the ASOR, AAA, and WAC.

Jon Price currently teaches Heritage and Cultural Management at Northumbria University, Newcastle, UK. His career in field archaeology began in 1974; since then he has also been a museum curator and run his own museum interpretation company. He is a founding member of No Man's Land, an organization working on the archaeology of Great War sites in northwest Europe. He has been carrying out fieldwork and research in the archaeology of modern conflicts for ten years. His grandfather fought at the Battle of First Ypres in 1914 and went on to serve in Flanders and on the Somme until 1918. His father served on a different battlefield in the Cold War.

Peter Read is a Professorial Research Fellow in the Department of History, University of Sydney, Australia. He has divided his professional career between research in Australian Aboriginal history, and the meaning and significance of Australian place. His three major works in place studies are *Returning to Nothing* (Cambridge University Press, 1996), *Belonging* (Cambridge University Press, 2000), and *Haunted Earth* (University of New South Wales Press, 2003).

Phillip Segadika is the Principal Curator of Archaeology and Monuments Division at the Department of National Museum, Monuments and Art Gallery in Gaborone, Botswana. He is a landscape archaeologist and has particular interest in the development of management plans and the monitoring of intangible heritage resources. A former consulting archaeologist, he received his MA in landscape archaeology from the University of Wales, Lampeter, UK.

Angèle Smith is Assistant Professor of Anthropology at the University of Northern British Columbia, Canada. Her research focuses on landscapes, place, the construction and negotiation of cultural identities, and the politics of representation, and bridges many subdisciplines, including cultural anthropology, ethnohistory, and historical archaeology. Her current ongoing work in Ireland, funded by the Social Science and Humanities Research Council of Canada, explores the articulation and negotiation of place and identity among communities of Nigerian asylum seekers.

Larry J. Zimmerman is Professor of Anthropology and Museum Studies and Public Scholar of Native American Representation at Indiana University-Purdue University, Indianapolis, and the Eiteljorg Museum of American Indians and Western Art. He is vice president of the World Archaeological Congress, has numerous publications about the relationships between Indigenous people and archaeologists, and has recently started a project on the archaeology of homelessness.